McGraw-Hill's

500

World History

Questions

Volume 2: 1500 to Present

Also in McGraw-Hill's 500 Questions Series

McGraw-Hill's

500

World History

Questions

Volume 2: 1500 to Present

Ace Your College Exams

Jon Sterngass, PhD

New York   Chicago   San Francisco   Lisbon   London   Madrid   Mexico City
Milan   New Delhi   San Juan   Seoul   Singapore   Sydney   Toronto

1 2 3 4 5 6 7 8 9 10   QFR/QFR   1 9 8 7 6 5 4 3 2

ISBN   978-0-07-178062-9
MHID   0-07-178062-9

e-ISBN   978-0-07-178063-6
e-MHID   0-07-178063-7

Library of Congress Control Number 2012933637

McGraw-Hill products are available at special quantity discounts to use as premiums and sales promotions or for use in corporate training programs. To contact a representative, please e-mail us at bulksales@mcgraw-hill.com.

This book is printed on acid-free paper.

CONTENTS

INTRODUCTION

Congratulations! You've taken a big step toward achieving your best grade by purchasing *McGraw-Hill's 500 World History Questions, Volume 2: 1500 to Present*. We are here to help you improve your grades on classroom, midterm, and final exams. These 500 questions will help you study more effectively, use your preparation time wisely, and get the final grade you want.

This book gives you 500 multiple-choice questions that cover the most essential course material. Each question has a detailed answer explanation. These questions give you valuable independent practice to supplement your regular textbook and the groundwork you are already doing in the classroom.

You might be the kind of student who needs to study extra questions a few weeks before a big exam for a final review. Or you might be the kind of student who puts off preparing until right before a midterm or final. No matter what your preparation style, you will surely benefit from reviewing these 500 questions that closely parallel the content, format, and degree of difficulty of the questions found in typical college-level exams. These questions and their answer explanations are the ideal last-minute study tool for those final days before the test.

Remember the old saying "Practice makes perfect." If you practice with all the questions and answers in this book, we are certain that you will build the skills and confidence that are needed to ace your exams. Good luck!

—Editors of McGraw-Hill Education

CHAPTER 1

European Renaissance

1. An important precondition for the European invention of movable-type printing was
   (A) renewed interest in classical Greek and Latin
   (B) commercial production of manuscripts in the scriptoria
   (C) increased production of parchment and vellum
   (D) patronage of rich nobles
   (E) interest in reading the Bible in vernacular languages

2. The word *Renaissance*
   (A) is Italian for "rebirth"
   (B) was invented during the 1700s to disparage the Middle Ages
   (C) was popularized by Jacob Burckhardt, who noted the similarities between medieval and Renaissance thought
   (D) was first used by Marsilio Ficino to express a general consciousness of modernity
   (E) originally referred to a rebirth in arts and literature

3. The Renaissance philosophy of humanism generally emphasized all of the following EXCEPT
   (A) the importance of human reason
   (B) Greco-Roman civilization as a model
   (C) concern for everyday problems rather than metaphysics
   (D) realism in art and literature
   (E) the superiority of a life of faith over involvement in the world

4. All of the following are true of the Italian Wars EXCEPT that they

(A) demonstrated the superiority of republican armies over mercenaries
(B) were marked by an increasing degree of alliances, counteralliances, and betrayals
(C) were ruinous to the Italian peninsula
(D) began with the invasion of Italy by Charles VIII of France
(E) ended with Spain as the premier power of Europe

5. Renaissance painting was characterized by all of the following EXCEPT

(A) an emphasis on individual people
(B) the use of perspective
(C) the use of themes from nature
(D) an emphasis on realism
(E) the popularity of frescoes

6. All of the following have at one time been cited as causes of the Renaissance EXCEPT the

(A) Black Death and subsequent plagues
(B) formation of nation-states with powerful monarchs
(C) increasing use of money rather than land as a medium of exchange
(D) weakening of the nobility because of the Thirty Years' War
(E) Western Schism from 1378 to 1417

7. What is one of the main differences between the Italian Renaissance and the Northern Renaissance?

(A) Painters in Italy often used perspective in their works, but northern painters preferred flatness to three-dimensionality.
(B) Writers in Italy tried to capture the personality of their subjects, but northern writers avoided realistic characters.
(C) Humanists in Italy were interested mainly in secular themes, but northern humanists' ideas were often religious.
(D) Italian artists were patronized by wealthy merchant families, but northern artists were patronized mostly by peasants.
(E) Governmental power was centralized in the Italian Renaissance, while the Northern Renaissance was dominated by independent city-states.

8. Around 1430, a new style of music appeared in the Low Countries that would dominate composition for the next two centuries. The style is known as
   (A) Gregorian chant
   (B) romanticism
   (C) baroque
   (D) chorales
   (E) polyphony

9. In Italian Renaissance culture, the social stigma of illegitimacy was placed on the
   (A) woman who bore the child
   (B) child born out of wedlock
   (C) father of the child
   (D) wife of the child's father
   (E) parish priest of the woman who bore the child

10. All of the following are true of Matthias Corvinus EXCEPT that
    (A) he united the Bohemian and Hungarian crowns
    (B) he achieved great military success through the use of a standing army
    (C) his library at Buda was one of the finest in Europe
    (D) the Ottomans defeated him at Mohács and destroyed his empire
    (E) he promoted Renaissance values in Hungary

11. The Florentine government opened the Ospidale degli Innocenti in 1445 in order to
    (A) deal with the large numbers of abandoned children in the city
    (B) supply the upper classes with a ready supply of wet nurses
    (C) provide an alternative for those who lost their money in the Dowry Fund
    (D) lower the high infant mortality rate
    (E) offer shelter to poor, pregnant, single women

12. All of the following authors wrote their most famous works in vernacular languages EXCEPT
    (A) Dante Alighieri—*The Divine Comedy*
    (B) Geoffrey Chaucer—*The Canterbury Tales*
    (C) François Rabelais—*Gargantua and Pantagruel*
    (D) Leonardo Bruni—*History of the Florentine People*
    (E) Luís de Camões—*The Lusiads*

13. An important factor in fostering the creativity of individual artists in the Renaissance was the
    (A) development of a market system for the visual arts
    (B) invention of sophisticated tools for art and architecture
    (C) spread of commissioned work paid for by powerful princes and nobles
    (D) decline of artists' involvement in workshops
    (E) increase in the number of individually signed paintings

14. Although Milan led the way in the use of diplomats, the city that became the diplomatic hub of Europe during the Renaissance was
    (A) Prague
    (B) Paris
    (C) London
    (D) Rome
    (E) Constantinople

15. All of the following were results of the War of the Roses EXCEPT
    (A) the cloth industry expanded in England
    (B) Henry Tudor became King of England
    (C) wool merchants gained a majority in the House of Commons
    (D) the English nobility suffered heavy casualties
    (E) changes in feudal society led to the movement towards the Renaissance

16. Giovanni Pico della Mirandola is famous for writing
    (A) *Oration on the Dignity of Man*
    (B) *Gargantua and Pantagruel*
    (C) *Three Books on Life*
    (D) *The Expulsion from Paradise*
    (E) *Tirant the White*

17. The trend of constructing urban palaces for the Florentine ruling elite was begun by
    (A) Filippo Brunelleschi
    (B) Andrea Mantegna
    (C) Leon Battista Alberti
    (D) Michelangelo Buonarroti
    (E) Lorenzo Ghiberti

18. The new demand for religious conformity in Spain led to the

(A) fall of Granada in 1478
(B) introduction of the Inquisition
(C) marriage of Isabella of Castile and Ferdinand of Aragon
(D) voyages of discovery in the Atlantic
(E) Moorish Revolt of 1497

19. All of the following were noted Renaissance painters EXCEPT

(A) Raphael
(B) Titian
(C) Diego Velázquez
(D) Michelangelo
(E) Leonardo da Vinci

20. "Since love and fear can hardly exist together, if we must choose between them, it is far safer [for a ruler] to be feared than loved."

The author of this famous quotation is

(A) Niccolò Machiavelli
(B) Petrarch
(C) Erasmus
(D) Cosimo de' Medici
(E) Lucrezia Borgia

CHAPTER 2

European Reformation and Wars over Religion

21. The book *In Praise of Folly* criticized the lack of spirituality in the Roman Catholic Church and urged a return to the basic message of Jesus. The author was

    (A) Desiderius Erasmus
    (B) Thomas More
    (C) Isaac Abravanel
    (D) Paracelsus
    (E) François Rabelais

22. The ideas presented in Martin Luther's *Freedom of a Christian* diverged from traditional Catholic teachings by stressing that salvation could be gained solely by

    (A) good works
    (B) faith
    (C) proselytizing for the church
    (D) strictly obeying church laws
    (E) performing works of charity

23. Unlike Catholic women, Protestant women could not

    (A) represent themselves in marital courts
    (B) petition for divorce
    (C) renounce marriage and family to live in a convent
    (D) marry without parental consent
    (E) study the Bible

24. The European city associated with John Calvin is
    (A) Geneva
    (B) Zurich
    (C) Münster
    (D) Strasbourg
    (E) Basel

25. All of the following were noted military leaders in the Thirty Years' War
    EXCEPT
    (A) Gustavus Adolphus
    (B) Johann Tserclaes, Count of Tilly
    (C) Albrecht von Wallenstein
    (D) Louis de Bourbon, Prince of Condé
    (E) Prince Eugene of Savoy

26. The impact of the Thirty Years' War on the population and economy
    of Europe can be described as
    (A) negligible
    (B) negative only in the Dutch Republic
    (C) equally devastating in almost all of continental Europe
    (D) most devastating in Spain and France
    (E) most devastating in Germany and Bohemia

27. The treaty that ended the Thirty Years' War is known as the
    (A) Treaty of Paris
    (B) Peace of Prague
    (C) Peace of Westphalia
    (D) Peace of Augsburg
    (E) Treaty of Cateau-Canbrésis

28. All of the following are true regarding the Peasants' War of 1524–1526
    EXCEPT that
    (A) it was supported by Martin Luther
    (B) a primary cause was the Reformation
    (C) an estimated 100,000 peasants died
    (D) it affected mostly southern and central Germany
    (E) it was the largest popular uprising in Europe before the French
        Revolution

29. In 1571, the Ottoman expansion into the western Mediterranean was checked in an enormous naval battle known as the

(A) Battle of Preveza
(B) Battle of Lepanto
(C) Battle of the Dunes
(D) Battle of Blenheim
(E) Battle of Djerba

30. All of the following were noted artists of the Northern Renaissance and Reformation EXCEPT

(A) Thomas Gainsborough
(B) Rembrandt
(C) Albrecht Dürer
(D) Jan van Eyck
(E) Pieter Bruegel

31. Which of the following statements is true regarding indulgences?

(A) Indulgences are no longer granted by the Roman Catholic Church.
(B) Indulgences always involve a payment of money.
(C) Indulgences are granted as a way to avoid confession and absolution.
(D) In 1516, money from the sale of indulgences had to stay within the diocese where they were sold.
(E) Martin Luther's *Ninety-Five Theses* specifically protested against the efficacy of indulgences.

32. All of the following are positions promulgated by the Council of Trent EXCEPT that

(A) both good works and faith provide salvation for individuals
(B) seven sacraments are essential to Christian theology
(C) the Eucharist is a ceremony symbolizing Christ's union with his believers
(D) bishops were required to live in their dioceses and oversee the clergy's education
(E) all weddings were to take place in churches and be registered by the parish clergy

33. One of the main causes of the Reformation in Europe was the

(A) widespread belief that the Catholic Church was corrupt
(B) domination of religious life by Europe's kings and scholars
(C) Catholic Church's teaching that even sinners could go to heaven
(D) opposition of most merchants and rulers to learning new ideas
(E) decline of nationalism in northern Europe

34. Although Martin Luther and Huldrych Zwingli shared many views, they diverged on the significance of

(A) Bible reading
(B) penance
(C) clerical celibacy
(D) the Eucharist
(E) pilgrimage

35. All of the following are true regarding the Edict of Nantes EXCEPT that it

(A) was issued by Henry IV
(B) reinstated the civil rights of Huguenots
(C) forbid Protestants to worship publicly in Paris
(D) ended the French Wars of Religion and permanently solved the issue of the rights of Huguenots
(E) was resented by Pope Clement VIII

36. One of the conclusions that can be drawn from the creation of the Anglican Church by Henry VIII was that

(A) Henry VIII was an excellent monarch
(B) Catherine of Aragon was unable to have children
(C) major historical changes are sometimes triggered by chance events
(D) Henry always intended to break with Rome and used the Anne Boleyn incident as an excuse
(E) if Pope Clement VII had been willing to compromise, England would still be Catholic today

37. All of the following are true of witchcraft in Europe EXCEPT that

(A) trials of witches peaked between 1560 and 1640
(B) in the Middle Ages (before 1400) women made up 80 percent of those accused
(C) more than 40,000 people were executed as witches in Europe
(D) the accused were often poor and socially marginal
(E) the majority of witch trials took place in the Holy Roman Empire

38. In the 17th century, the Baroque style

(A) reaffirmed that emotionalism was an important part of Catholicism
(B) continued to emphasize the Renaissance focus on unity and clarity
(C) developed initially in the German states
(D) was rejected by monarchs as too bizarre to patronize
(E) typically displayed the moment before a dramatic event took place rather than be accused of sensationalism

39. "The German Jews managed to come together [in Hamburg] and hold prayers in private houses, as best they could. . . . When the clergy discovered it, they became intolerant and drove us forth, and then like timid sheep we had to betake ourselves to the synagogue in Altona. This lasted a good while, till we crept back to our little Hamburg prayer-rooms. So from time to time we enjoyed peace, and again were hunted forth; and so it has been to this day."

The author of this quotation was

(A) Glückel of Hameln
(B) Christine de Pisan
(C) Julian of Norwich
(D) Mary Wollstonecraft
(E) Margery Kempe

40. All of the following were results of the Protestant Reformation EXCEPT that it

(A) broke the religious unity of Europe
(B) led to the stagnation of European Catholicism
(C) increased the literacy rate
(D) strengthened the growth of nation-states
(E) began a century of religious wars

41. The so-called Little Ice Age

(A) began suddenly in 1316
(B) is not supported by dendroclimatology
(C) followed a Medieval Warm Period
(D) affected winter temperatures, but not glaciation
(E) led to famine and disease

42. Katharina Zell was

(A) an outspoken Protestant reformer
(B) the wife of Martin Luther
(C) a Catholic nun who was declared a saint within 25 years of her death
(D) the most famous writer of Protestant chorales
(E) the author of the first novel ever written in German

43. The Fuggers were
- (A) a new class of royal officials established by Henry IV to counterbalance the traditional nobility
- (B) a group of neutral Catholics and Calvinists during the French Wars of Religion
- (C) the name taken by young humanists and clerics who shared Martin Luther's critical attitude toward the Catholic Church
- (D) a radical Protestant sect that believed in adult baptism
- (E) a famous family of merchant princes and bankers

44. The Anabaptists, who stressed adult baptism and the separation of church and state, split into a number of denominations that still exist today. These denominations include all of the following EXCEPT
- (A) Schwarzenau Brethren (Dunkers)
- (B) Hutterites
- (C) Amish
- (D) Mennonites
- (E) Methodists

45. The ruler of England during the time of the Spanish Armada was
- (A) Henry VIII
- (B) Edward VI
- (C) Mary I
- (D) Elizabeth I
- (E) James I

CHAPTER 3

Islamic Gunpowder Empires: Ottoman, Safavid, and Mughal

46. All of the following are true of the so-called gunpowder empires (Mughal, Ottoman, and Safavid) EXCEPT that

    (A) they were all Islamic
    (B) each made use of newly developed firearms
    (C) they all developed highly centralized states
    (D) the main language of each empire was Arabic
    (E) they all were extremely powerful in the 1600s

47. The Safavid Empire is associated with present-day

    (A) India
    (B) Iran
    (C) Egypt
    (D) Turkey
    (E) Indonesia

48. Under Abbas I (reigned 1587–1629), the Safavids

    (A) ignored Europe
    (B) made an alliance with Ivan the Terrible
    (C) worked with England to counter the Portuguese
    (D) were not a factor in great-power diplomacy
    (E) forged an alliance with the Ottomans to counter European expansion into Asia

49. All of the following are true of the Battle of Chaldiran (1514) EXCEPT
that
   (A) Ottoman guns and artillery were the deciding factor in the battle
   (B) it destroyed Ismail I's aura of invincibility
   (C) it essentially ended warfare between the Ottomans and the Safavids
   (D) the Safavids lost Iraq as well as the Kurdish and Armenian parts
        of eastern Anatolia
   (E) it led to the present-day border between Turkey and Iran

50. All of the following are true of Isfahan EXCEPT that
   (A) Abbas I moved the capital there from Qazvin
   (B) Naghsh-e Jahan Square, constructed between 1598 and 1629, is
        a UNESCO World Heritage Site
   (C) it was once one of the world's largest cities
   (D) it was a meeting place of many different cultures and nationalities
   (E) its heyday ended when it was sacked by the Ottomans in 1642

51. The Mughal Empire was founded by
   (A) Aurangzeb
   (B) Akbar
   (C) Babur
   (D) Bayezid I
   (E) Humayun

52. Muslim rule in India led to the appearance of a new language known as
   (A) Urdu
   (B) Tamil
   (C) Telkugu
   (D) Marathi
   (E) Gujarati

53. The Delhi Sultanate
   (A) checked Timur's (Tamerlane's) advance into India
   (B) replaced the Mughal dynasty as the major power on the subcontinent
   (C) united India under strong centralized government
   (D) was a single dynasty with great cultural prestige
   (E) introduced the dome and the pointed arch to India

54. Akbar strengthened his rule over India by all of the following EXCEPT

(A) restricting office holding to loyal Mughals
(B) using marriage alliances to strengthen his empire
(C) allowing Hindus to rebuild temples
(D) force of arms
(E) eliminating the jizya tax

55. The Mughal Empire reached its greatest extent under

(A) Babur
(B) Akbar
(C) Aurangzeb
(D) Jahangir
(E) Furrukhsiyar

56. The 18th century in India is often characterized as

(A) the Golden Age
(B) the Great Anarchy
(C) the British Conquest
(D) the age of the Delhi Sultanate
(E) the Collapse of the Marathas

57. Which of the following statements refers to Mehmed II?

(A) Although greatly outnumbered, his forces won a surprising victory on the Byzantine frontier.
(B) By conquering Constantinople, he paved the way for the expansion of the Ottoman Empire.
(C) He established Ottoman domination of the eastern Mediterranean by conquering the island of Rhodes.
(D) He claimed to be descended from Genghis Khan and conquered both Russia and Persia.
(E) His conquest of Belgrade allowed the Ottomans to rule almost all of Hungary.

58. Sultan Suleiman I shocked Europe by making an alliance with

(A) Henry VIII
(B) Charles V
(C) Francis I
(D) Gustavus Adolphus
(E) Ismail I

59. In the second half of the 17th century, the Ottoman sultans avoided revolt by

    (A) granting elites an equal role in government
    (B) playing different elite groups off against each other
    (C) diverting the elites with lavish entertainment
    (D) imposing serfdom on Anatolian peasants
    (E) suppressing bandit mercenaries by force

60. All of the following were included in the Ottoman Empire at one time EXCEPT

    (A) northern Africa
    (B) Sicily
    (C) Anatolia
    (D) Hungary and Austria
    (E) the Balkans

61. All of the following are true of Valide Sultans EXCEPT that

    (A) the period in the late 1500s and early 1600s was known as the Sultanate of Women
    (B) they often sat behind a curtain at the Divan because they could not speak to men
    (C) three famous Valide Sultans were Nurbanu Sultan, Safiye Sultan, and Kosem Sultan
    (D) their quarters were centrally located in the harem
    (E) the Valide Sultan had tremendous power because she was the sultan's favorite consort

62. The weakening of the Ottoman Empire was caused by all of the following EXCEPT

    (A) the eventual disparity between western European and Ottoman technology
    (B) limited agricultural resources to support the growing population
    (C) the high costs of maintaining a large military
    (D) overly conservative and traditional attitudes among Ottoman leadership
    (E) the failure to establish widespread trading outposts

63. Domestic women in the Ottoman Empire
- (A) played an important role in the production of firearms
- (B) did not face the same restrictions on their mobility as women in other Islamic areas
- (C) constituted a majority of the members of the Ottoman textile guilds
- (D) used embroidery as a way to gain financial independence
- (E) dominated the Bursa silk industry

64. Under Ottoman rule
- (A) religious freedom was denied to Jews and Christians
- (B) millets promoted unity in the empire
- (C) non-Muslim girls were educated in the principles of Islam
- (D) millets helped promote peaceful relationships between the sultan and his subjects
- (E) minority ethnic groups were subject to Shari'ah-based law

65. Ultimately, the Janissary corps was
- (A) converted to Christianity
- (B) defeated by the Russians in the Crimean War and disbanded
- (C) massacred by Sultan Mahmud II
- (D) assimilated into a new western-style conscript army
- (E) reformed by the teenage sultan Osman II

CHAPTER 4

The Rise and Expansion of European Nation-States

66. One of the reasons the Dutch prospered in the 1600s was because

(A) of their attachment to the ascendant Spanish Empire
(B) the Low Countries became a center of trade and banking
(C) of the intelligent leadership of King Vermeer
(D) they were a homogenous Protestant population
(E) they refused to trade in weapons and so did not alienate commercial partners throughout Europe

67. All of the following were part of the Columbian Exchange EXCEPT

(A) horses and llamas
(B) smallpox and syphilis
(C) corn and rice
(D) potatoes and wheat
(E) bison and dogs

68. The concept of *raison d'état* is usually associated with

(A) Cardinal Richelieu
(B) Louis XIV
(C) D'Artagnan
(D) Madame de Lafayette
(E) Cardinal Mazarin

69. When Philip II died in 1598, Spain

(A) was at the height of its power
(B) was at peace with the rest of the world
(C) was facing severe economic problems
(D) underwent a succession crisis because he died childless
(E) had definitively ended the revolt in the Netherlands

70. All of the following are true about the growth of nation-states in Europe EXCEPT that
- (A) the Holy Roman Empire coalesced into a powerful nation-state
- (B) the strongest states in Europe in the 1700s were France, England, and Spain
- (C) nation-states developed centralized governments with large bureaucracies
- (D) nation-states often acquired power over the church
- (E) England and the Netherlands developed constitutional monarchies

71. Capitalism is characterized by all of the following EXCEPT
- (A) the elimination of financial risks
- (B) private ownership
- (C) the ability to make profits
- (D) the laws of supply and demand
- (E) the ability to make private decisions regarding production

72. All of the following were Portuguese outposts along the African coast EXCEPT
- (A) Ceuta
- (B) São Tomé and Príncipe
- (C) São Jorge da Mina
- (D) Goa
- (E) Fort Santo Antonio

73. The statement "*L'état c'est moi*" ("I am the state") is attributed to
- (A) Louis XIV
- (B) Louis XV
- (C) Cardinal Richelieu
- (D) Cardinal Mazarin
- (E) Henry IV

74. All of the following are true of salons EXCEPT that they were
- (A) informal gatherings
- (B) usually presided over by socially eminent women
- (C) a primary means by which courtly manners spread through the upper classes of society
- (D) concerned with conversation about love, literature, and philosophy
- (E) unique to France

75. Sweden ceased to be a major power in Europe after the Battle of

- (A) Narva
- (B) Culloden
- (C) Breitenfeld
- (D) Poltava
- (E) Naseby

76. The Levellers

- (A) were a French Huguenot sect that preached equality
- (B) were the soldiers and farmers drafted by Oliver Cromwell to modernize the country by building the Exeter Canal and the Stamford Canal
- (C) were English intellectuals who attacked John Lilburne's role in the government of Charles I
- (D) were English Puritans who wanted Parliament to meet regularly and its members to be paid
- (E) inspired the Los Angeles Diggers

77. The virtues that Louis XIV attempted to instill in the aristocracy included

- (A) order and self-control
- (B) freedom and self-determination
- (C) materialism and competition
- (D) love of luxury and promiscuity
- (E) asceticism and devotion to God

78. All of the following are true regarding the Navigation Act of 1651 EXCEPT that it

- (A) was a mercantilist measure
- (B) was meant to target French competition
- (C) led to the First Anglo-Dutch War
- (D) banned foreign ships from transporting goods from outside Europe to England or its colonies
- (E) banned third-party country's ships from transporting goods from another European country to England

79. In the 1600s and 1700s, the upper classes increasingly considered popular culture
    (A) vulgar and unsuitable for those who aspired to nobility
    (B) curious and worthy of study to be incorporated into so-called high culture
    (C) a positive influence on the lives of people who did not have access to court culture
    (D) a model for their own behavior
    (E) a basis on which to build feelings of nationalism among the illiterate

80. Rococo was an art style that
    (A) emphasized severe lines and classical forms
    (B) predominantly influenced painting
    (C) was popular in the 18th century
    (D) originated in Venice and spread widely through the Hapsburg lands
    (E) allowed Thomas Chippendale to paint understated portraits of King George I

81. At the end of the Thirty Years' War, European monarchs built magnificent palaces filled with artwork because
    (A) war had enriched the countries of Europe
    (B) the slave trade had grown tremendously during the war
    (C) they wanted to celebrate the peace
    (D) they needed to justify the increase in state power
    (E) they needed to spend money that had previously gone to warfare

82. Inflation in Spain in the early 1500s was primarily caused by the
    (A) increase in the price of slaves
    (B) cost of fighting wars all over Europe
    (C) amount of gold and silver imported into Spain
    (D) luxury-loving Spanish court
    (E) booming Spanish economy

83. Almost half of all African slaves went to
    (A) domestic servitude in Europe
    (B) raising sugar in Spanish America
    (C) mining silver in central Mexico
    (D) cultivating Dutch, French, Danish, or British sugar plantations in the Caribbean
    (E) producing tobacco, rice, and indigo in the British colonies of North America

84. Historians estimate that between 1400 and 1900, the number of kidnapped Africans who were carried across the ocean in the transatlantic slave trade was about

(A) 5 million
(B) 11 million
(C) 17 million
(D) 23 million
(E) 29 million

85. All of the following are true about the armies of European nation-states in the 1600s EXCEPT that

(A) European armies grew much larger
(B) the use of mercenaries began to decline
(C) musket-wielding soldiers were set up in long lines of three to five ranks
(D) governments introduced uniforms during the Thirty Years' War
(E) the pike square dominated most battles

86. According to estimates of slave mortality, about what percentage of slaves died in the Middle Passage from 1590 to 1867?

(A) 4 percent
(B) 12 percent
(C) 20 percent
(D) 28 percent
(E) 36 percent

87. "The person of the king is sacred, and to attack him in any way is an attack on religion itself. . . . The respect given to a king is religious in nature. Serving God and respecting kings are bound together."

The author(s) of this statement was/were

(A) Jean Jacques Rousseau
(B) Oliver Cromwell
(C) Jacques-Bénigne Bossuet
(D) a committee of the Rump Parliament of England
(E) François Ravaillac

88. Which event came last chronologically?

(A) Amerigo Vespucci explores the east coast of South America.
(B) John Cabot lands on Newfoundland.
(C) Henry Hudson sails up the Hudson River.
(D) Pedro Álvares Cabral lands in Brazil.
(E) Jacques Cartier sails up the St. Lawrence River.

89. The doctrine of constitutionalism was first proposed in France by

(A) Enlightenment thinkers
(B) University of Paris professors
(C) the urban bourgeoisie
(D) Jansenist writers
(E) Huguenot resisters

90. The first Portuguese explorer to successfully reach the Cape of Good Hope at the southern tip of Africa was

(A) Vasco da Gama
(B) Bartolomeu Dias
(C) Ferdinand Magellan
(D) Christopher Columbus
(E) Nicolau Coelho

91. A visitor to this country in 1658 wrote, "there is no order in the state, and the subjects are not afraid either of the king or the judge. Everybody who is stronger thinks to have the right to oppress the weaker. . . . Such abominable depravity is called . . . 'aristocratic freedom.'"

The country in question is

(A) the Dutch Republic
(B) England
(C) France
(D) Sweden
(E) Poland

92. The Treaty of Utrecht

(A) confirmed French ambitions in Europe
(B) ended the Thirty Years' War
(C) is associated with the idea of balance of power
(D) barred Philip, Duke of Anjou, from ever becoming King of Spain
(E) awarded France the areas around the Hudson Bay, Newfoundland, and Acadia in exchange for territory lost in Europe

93. All of the following were examples of Peter the Great's Westernization policy EXCEPT

(A) instituting parliamentary government
(B) modernizing the army
(C) limiting the power of the nobility
(D) placing religion under state control
(E) cutting off the beards of his nobles

94. *The Fable of the Bees* argued that the desire for material goods promoted economic prosperity. It was written by

(A) Jeremy Bentham
(B) Jethro Tull
(C) David Hume
(D) George Berkeley
(E) Bernard Mandeville

95. Most Europeans in the early 1700s believed all of the following about slavery EXCEPT that it

(A) was justified by the supposed primitive nature of Africans
(B) was simply a by-product of commercial progress
(C) did not contradict beliefs concerning the importance of liberty and natural rights
(D) was not justified because of the spiritual equality between whites and blacks before God
(E) was essential to maintaining a prosperous European standard of life

96. The *Atlantic system* was the name given to the

(A) alliance of Spain and Portugal after the Treaty of Tordesillas
(B) interconnected economic systems of Europe, Africa, and North and South America between 1600 and 1800
(C) set of Parliamentary laws to impose British mercantilist policy on the regions bordering the Atlantic Ocean
(D) series of Portuguese coastal forts stretching along the western coast of Africa
(E) alliance of France and Spain after the Treaty of Utrecht to prevent further Hapsburg expansion to the west

97. The Portuguese admiral whose military and administrative activities conquered and established the Portuguese colonial empire in the Indian Ocean was

(A) Bartolomeu Dias
(B) Alfonso de Albuquerque
(C) Ferdinand Magellan
(D) Prince Henry the Navigator
(E) Diogo Gomes

98. In the early 1700s, the new literate public gathered together to exchange opinions in

(A) churches
(B) coffeehouses
(C) public parks
(D) Parliaments
(E) pipe shops

99. In 1802, the nation of Great Britain included all of the following EXCEPT

(A) the Faroe Islands
(B) Wales
(C) Scotland
(D) Ireland
(E) England

100. An example of the influence of Pietism on Judaism can be seen in the life of

(A) Elijah ben Solomon, the Vilna Gaon
(B) Moses Mendelssohn
(C) Jacob Frank
(D) Israel ben Eliezer, the Baal Shem Tov
(E) Sabbatai Zevi

CHAPTER 5

The Scientific Revolution and the Enlightenment

101. In 1633, the Catholic Church forced Galileo Galilei to appear before the Inquisition. This incident is probably still remembered because it

   (A) symbolizes the historic mistrust between science and religion
   (B) reminds people that the sun is actually the center of the universe
   (C) shows that Galileo was actually a better scientist than Copernicus
   (D) demonstrates the weakness of the Inquisition in the 1600s
   (E) reveals the limitations of the scientific method

102. "There was a very famous dervish in the neighborhood who was supposed to be the best philosopher in Turkey; they went to consult him . . . . 'Reverend Father,' said Candide, 'there is a horrible lot of evil in the world.'
   " 'What does it matter,' said the dervish, 'whether there is evil or good? When His Highness sends a ship to Egypt, does he wonder whether the mice in the ship are comfortable or not?' "

   The author of this passage is

   (A) Gottfried Leibniz
   (B) David Hume
   (C) Voltaire
   (D) Madame de Lafayette
   (E) Aphra Behn

103. Which man was the virtual inventor and master of the essay as a literary form?

   (A) Michel de Montaigne
   (B) Jean Bodin
   (C) William Harvey
   (D) Tycho Brahe
   (E) Baruch Spinoza

104. Which of the following refers to an important scientific discovery of the 1600s?

(A) Antoine Lavoisier and the discovery of hydrogen
(B) Isaac Newton and universal gravitation
(C) Carl Linnaeus and taxonomy
(D) William of Ockham's razor
(E) Gregor Mendel and heredity

105. All of the following made important discoveries in medicine in the 16th and 17th centuries EXCEPT

(A) Galen
(B) Andreas Vesalius
(C) Paracelsus
(D) William Harvey
(E) Jean Fernel

106. Witchcraft trials declined when

(A) popular attitudes toward witches began to change
(B) Catholic and Protestant clergy stopped associating disorder with female sexuality
(C) scientific thinking raised questions about evidence presented in witchcraft trials
(D) governments decided that witch trials created too much popular disorder
(E) the Peace of Augsburg (1555) settled the religious differences in the Holy Roman Empire

107. Deists often used the simile that God was like a

(A) shepherd
(B) watchmaker
(C) puppeteer
(D) father
(E) king

108. In *Two Treatises of Government*, John Locke

(A) argued that the king was a representative of God on earth
(B) contended that slavery violated the natural rights possessed by all humans
(C) stated that the purpose of government was to control the negative impulses that drove human nature
(D) celebrated the Glorious Revolution of 1688
(E) repudiated the blank slate metaphor of knowledge

109. Montesquieu is associated with

(A) the spread of the scientific method
(B) the compromise solution to Reformation arguments over the Eucharist
(C) support for the divine right theory of government
(D) logic-based Huguenot petitions for the restoration of their civil liberties
(E) the separation of the powers of government

110. The phrase "I think, therefore I am" is associated with

(A) Nicolas de Malebranche
(B) Pierre Bayle
(C) Gottfried Leibniz
(D) René Descartes
(E) Francisco Suárez

111. Pascal's wager refers to

(A) the agreement between Blaise Pascal and Louis XIV to cease the persecution of the Jansenists
(B) the offer of a reward to anyone who could prove empirically that Kepler's laws were true
(C) Blaise Pascal's declaration that scientific theories can only be considered disproved if they are empirically false
(D) the controversy over the veracity of Boyle's Law (1662)
(E) the application of probability theory to the question of the existence of God

112. John Locke's *blank slate* metaphor argued that

(A) governments were only as good as the people who were in them
(B) society could never be perfected because of flaws in human nature
(C) all people are essentially equal at birth
(D) human beings have certain innate ideas such as "love" and "God"
(E) the British government needed to jettison its preconceptions and reorganize according to Enlightenment principles

113. All of the following are true of Francis Bacon EXCEPT that he

(A) believed that science and politics were incompatible
(B) predicted that the scientific method would lead to social progress
(C) is sometimes considered the founder of empiricism
(D) spread the prestige of the scientific method
(E) wrote *The New Atlantis*, a scientific utopia

114. Women's involvement in European science in the 1600s was

(A) seen in every institution as increasing numbers of women were trained as scientists

(B) encouraged by monarchs who wished to foster scientific studies

(C) limited to biology and chemistry

(D) limited by women's lack of access to university education

(E) epitomized by the work of Elena Cornaro Piscopia

115. Hugo Grotius is associated with the

(A) concept of natural law

(B) invention of the microscope

(C) solution to Kepler's problem

(D) classification system for species of plant and animal life

(E) discovery of phosphorus in 1669

116. All of the following were improvements in nautical technology that aided the European age of exploration (c. 1400–1600) EXCEPT

(A) the metal astrolabe

(B) the magnetic compass

(C) caravels

(D) lateen sails

(E) the sextant

117. Nicolaus Copernicus

(A) discovered that the orbits of the planets were elliptical, rather than circular

(B) addressed his written work to a broad audience of nobles and merchants

(C) was forced into exile in the Dutch Republic for his views

(D) began the astronomical revolution by arguing that the earth and planets revolved around the sun

(E) attacked the Ptolemaic account of heliocentrism

118. Enlightenment thinkers generally believed all of the following EXCEPT

(A) even social problems can be solved using a scientific approach

(B) individuals have the power to judge the world using reason

(C) a society's laws exist to avenge crimes

(D) what is natural is also good and reasonable

(E) human nature can be improved through further education

119. All of the following are true of the *Encylopédie* EXCEPT that

(A) Denis Diderot played a major role in its creation
(B) it helped prepare the intellectual climate for the French Revolution
(C) the support of Louis XV played a key role in its publication
(D) it infuriated the Jesuits, who attacked it as irreligious
(E) the first volume appeared in 1751

120. "During the time men live without a common power to keep them all in awe, they are in that condition which is called war; and such a war, as is of every man, against every man. . . . In such condition, there is no place for industry, . . . no arts, no letters, no society, and which is worst of all, continual fear, and danger of violent death. And the life of man solitary, poor, nasty, brutish, and short."

The author of this quotation is

(A) John Locke
(B) Jean-Jacques Rousseau
(C) George Berkeley
(D) Montesquieu
(E) Thomas Hobbes

CHAPTER 6

Colonial North and South America

121. From 1700 to 1709, people in Great Britain used 4 pounds of sugar per person per year. From 1800 to 1809, they were using 18 pounds of sugar per person per year. Most of this sugar was produced by

(A) slave labor in Brazil
(B) indentured servants in the Chesapeake
(C) free labor in Louisiana
(D) slave labor on Caribbean plantations
(E) haciendas in New Granada

122. All of the following are true of the Treaty of Tordesillas EXCEPT that it

(A) was widely ignored by England, France, and the Dutch Republic
(B) awarded all of South America to Spain
(C) was based on a papal bull issued by Pope Alexander VI
(D) was signed a few years after Christopher Columbus's first voyage
(E) awarded Africa and India to Portugal

123. The incident that gave the Spanish control over Peru is known as the

(A) Battle of Pichincha
(B) Battle of Tenochtitlán
(C) Battle of Ayacucho
(D) First Battle of Guararapes
(E) Battle of Cajamarca

124. The *encomienda* was a system that

(A) was used by the Spanish crown in the early 1600s
(B) attempted to protect Native workers from local exploitation
(C) was supposed to instruct Natives in the Spanish language and the Catholic faith
(D) was effectively suppressed by the New Laws of 1542
(E) was initiated by Spanish colonists without authority from Spain

125. In 1680, the wealthiest British colony in the Western Hemisphere was

(A) Barbados
(B) Jamaica
(C) Virginia
(D) Massachusetts
(E) Canada

126. Bartolomé de Las Casas

(A) was a Jesuit who investigated the flora and fauna of New Granada
(B) worked all his life to end the enslavement of Africans
(C) lobbied for the New Laws of 1542 as a way to help Native peoples
(D) advocated the expansion of the *encomienda* system as the best way to achieve equality in Spanish America
(E) wrote books arguing that the subjugation of the Indians was warranted because of their sins as pagans and their low level of civilization

127. The *repartimiento* system

(A) was replaced by the *encomienda* system
(B) forbade the payment of wages to Natives in Spanish America
(C) created slavery-like conditions in the silver mines of 16th-century Peru
(D) was a tribute-labor system unique to Spanish South America
(E) thrived in the early 1500s

128. All of the following are true of indentured servants in the Chesapeake EXCEPT that

(A) most of them were female
(B) they made up about three out of every four English migrants to the Chesapeake during the 1600s
(C) half of all indentured servants died before receiving their freedom
(D) they usually agreed to work for a master for four to seven years
(E) an indentured servant could produce as much as five times his or her purchase price in a single year

129. In the complex caste system devised by the Spanish in colonial Latin America, the order of the hierarchy, from highest to lowest, was

(A) *criollos, peninsulares, mulattos, indios, mestizos*
(B) *peninsulares, mestizos, criollos, indios, mulattos*
(C) *peninsulares, mestizos, criollos, mulattos, indios*
(D) *peninsulares, criollos, mestizos, indios, mulattos*
(E) *peninsulares, criollos, mestizos, mulattos, indios*

130. "For we must consider that we shall be as a city upon a hill. The eyes of all people are upon us, so that if we shall deal falsely with our God in this work we have undertaken, . . . we shall be made a story and a byword throughout the world."

The author of this statement is

(A) William Bradford
(B) Roger Williams
(C) Jonathan Edwards
(D) John Winthrop
(E) Cotton Mather

131. All of the following are true about maroons EXCEPT that

(A) they were runaway slaves who formed independent settlements
(B) the Black Seminoles were an example of a maroon community in North America
(C) the maroon settlement of Palmares in Brazil had more than 20,000 residents
(D) they formed long-lasting communities in the rugged interior of Jamaica
(E) they were common in Brazil but rarely existed in Spanish America

132. New England colonists differed from Chesapeake colonists in that

(A) New England settlers were not members of the Church of England
(B) the New England colonies were settled purely for religious reasons
(C) the Chesapeake colonies were less tolerant of religious differences
(D) there were fewer women in Chesapeake colonies
(E) no Africans were brought to New England as slaves

133. The Revolt of the Comuneros (c. 1717–c. 1735)

(A) was the only revolt against Spanish colonial administration in South America in the 18th century

(B) led to the collapse of the New Granada government and its replacement of *peninsulares* with *mestizos*

(C) was a serious rising in Paraguay against Spanish authority in South America

(D) was an attack by the Jesuit *reducciones* against the viceroys of Peru

(E) overthrew the rule of Ferdinand Momp' de Zayas, leading to two centuries of anarchy in Panama

134. All of the following are true of the Dominion of New England EXCEPT that

(A) it included New Jersey

(B) its formation was instigated by James II

(C) it abolished existing charters and legislative assemblies

(D) it had no permanent effects

(E) it fell apart after the Glorious Revolution of 1688

135. The Spanish-Colombian naturalist who in the 1700s assembled one of the richest botanical collections in the world was

(A) José Celestino Mutis

(B) Pedro Mesia de la Cerda

(C) Alexander von Humboldt

(D) José de Acosta

(E) Ignacije Szentmartony

136. All of the following are associated with the Spanish conquest of the Aztec Empire EXCEPT

(A) Hernán Cortés

(B) Montezuma II

(C) Bernal Díaz del Castillo

(D) La Malinche

(E) Juan de Betanzos

137. In 1654, 23 Dutch Jews fled to New York and became the first Jews in North America. The area they fled from was

(A) Surinam

(B) Dutch Guyana

(C) Brazil

(D) Aruba

(E) Curaçao

138. How did Puritans differ from Pilgrims?

    (A) Puritans were not Protestants.

    (B) Puritans remained members of the Church of England.

    (C) Puritans believed in antinomianism.

    (D) Puritans were not persecuted in England.

    (E) Puritans tolerated religious dissent.

139. Native populations of Central and South America

    (A) endured hard economic times because of the mestizo system

    (B) avoided the worst effects of European colonization because Europeans enslaved Africans

    (C) suffered massive population declines because of the European invasion

    (D) supported the *encomienda* system as their best way to advance in difficult circumstances

    (E) initially suffered huge population declines but saw a considerable rebound after 1550

140. The first slaves came to British North America in

    (A) 1589

    (B) 1619

    (C) 1649

    (D) 1679

    (E) 1709

141. The first important cash crop in British North America was

    (A) cotton

    (B) indigo

    (C) rice

    (D) tobacco

    (E) sugar

142. The economic philosophy of mercantilism holds that economic power resides primarily in

    (A) surplus manpower and control over raw materials

    (B) control of hard currency and a positive trade balance

    (C) the ability to extend and receive credit at favorable interest rates

    (D) domination of the slave trade and control of the Atlantic system

    (E) the ability to compete successfully in free markets

143. In about 1800, the population of Spanish America was approximately 17 million. How many do historians estimate were *mestizos* and *mulattos*?

(A) 1.5 million
(B) 3.5 million
(C) 5.5 million
(D) 7.5 million
(E) 9.5 million

144. The Great Awakening in British North America was significant because it

(A) unified Protestants under one denomination
(B) emphasized rationalism over emotionalism
(C) was a unifying experience for colonists
(D) led to a decline in church membership
(E) detracted from the demand for higher education

145. All of the following statements are true regarding cities in North America during the colonial era EXCEPT

(A) poor sanitation left colonial cities vulnerable to epidemics
(B) religious and ethnic diversity was greater in colonial cities than in the countryside
(C) most large colonial cities grew around a seaport
(D) cities served as the cultural centers of America
(E) as commerce expanded, the wealth of artisans and laborers grew more rapidly than that of merchants

CHAPTER 7

An Age of Revolutions

146. The Grito de Dolores ("Cry of Dolores") was uttered by

(A) Miguel Hidalgo
(B) José Maria Morelos
(C) Agustín de Iturbide
(D) Benito Juárez
(E) Francisco Madero

147. Before 1787, the French monarchy

(A) showed many signs that it was in trouble
(B) seemed just as securely established as ever
(C) was suffering because of a century-long decline in living standards
(D) was becoming increasingly authoritarian under Louis XVI
(E) was regularly denounced by patriots throughout Europe

148. On 9 Thermidor, Year II,

(A) Maximilien Robespierre was arrested
(B) the French Republic was established
(C) the French citizen army showed its worth by defeating the Austrians at Valmy
(D) the Bastille was stormed
(E) Napoleon Bonaparte staged a coup that overthrew the Directory

149. The turning point of the American Revolution was the Battle of

(A) Trenton
(B) Lexington
(C) Yorktown
(D) Bunker Hill
(E) Saratoga

150. The Tennis Court Oath

 (A) occurred after the attack on the Bastille

 (B) was affirmed in a voice vote by the Estates General

 (C) stated that political authority derived from the people and not the king

 (D) was a declaration by the French nobility in support of Louis XVI

 (E) took place at the opening meeting of the Estates General in the royal tennis court in the Versailles Palace

151. Which of the following remained constant in France during the ancien régime, the French Revolution, and rule by Napoleon?

 (A) legal privileges for the nobility

 (B) centralization of the state

 (C) universal male suffrage

 (D) public executions by guillotine

 (E) special privileges for the Catholic Church

152. All of the following are true regarding the French Declaration of the Rights of Man (1789) EXCEPT that it

 (A) asserted that excessive private property violates the equality of men

 (B) stated that men are born free and remain free and equal in rights

 (C) declared that the rule of law is necessary for the proper functioning of society

 (D) endorsed the principle that all citizens are presumed innocent until proven guilty

 (E) did not make any explicit statement about the rights or status of women

153. "Till women are more rationally educated, the progress in human virtue and improvement in knowledge must receive continual checks. . . . If women be educated for dependence; that is, to act according to the will of another fallible being, and submit, right or wrong, to power, where are we to stop?"

The 18th-century author of this quotation was

 (A) Jean Elliot

 (B) George Sand

 (C) Germaine de Staël

 (D) Mary Wollstonecraft

 (E) Marie-Antoinette

154. In his essay "On Liberty" (1859), John Stuart Mill wrote, "If all mankind minus one were of one opinion, mankind would be no more justified in silencing that one person than he, if he had the power, would be justified in silencing mankind." This idea is best represented in the

(A) Declaration of the Rights of Man
(B) Fifth Amendment to the US Constitution
(C) Declaration of Independence
(D) First Amendment to the US Constitution
(E) Articles of Confederation

155. Napoleon might be called an heir of the French Revolution because he

(A) spread the ideas of equality of law and religious toleration throughout Europe
(B) created an absolute monarchy in France
(C) gave the Catholic Church control over European religious matters
(D) stressed the importance of birth as a criterion for advancement
(E) denounced the idea of an aristocracy of merit

156. Which estate began the French Revolution against the monarchy?

(A) First Estate
(B) Second Estate
(C) Third Estate
(D) Fourth Estate
(E) Fifth Estate

157. All of the following are true regarding Simón Bolívar EXCEPT that

(A) he declared himself dictator in 1828 and barely escaped assassination the next night
(B) his victory at Boyacá in 1819 capped one of the greatest military campaigns in history
(C) he advocated a united South America
(D) he detested the French Revolution as an example of what might happen if the masses gained power
(E) he wrote *La Carta de Jamaica* to justify revolution and republican government in Spanish America

158. All of the following were results of the French Revolution EXCEPT

(A) the Declaration of the Rights of Man
(B) the end of feudalism in France
(C) restrictions on the independence of the Catholic Church
(D) creation of a stable, limited monarchy in France
(E) the emancipation of the Jews of France

159. Eric Williams's thesis suggested that the

(A) history of the world is a result of impersonal economic forces with the sole exception of Napoleon

(B) abolition of the slave trade was a result of the superior morality of the British

(C) slave trade and Caribbean sugar plantations created the Industrial Revolution

(D) United States already possessed the dominant economy in the world in 1800

(E) British opposition to Napoleon was primarily economic and not political

160. One of the major goals of the authors of the Articles of Confederation was to

(A) weaken the American people's primary loyalty to their individual states

(B) give the legislative branch control of interstate commerce

(C) model the new government after the successful system in Great Britain

(D) limit the ability of the national government to oppress the people

(E) ensure the easy movement of commerce between states

161. Under the Napoleon's Civil Code, women

(A) were worse off than they had been before the Revolution

(B) were better off than they had been before the Revolution

(C) were about the same as they had been before the Revolution

(D) could no longer divorce their husbands

(E) could now sue in court, and sell their own property

162. The Preamble to the United States Constitution

(A) established the principle of checks and balances

(B) proclaimed a Bill of Rights

(C) created a basic framework for the separation of powers

(D) listed the positive goals of the new constitution

(E) announced that the national government would draw its power directly from the states

163. All of the following were causes of the Industrial Revolution in England EXCEPT that

(A) England possessed excellent supplies of iron and coal

(B) the agricultural revolution in England led to surplus farm population

(C) the English elite had excess capital to invest as well as entrepreneurial talent

(D) the political system was stable because it was built on universal male suffrage

(E) England possessed good harbors and excellent access to trade routes

164. All of the following are associated with the liberation of South American colonies from Spanish rule in the early 1800s EXCEPT

(A) Simón Bolívar

(B) José de San Martín

(C) Bernardo O'Higgins

(D) Antonio José de Sucre

(E) Valeriano Weyler

165. All of the following are true of the Haitian Revolution EXCEPT that

(A) it received support from US President Thomas Jefferson

(B) it culminated in an independent Haiti and an end to slavery in the nation

(C) it is the only example of a successful long-term slave revolt

(D) the hero of the revolt was François-Dominique Toussaint Louverture

(E) Napoleon sent a 20,000-man army to Haiti but failed to retain the colony

166. The Treaty of Paris (1783) contained all of the following provisions EXCEPT

(A) American retention of colonial fishing rights off the Canadian coast

(B) British unconditional recognition of America as an independent country

(C) the Mississippi River as the western boundary of America

(D) a promise by America to honor land claims by Loyalists

(E) forgiveness of all colonial American debts owed to Great Britain

167. The person most responsible for devising the settlement at the Congress of Vienna was the

(A) French prince Talleyrand
(B) Austrian prince Metternich
(C) British prime minister Castlereagh
(D) Russian king Alexander I
(E) Austrian emperor Francis I

168. The founder of modern chemistry was

(A) Carl Linnaeus
(B) Antoine Lavoisier
(C) Mary Anning
(D) Georges Cuvier
(E) Charles Lyell

169. All of the following are true regarding the early Industrial Revolution in the late 1700s EXCEPT that

(A) James Hargreaves invented the spinning jenny in 1765
(B) in 1769, Richard Arkwright invented the spinning frame
(C) Samuel Crompton invented the spinning mule in 1779
(D) the operation and maintenance of spinning jennies often became the work of child laborers
(E) textile factories first appeared in the United States in Lowell, Massachusetts, in the 1820s

170. All of the following were grievances against King George III listed in the American Declaration of Independence EXCEPT that he had

(A) imposed taxes without colonial assent
(B) used merciless Indian savages against the colonists on the frontier
(C) burnt colonial towns and destroyed the lives of Americans
(D) forced the slave trade on the American colonies
(E) kept standing armies in the colonies in times of peace without the consent of colonial legislatures

171. The slave trade to North America

(A) decreased every decade in the 1700s
(B) increased in the beginning of the 1700s, but decreased as the American Revolution grew closer
(C) ended after the American Revolution brought freedom to the people of North America
(D) peaked in the decade from 1761 to 1770
(E) rivaled the slave trade to the British Caribbean in the 1700s

172. All of the following characteristics are associated with Romanticism in literature EXCEPT

(A) a fascination with history

(B) the beauty and mystery of nature

(C) an emphasis on clarity, order, and balance

(D) a fixation on death

(E) a stress on the irrational depths of human nature

173. The American colonists objected to taxation by Parliament in the 1760s because

(A) they were paying more than their British counterparts

(B) the new taxes were permanent

(C) they desired to break away from Great Britain

(D) they viewed it as an internal tax

(E) colonial tax collectors were getting rich

174. Among elites in 18th-century Europe and the United States, children were

(A) seen and not heard; harsh discipline was the favored method of child rearing

(B) considered miniature adults with no specific needs of their own

(C) left to their own devices to develop freely without much supervision

(D) a topic of increasing interest because it was believed that an adult's character was formed in childhood

(E) demonstrating increasing self-discipline because of the pervasive republican ideology of the late 1700s

175. Which of the following statements is true regarding the role of patriot women in the 1760s and 1770s in America?

(A) Because the Boston Tea Party primarily affected Massachusetts, women's tea boycotts were restricted to New England.

(B) Women produced so much homespun that it compensated for the loss of British imports.

(C) Patriot women opposed both the Townshend Acts and the Tea Act.

(D) The Daughters of Liberty were organized in response to the Sugar Act of 1764.

(E) The use of homespun played a crucial role in the ability of the Continental Congress to supply uniforms for patriot forces.

176. The Berbice Slave Uprising began in 1763 when slaves on two plantations rebelled and took control of the region. Many plantations fell to the slaves, led by Cuffy (now the national hero of the country), and half the white European population fled. The country is

(A) Guyana
(B) Brazil
(C) Barbados
(D) Haiti
(E) Colombia

177. The British leader of the movement to abolish the slave trade was

(A) John Wilkes
(B) George Grenville
(C) George Canning
(D) John Wesley
(E) William Wilberforce

178. The British Petition of Right guaranteed all of the following rights EXCEPT

(A) no imprisonment without due cause
(B) no taxation without consent of Parliament
(C) no use of martial law in time of peace
(D) no trial without the right to legal counsel
(E) no housing of the military in private homes

179. All of the following were major battles of the Napoleonic Wars EXCEPT

(A) Austerlitz
(B) Sedan
(C) Trafalgar
(D) Jena
(E) Marengo

180. The enclosure movement that was part of the agricultural revolution of the late 1600s and 1700s

(A) led to a decline in population as people lost their land
(B) created enormous political instability, sometimes leading to vast riots
(C) enabled wealthy bourgeoisie to steal the common lands of England in the name of increased agricultural production
(D) did not have a significant impact on the social composition of the countryside
(E) discouraged landless peasants from moving to the cities

CHAPTER 8

19th-Century United States and Europe

181. All of the following were stipulations of the Congress of Vienna EXCEPT

  (A)   France lost all territory conquered by Napoleon
  (B)   Switzerland was declared neutral
  (C)   Russia was given Finland and the Duchy of Warsaw (Poland)
  (D)   a large United Kingdom of the Netherlands was created for the Prince of Orange
  (E)   the Holy Roman Empire was restored as a check to French and Russian power

182. Adam Smith argued that the manufacturing process could be improved when

  (A)   all men possessed individual rights such as freedom of religion
  (B)   men worked in factories on steam-powered machinery
  (C)   the process was broken down into separate operations
  (D)   government played a strong role in overseeing production
  (E)   people abandoned self-interest and instead trusted the "invisible hand" of the market

183. In the *Communist Manifesto*, Karl Marx and Friedrich Engels

  (A)   supported the use of worker's petitions to lead to gradual reform
  (B)   encouraged communists to help the bourgeoisie destroy feudalism
  (C)   advocated the creation of cooperative utopian socialist communities
  (D)   called for communists to work for the downfall of the bourgeoisie
  (E)   opposed industrial capitalism and advocated a return to medieval values

184. All of the following were Union victories in the US Civil War EXCEPT

(A) Vicksburg
(B) Gettysburg
(C) Bull Run
(D) Antietam
(E) New Orleans

185. All of the following are true of the Louisiana Purchase EXCEPT that

(A) Napoleon decided to sell Louisiana after his troops were defeated by the Haitians
(B) the United States originally offered $50 million for the entire Louisiana Purchase
(C) the United States bought one-third of the continent for about 3.5 cents an acre
(D) President Jefferson reversed his previous position on the necessity for strict construction of the US Constitution
(E) the commerce of the United States west of the Appalachians depended on the Mississippi River

186. In Russia, the system of serfdom

(A) impeded the movement of free labor necessary for industrialization
(B) provided labor for industry and the construction of railroads
(C) became less restrictive in the 1830s and 1840s
(D) was accepted by almost everyone as the natural order of things
(E) had basically died out by the 1850s

187. According to Thorstein Veblen, the pursuit of fashion in clothing

(A) was of equal concern to women and men in the "best" circles
(B) was less important in the 1800s than in the 1700s
(C) was time-consuming, expensive, and pointless, and so a sign of leisured wealth
(D) was not considered appropriate for unmarried women
(E) proved that women were not susceptible to the appeal of "conspicuous consumption"

188. All of the following are essential in a modern industrial economy EXCEPT

(A) labor
(B) natural resources
(C) markets
(D) free trade
(E) all of the above

189. What do Brook Farm, the Oneida Community, and New Harmony have in common?

(A) They were religious communities inspired by the Second Great Awakening.

(B) They demonstrated the attraction of socialism to many Americans.

(C) They failed because they practiced political and social equality in their own communities.

(D) They were stops along the Underground Railroad that aided fugitive slaves.

(E) They were utopian communities designed to ameliorate the negative effects of the Industrial Revolution.

190. Employers began using managers to supervise workers in the 1800s because

(A) workers were losing respect for employers and were increasingly difficult to discipline

(B) employers, now exceedingly wealthy, preferred to spend their time in leisure pursuits

(C) businesses had increased in size and complexity and so tasks had to be divided

(D) employers thought that the use of managers would lessen labor friction

(E) managers took over roles previously determined by the market, such as the coordination and allocation of resources

191. All of the following are true of the Mexican-American War EXCEPT that

(A) about 65,000 Americans died, more than in the Vietnam and the Iraq/Afghanistan Wars combined

(B) although the war began over the disputed boundary of Texas, the United States took one-third of Mexican territory that was unconnected with the dispute

(C) the United States invaded Mexico and occupied Mexico City

(D) it was indirectly a major cause of the Civil War

(E) the Treaty of Guadalupe Hidalgo opened the door to American trade with Asia

192. The Peterloo Massacre was

    (A) a labor dispute that led to four days of bloody rioting in Great Britain

    (B) an anti-British protest in Ireland that was brutally suppressed by British troops

    (C) the result of a demonstration in Britain to reform parliamentary representation

    (D) an assault by the British army against supporters of the Paris Commune in 1871

    (E) an ironic term for the filibuster against debates to end the Corn Laws

193. The War of 1812 led to all of the following results EXCEPT

    (A) the end of the possibility of Native American military resistance to the American invasion of their lands

    (B) a heightened feeling of American nationalism

    (C) the strengthening of the American militia system after the militias' superior performance in the war

    (D) the growth of American industry

    (E) a stronger sense of Canadian nationalism

194. The birthrate fell in 19th-century Europe and the United States partially because

    (A) governments were urging people to have smaller families

    (B) large numbers of young men were dying in wars

    (C) birth control was more widely available

    (D) contagious diseases for children were spreading at unprecedented rates

    (E) men no longer accepted the basic ideas of the cult of domesticity

195. All of the following are true of the Reconstruction Era EXCEPT that

    (A) it resulted in the one-party "solid South"

    (B) African Americans were awarded land as reparations for their enslavement

    (C) it failed to reorder the social and economic structure of the South in a meaningful way

    (D) it led to the passage of three major amendments to the Constitution

    (E) it was incredibly lenient

196. The invention of the Bessemer process in 1856 and the open-hearth furnace in 1868 led to all of the following EXCEPT

(A) locating large steel mills by rivers to make it easier to transport the steel

(B) an increase in the scale of business, requiring enormous amounts of capital

(C) the obsolescence of the skilled jobs of the puddler, heater, and hand roller

(D) the increased production of harder and more durable steel with less labor

(E) the acceleration of the managerial revolution

197. In the United States and Europe, lithographs

(A) were produced in very small numbers during the 1830s and 1840s

(B) were concerned primarily with political subjects

(C) helped increase awareness of social and political issues

(D) were of little interest to most middle-class people except as a curiosity

(E) were unprofitable for the American firm of Currier and Ives, who instead made a fortune by producing stereographs

198. All of the following were examples of massive labor unrest in the United States in the late 1800s EXCEPT the

(A) New York City Orange Riots (1870–1871)

(B) railroad strikes of 1877

(C) Haymarket Affair, in Chicago (1886)

(D) Homestead Affair, in Pennsylvania (1892)

(E) Pullman strike (1894)

199. All of the following are true of Giuseppe Mazzini EXCEPT that he

(A) played a major role in the revolutions of 1848

(B) founded Young Italy

(C) supported Giuseppe Garibaldi's expedition to Sicily

(D) agreed with Camillo Benso di Cavour on the best strategy to unify Italy

(E) was an outstanding figure of the Risorgimento

200. The Monroe Doctrine

    (A) is standing international law and must be obeyed

    (B) is an American foreign policy position and nothing more

    (C) was cosigned by other countries in the Western Hemisphere

    (D) was approved by the US Congress

    (E) demonstrated the military power of the United States under President James Monroe

201. The British Reform Bill of 1832

    (A) allowed all adult men to vote

    (B) abolished most rotten boroughs

    (C) allowed most adult men to vote

    (D) allowed wealthy women to vote

    (E) removed the ownership of property as a prerequisite for voting

202. The Hudson River School refers to

    (A) a utopian educational experiment in upstate New York

    (B) a faction of New York politicians who helped form the Second Party System

    (C) an informal association of Knickerbocker writers from east-central New York who attacked their more liberal opponents in jointly written satirical verses

    (D) a collection of ministers aligned with the Second Great Awakening who spread reform throughout the Burned Over District

    (E) an informal group of painters who glorified the beauties of American scenery

203. The 1871 Paris Commune

    (A) energized the worker's movement, making it stronger than ever

    (B) was widely imitated throughout western Europe

    (C) was peacefully put down by the French government

    (D) developed a wide array of political clubs and self-managed, cooperative workshops

    (E) was violently destroyed by Prussian troops

204. All of the following were characteristics of the walking city of the early 1800s EXCEPT

(A) congestion
(B) a clear distinction between city and country
(C) a mixture of commercial, office, or residential functions
(D) a short commute for most workers
(E) the most fashionable addresses were located farthest from the center of the city

205. All of the following are true of the Crimean War EXCEPT that

(A) the British, French, and Ottoman Empire fought on the same side
(B) the war drew Austria and Russia, Europe's two conservative powers, closer together
(C) more than 700,000 men died, two-thirds from disease and starvation
(D) the peace of Paris checked Russian expansion into southeastern Europe
(E) the US government and most Americans were anti-British

206. The popularity of Lourdes as a site of Christian pilgrimage revealed

(A) the strong hold that Catholicism still had on almost the entire European population
(B) the strength of religious belief among women
(C) the positive impact of Pope Pius IX's *Syllabus of Errors*
(D) the inability of the church to adapt to the modern world
(E) the continuing anti-Semitism of Catholicism for promoting the "blood libel"

207. All of the following composers used music to encourage nationalistic feeling in the 1800s EXCEPT

(A) Richard Wagner
(B) Antonín Dvorák
(C) Edvard Grieg
(D) Luigi Cherubini
(E) Isaac Albéniz

208. The *cult of domesticity*
- (A) referred to a woman's role as homemaker and mother
- (B) expanded the influence of women outside the house into law and medicine
- (C) led to the creation of communal societies devoted to domestic improvement
- (D) implied a religious belief in perfectibility
- (E) naturally degraded women

209. When European and American governments allowed professions such as medicine and law to regulate themselves,
- (A) the number of abuses in those fields rose dramatically
- (B) they became more exclusive and more specialized
- (C) they became more open (especially to women) because they were based on merit
- (D) they were less likely to require training or specialized knowledge
- (E) they tried to return to the older middle-class emphasis on status through family position and local reputation

210. In the 1800s, American businessmen exalted individual initiative and laissez-faire economics. However, they demanded all of the following from the government EXCEPT
- (A) high tariffs
- (B) generous land grants to railroads
- (C) loan programs with low interest rates specifically for large businesses
- (D) state power to break strikes and impose labor discipline
- (E) constitutional protection for corporations

211. "The world is too much with us; late and soon,
Getting and spending, we lay waste our powers
Little we see in Nature that is ours;
We have given our hearts away, a sordid boon!"

The author of this quotation is
- (A) William Wordsworth
- (B) Alfred Tennyson
- (C) Henry Wadsworth Longfellow
- (D) John Clare
- (E) Robert Burns

212. Urbanization in the 1800s

(A) was a major cause of the temporary decline of international migration

(B) took place in Germany before Great Britain

(C) resulted primarily from a decline in the death rate due to improved public health and knowledge of the germ theory

(D) led to cholera epidemics

(E) affected western Europe but not eastern Europe

213. "Brothers, the white men want more than our hunting grounds; they wish to kill our warriors; they would even kill our old men, women and little ones. . . . Brothers, if you do not unite with us, they will first destroy us, and then you will fall an easy prey to them. They have destroyed many nations of red men because they were not united, because they were not friends to each other."

The author of this quotation is

(A) Crazy Horse

(B) Chief Joseph

(C) Geronimo

(D) Osceola

(E) Tecumseh

214. Florence Nightingale

(A) was a model of female domesticity because she cared for others

(B) escaped the role of female domesticity by organizing a nursing service in the Crimea

(C) presented herself as an exceptional woman and urged other women to avoid nursing for the military

(D) was widely despised for acting in an unladylike manner

(E) was famous because she was the only woman to serve as a battlefield nurse in the Crimean War

215. The decision of seven Southern states to secede from the United States between December 1860 and February 1861 was

(A) precipitated by the election of Abraham Lincoln to the presidency

(B) supported by specific references to the United States Constitution

(C) cheered by most Republicans who believed "let erring sisters depart in peace"

(D) applauded by all remaining states in which slavery was legal

(E) led by Stephen Douglas, who believed Abraham Lincoln had turned into a tyrant

216. All of the following are true of Otto von Bismarck EXCEPT that he

(A) presided over the unification of Germany

(B) drove Austria from the German Confederation

(C) was known as the Iron Chancellor

(D) consistently opposed all liberal positions

(E) published the Ems Dispatch in order to manipulate France into a war with Prussia

217. The term *vertical integration* refers to

(A) Reconstruction-era efforts to assimilate newly freed slaves into American society at various social class levels

(B) an architectural school of the late 1800s that hoped to blend skyscrapers with the natural landscape

(C) the industrial practice of assigning workers a single, repetitive task in order to maximize productivity

(D) a business's control of all aspects of an industry, from production of raw materials to delivery of finished goods

(E) the belief that wealthy citizens have a moral obligation to engage in philanthropic acts and not just opt out of society

218. The Declaration of Sentiments, written in Seneca Falls in 1848, complained that men had oppressed women in all the following ways EXCEPT that

(A) women suffered taxation without representation

(B) women were unable to obtain a legal divorce

(C) married men had more economic and legal rights than married women

(D) women were unable to obtain an equal education as men

(E) women were denied the right to vote

219. In 1859, cotton production made up approximately what percentage of American exports (by dollar value)?

(A) 15 percent

(B) 30 percent

(C) 45 percent

(D) 60 percent

(E) 75 percent

220. "What good man would prefer a country covered with forests and ranged by a few thousand savages to our extensive Republic, studded with cities, towns, and prosperous farms? . . . The waves of population and civilization are rolling to the westward, and we now propose to acquire the countries occupied by the red men of the South and West by a fair exchange, and, at the expense of the United States, to send them to a land where their existence may be prolonged and perhaps made perpetual."

The author of this quotation is

(A) Henry Clay
(B) Davy Crockett
(C) Andrew Jackson
(D) Sequoyah
(E) Abraham Lincoln

221. All of the following made instrumental contributions to the development of the germ theory EXCEPT

(A) Louis Pasteur
(B) Ignaz Semmelweis
(C) Robert Koch
(D) Karl Friedrich Schinkel
(E) Joseph Lister

222. Jim Crow laws were

(A) declared unconstitutional in the US Supreme Court case of *Plessy v. Ferguson*
(B) passed by southern whites after Reconstruction
(C) common in the northern states
(D) initially instituted so that white southerners could steal black land
(E) detrimental, but did create good schools for former slaves

223. All of the following were part of the realist movement in the 1800s and early 1900s EXCEPT

(A) Émile Zola
(B) Honoré de Balzac
(C) Stephen Crane
(D) Theodore Dreiser
(E) Herman Melville

224. All of the following are true of Poland in the 1800s EXCEPT

   (A) Polish national identity always trumped class interests
   (B) present-day Poland was divided between Prussia, Russia, and Austria
   (C) the Russians constantly feared the outbreak of Polish nationalist agitation
   (D) only in Austrian Galicia did Poles enjoy meaningful autonomy
   (E) the center of the Polish nationalist movement was in Paris

225. The 1848 revolutions in Italy, Hungary, Austria, and the German states

   (A) differed from the revolution in France in that they were successful
   (B) differed from the revolution in France because they did not call for greater political participation
   (C) followed a similar pattern to the revolution in France, with early success followed by repression
   (D) were similar to the revolution in France in that they were primarily concerned with issues affecting the working classes
   (E) were similar to the revolution in France because they were doomed by ethnic divisions

226. The Russian novelist Leo Tolstoy believed that regeneration in Russia could only come about through

   (A) revolution
   (B) absolute obedience to the tsar
   (C) spiritual renewal
   (D) modernization
   (E) adhering closely to the traditional Russian Orthodox Church

227. Georges Haussmann's renovations in Paris

   (A) fostered harmony between the classes because they involved the construction of new housing for the rich and poor
   (B) encouraged greater interaction between rich and poor as boulevards joined neighborhoods
   (C) created a city that was intended to serve as a symbol of the grandeur of the regime
   (D) did not interest realist painters
   (E) preserved much of medieval Paris in an attempt to foster the newly developing tourist trade in the late 1800s

228. The man most responsible for the development of the steam railroad was

(A) Peter Cooper
(B) Henry Fox Talbot
(C) James Watt
(D) Jethro Tull
(E) George Stephenson

229. In the 1800s, the "Sick Man of Europe" refers to

(A) Russia
(B) the Ottoman Empire
(C) Germany
(D) Italy
(E) Spain

230. All of the following are true regarding department stores EXCEPT that

(A) they encouraged a capitalist ideology such as bargaining over prices
(B) they encouraged impulse buying
(C) their presence moved women out of the domestic sphere into a new public role
(D) they promoted a luxurious world open to everyone
(E) many people's first experience of elevators and plate glass was at a department store

CHAPTER 9

Southeastern Asia

231. All of the following are true regarding Captain James Cook EXCEPT that he

(A) searched for the Northwest Passage near the Bering Strait in Alaska

(B) played a major role in overcoming the problem of scurvy

(C) was the first European to land on Antarctica

(D) was killed in an incident in Hawaii

(E) mapped lands from New Zealand to Hawaii in greater detail and on a scale not previously achieved

232. Zheng He

(A) explored new lands for the Qing dynasty

(B) discovered entirely new trade routes in the Pacific and Indian Oceans

(C) was the last Chinese navigator to sail in the Indian Ocean until the 1800s

(D) landed in America in 1421

(E) began regular commercial contact between China and eastern Africa

233. The time of creation in the mythology of the Australian Aborigines is called

(A) the Dreaming

(B) the Popol Vuh

(C) the Stolen Mist

(D) the Doll'i

(E) the Water Light Time

234. The center of Portuguese India was in

(A) Puducherry (formerly Pondicherry)
(B) Goa
(C) Kochi (formerly Cochin)
(D) Coromandel
(E) Tharangambadi (formerly Tranquebar)

235. All of the following are true regarding Ferdinand Magellan's expedition EXCEPT that

(A) it claimed the Philippines for Portugal
(B) Magellan did not survive to complete the expedition
(C) it was the first European expedition to circumnavigate the earth
(D) only one ship and 18 men who set out returned to Spain
(E) it took place between 1519 and 1522

236. The author of the novel *Max Havelaar*, which exposed the abuses of Dutch colonial rule in Indonesia, was

(A) Muhammad Yamin
(B) Marah Roesli
(C) Merari Siregar
(D) Multatuli
(E) Nur Sutan Iskandar

237. Which of the following statements is true regarding the use of Australia as a penal colony?

(A) By 1871, the majority of people in Australia were the descendants of convicts.
(B) The British sent more than 1.6 million convicts to settle Australia.
(C) The First Fleet established the first permanent European colony on Australia.
(D) The first convicts arrived in Australia in 1824.
(E) The initial reason for settling convicts in Australia was Charles Dickens's depictions of the correctional facilities of England.

238. The Maluku Islands (Moluccas)

(A) were the place of origin of salt and pepper
(B) eventually became part of British Malaysia
(C) dominated the spice trade into the late 20th century
(D) were uninhabited until settled by the Portuguese in the 1500s
(E) were conquered by the Dutch in the 1600s

239. The Hawaiian ruler who conquered the Hawaiian Islands, formally established the kingdom of Hawaii, and helped preserve Hawaii's independence was

(A) Kamehameha I
(B) Kaahumanu II
(C) Keouawahine I
(D) Liliuokalani
(E) Kapaakea (Caesar Kaluaiku Kapaakea)

240. All of the following were Europeans who played a role in the European exploration of Australia EXCEPT

(A) Dirk Hartog
(B) Willem Janszoon
(C) William Barents
(D) Abel Tasman
(E) William Dampier

241. The Second Burmese Empire ruled Burma between about 1500 and 1752 and briefly created the largest empire in the history of southeastern Asia. Its capital was at

(A) Rangoon (Yangon)
(B) Toungoo
(C) Shwebo (Ratanasingha)
(D) Mandalay
(E) Sittwe (formerly Akyab)

242. The Manila-Acapulco galleon trade

(A) provided the food necessary for the colonists of New Spain
(B) led to inflation in Ming China
(C) used ships that took about a month to sail across the Pacific
(D) revealed China's inward turn after the expeditions of Zheng He
(E) carried Chinese silks and porcelain around the Cape of Good Hope to Europe

243. All of the following are true of Sikhism EXCEPT that

(A) it is a polytheistic religion
(B) the holy city is Amritsar
(C) the vast majority of Sikhs live in the Punjab region of India
(D) it is the world's fifth-largest organized religion
(E) the holy scripture is known as the Adi Granth

244. A musical ensemble from Indonesia that features a variety of instruments such as xylophones, drums, and gongs is known as a

(A) batik
(B) silat
(C) randai
(D) gamelan
(E) wayang

245. The battle that led to English dominance over Bengal and ultimately England's dominance over all of India was the

(A) Battle of Plassey
(B) Battle of Colachel
(C) Third Battle of Carnatic
(D) siege of Seringapatam
(E) Battle of Jamrud

246. Which of the following statements is true regarding the societies of Oceania?

(A) The Australians based their society on the cultivation of various grains.
(B) The Australians remained isolated from other people.
(C) The Polynesians maintained their prosperous society without the knowledge of metallurgy.
(D) New Zealanders carried on active long-distance trade.
(E) Polynesian societies developed few class distinctions.

247. All of the following are true regarding the Ayutthaya kingdom EXCEPT that

(A) it lasted for more than four centuries
(B) its capital was located at present-day Bangkok
(C) it expanded to roughly the borders of modern Thailand
(D) the main religion was Theravada Buddhism
(E) it was destroyed by the Burmese in 1767

248. Moai are associated with

(A) Samoa
(B) Tuvalu
(C) Easter Island
(D) New Caledonia
(E) Papua/New Guinea

249. All of the following are true regarding the Joseon (Chosun) dynasty of Korea EXCEPT that it

(A) was known as the Hermit Kingdom
(B) lasted for more than five centuries
(C) fought off an invasion by Toyotomi Hideyoshi
(D) established a new capital at Seoul in 1394
(E) rejected Confucianism in order to encourage a return to Theravada Buddhism

250. The historic city of Malacca (Melaka), once one of the leading commercial centers of southeastern Asia, is in the present-day nation of

(A) Laos
(B) Thailand
(C) Singapore
(D) Malaysia
(E) Indonesia

CHAPTER 10

Imperialism

251. All of the following are types of imperialistic dominance EXCEPT

(A) colonies
(B) protectorates
(C) spheres of influence
(D) economic imperialism
(E) garrison states

252. The number of Congolese killed in the Belgian Congo under the rule of Leopold II is estimated at

(A) 10,000
(B) 100,000
(C) 500,000
(D) 5 million
(E) 10 million

253. All of the following were causes of the so-called Sepoy Mutiny EXCEPT

(A) British land policies
(B) British insensitivity to local customs and religions
(C) the introduction of free market competition undermined traditional power structures and bonds of loyalty
(D) local rivalries between Hindus and Muslims that fanned nationalistic feelings against the raj
(E) the contempt Britain showed for traditional Indian leaders

254. The most famous missionary working in Africa in the 1800s was

(A) Henry Stanley
(B) David Livingstone
(C) Charles Gordon
(D) Anthonio Barroso
(E) Mary Slessor

255. Spectacular victories by indigenous forces over imperialist armies took place at

(A) Plassey and Khartoum
(B) Little Bighorn and Omdurman
(C) Adowa and Isandlwana
(D) Nanking and Kanpur
(E) Khartoum and Wounded Knee

256. All of the following European nations were involved in imperialistic enterprises in New Guinea and New Ireland at the end of the 1800s EXCEPT

(A) Portugal
(B) the Netherlands
(C) Germany
(D) Great Britain
(E) France

257. All of the following were true of the Berlin Conference EXCEPT

(A) no African representatives were present
(B) the signatories called for free trade on the Congo and Niger Rivers
(C) the Principle of Effectivity intensified the scramble for Africa
(D) Portugal's modern weakness as an imperialist power led the delegates to refuse to grant it any colonies
(E) King Leopold II's private claim to the entire Congo Free State was accepted

258. The Anglo-Saxon is "divinely commissioned to be, in a peculiar sense, his brother's keeper. . . . Another marked characteristic of the Anglo-Saxon is what may be called an instinct or genius for colonizing. His unequaled energy, his indomitable perseverance, and his personal independence, made him a pioneer."

The author of this statement is

(A) Mark Twain
(B) Booker T. Washington
(C) Samuel Gompers
(D) Andrew Carnegie
(E) Josiah Strong

259. All of the following nations received so-called spheres of influence in China EXCEPT

(A) Great Britain
(B) the United States
(C) France
(D) Germany
(E) Russia

260. The precipitating incident in the Boer War was the

(A) Fashoda Incident
(B) Muldergate Scandal
(C) Jameson Raid
(D) Natives Land Act
(E) slaughter at Omdurman

261. The primary impulse behind American expansion in the late 1800s was the

(A) aspiration to be a world power like Great Britain
(B) need to find a place to invest surplus capital
(C) desire to find cheap labor to manufacture products
(D) wish to spread democracy to underdeveloped nations
(E) need to find markets for surplus production

262. All of the following concepts were used to justify American and European imperialism EXCEPT

(A) racialism
(B) Social Darwinism
(C) the white man's burden
(D) root hog, or die
(E) ontogeny recapitulates phylogeny

263. "I contend that we are the first race in the world and that the more of the world we inhabit, the better it is for the human race. . . . I believe it to be my duty to God, my Queen and my country to paint the whole map of Africa red, red from the Cape to Cairo. That is my creed, my dream, and my mission."

The author of this quotation is

(A) Theodore Roosevelt
(B) Benjamin Disraeli
(C) William Gladstone
(D) Cecil Rhodes
(E) Paul Kruger

264. All of the following were ideas voiced in the Philippines annexation debate EXCEPT

(A) the role of the United States as God's chosen people to lead in the regeneration of the world

(B) the disadvantages of adding "inferior" people and races to the United States

(C) that if the United States did not annex the Philippines, some other imperialist power would take it

(D) that the area lacked any strategic value

(E) by annexing territories never intended to be states, the United States violated its core belief in self-determination and liberty

265. All of the following were results of European colonialism in Africa EXCEPT that

(A) hospitals were constructed and sanitation improved

(B) there was an increase in the number of Christians in Africa

(C) Africans lost control over their traditional lands

(D) artificial boundaries formed by imperialist powers created ongoing political problems

(E) there was an increase in African food supplies for local consumption

266. All of the following statements are true regarding American economic imperialism in Latin America EXCEPT

(A) The United States exports to Latin America increased from $50 million in 1870s to $300 million in 1914.

(B) The American-owned United Fruit Company owned more than 1 million acres of Central America in 1913.

(C) Porfirio Diaz fought against American economic imperialism and was assassinated in mysterious circumstances.

(D) American-controlled investments in Latin America totaled more than $1 billion in 1914.

(E) By 1910, Americans owned about 43 percent of Mexican property and produced half of Mexico's oil.

267. The British expanded this Asian city in the 1800s until it became one of the leading ports in the world for the export of tin and rubber.

(A) Singapore

(B) Penang

(C) Malacca

(D) Canton

(E) Kuantan

268. The Platt Amendment

(A) declared that the United States would not annex Cuba if it won the Spanish-American War

(B) allowed the United States to intervene in Cuban domestic affairs

(C) was a statement of American policy and nothing more

(D) represented the triumph of the beliefs of José Martí

(E) established political rules that are still in effect

269. By 1914, all of Africa had been divided among European powers except for Liberia and

(A) Ethiopia

(B) Egypt

(C) South Africa

(D) Kenya

(E) Ghana

270. The First Opium War (1839–1842) was caused by

(A) the Chinese refusal to stop the export of opium to British colonies

(B) the British insistence on the need for other European powers to respect Chinese law

(C) the clash in values because of the British insistence on the evils of opium

(D) the restriction of British traders to Shanghai and Guangzhou

(E) China's prohibitions on the importation of opium

271. All of the following are reasons for the New Imperialism EXCEPT

(A) a desire for captive markets

(B) the need for raw materials

(C) intensified nationalism

(D) the increasing need for slaves

(E) advances in medicine and technology

272. Extraterritoriality was an imperialist tool in China because it

(A) allowed European nations to annex parts of China like Hong Kong and Macao

(B) guaranteed that Chinese citizens could be tried in European courts, ensuring they would always be declared guilty if politically expedient

(C) assured that in a dispute with a Chinese person, Europeans had the right to be tried in a court under the laws of his or her own country

(D) permitted imperialist powers to set up governments in treaty ports

(E) sanctioned the purchase of Chinese surplus property and territory by imperialist nationals

273. All of the following were successes of Japanese imperialism EXCEPT the

(A) Sino-Japanese War
(B) Russo-Japanese War
(C) March First Movement
(D) annexation of Korea
(E) annexation of Taiwan

274. The concept of *unequal treaties* is primarily associated with

(A) Mexico
(B) Egypt
(C) South Africa
(D) China
(E) Meiji Japan

275. The Mahdi

(A) formed a democratic Islamic government in the Sudan
(B) revolutionized warfare in the Sudan
(C) was rejected by the Wahhabis because he claimed to be a messianic figure
(D) was defeated by Charles "Chinese" Gordon at Omdurman
(E) won a stunning victory at Khartoum in 1885

276. Who is considered to be the founder of Indian nationalism in the early 1800s?

(A) Vallabhbhai Patel
(B) Ram Mohan Roy
(C) Jawaharlal Nehru
(D) Rajendra Prasad
(E) Badshah Khan

277. Under Benito Juárez, Mexican forces defeated the soldiers of this nation, who attempted to set up a monarchy in Mexico under Maximilian I.

(A) Austria
(B) France
(C) Spain
(D) England
(E) Belgium

278. The Herero and Namaqua genocide, the first genocide of the 20th century, took place in present-day

(A) Namibia
(B) Lesotho
(C) Sierra Leone
(D) Cameroon
(E) South Africa

279. The problem of colonial boundaries is demonstrated by these two nations, who share many cultural values yet have an international border that wedges one country into the middle of the other.

(A) Benin and Togo
(B) Gabon and Equatorial Guinea
(C) Senegal and Gambia
(D) Uganda and Kenya
(E) Lesotho and Swaziland

280. "Any country whose people conduct themselves well can count on our hearty friendship. . . . Chronic wrongdoing, or an impotence which results in a general loosening of the ties of civilized society, may in America, as elsewhere, ultimately require intervention by some civilized nation, and in the Western hemisphere the adherence of the United States to the Monroe Doctrine may force the United States, however reluctantly, in flagrant cases of wrongdoing or impotence, to the exercise of an international police power. . . . Our interests and those of our southern neighbors are in reality identical."

The author of this quotation is

(A) Philander Knox
(B) William Howard Taft
(C) William Jennings Bryan
(D) Theodore Roosevelt
(E) William McKinley

281. Which of the following statements is true regarding the kingdom of Hawaii?

(A) Hawaii was valuable to the United States solely as a coaling station.

(B) By 1884, Americans owned 10 percent of Hawaii's wealth but made up less than 1 percent of the population.

(C) The McKinley Tariff of 1890 gave favorable tariff rates for the sale of Hawaiian products in the United States.

(D) Queen Liliuokalani supported the so-called Bayonet Constitution.

(E) The American ambassador to Hawaii ordered the US Marines to help overthrow the legal government of Hawaii.

282. Which of the following present-day nations was a part of French Indochina?

(A) Singapore

(B) Laos

(C) Burma

(D) Malaysia

(E) Thailand

283. All of the following are true regarding Samoa EXCEPT that

(A) the island was valuable because of its fine harbor and its strategic position

(B) the Samoan crisis was temporarily resolved at the Berlin Conference

(C) the United States, France, and Germany all jockeyed for position in Samoa

(D) a timely hurricane helped prevent hostilities at Samoa in 1889

(E) as of 2012, the American part of Samoa remains a colony of the United States

284. In order to build a canal in Panama, the United States

(A) overthrew the government of Panama

(B) reneged on the Hay-Pauncefote Treaty with Britain

(C) negotiated with Panamanian representatives of the new government

(D) ensured the success of the Panamanian revolt against Colombia

(E) refused to acquire any land in Panama as long as the Panamanian government gave the United States the right to build a canal

285. The Boxer Rebellion

(A) resulted in huge indemnities and foreign troops stationed in Beijing
(B) was opposed by Empress Dowager Cixi, who believed it could not succeed
(C) marked the end of extraterritoriality in China
(D) represented the desires of the growing urban middle classes, who desired secular modernization for China
(E) led to a virtual civil war in southern China

286. All of the following are true regarding the Philippine-American War EXCEPT that

(A) more than 40,000 Filipinos died
(B) Filipinos would not have demanded independence if not for the Spanish-American War
(C) Americans used the same "reconcentration camp" policy that they had condemned in Cuba
(D) the leader of Filipino independence forces was Emilio Aguinaldo
(E) 10 times as many Americans died in the Philippine-American War as in the Spanish-American War

287. The Maori

(A) came to New Zealand from Polynesia in the 1600s
(B) developed a noteworthy warrior culture
(C) fought to preserve their cattle- and sheep-raising lands
(D) played a major role in the independence movement in New Zealand in the early 1900s
(E) were reduced to less than 1,000 people by the British

288. All of the following are true regarding the Cuban Revolution of 1895 EXCEPT that

(A) Cuba and Puerto Rico were the last of Spain's once-extensive Latin American empire
(B) Cuban rebels adopted a deliberate policy of devastating the island so completely that the Spanish would want to leave
(C) the Spanish refused to allow Cuba to trade with the United States
(D) United States popular opinion generally supported the Cuban revolution
(E) the Spanish used a brutal "reconcentration" policy that led to thousands of Cuban deaths

289. The so-called Sepoy Mutiny began in

(A) 1777
(B) 1797
(C) 1817
(D) 1837
(E) 1857

290. All of the following are true regarding the Boer War (South African War) EXCEPT that

(A) the British used reconcentration camps to defeat the Boers
(B) the Boers won a series of early victories
(C) the war left much bitterness that affected South Africa's political history
(D) it was fought between the Orange Free State and the Transvaal
(E) it was the longest, bloodiest, and most expensive conflict the British fought between 1815 and 1914

CHAPTER 11

Ming and Qing China

291. Why did the Qing dynasty allow China to trade with the Europeans in the 1600s and 1700s?

    (A) The Qing dynasty was eager to adopt European culture.

    (B) Some important goods, like silk and tea, came from Europe.

    (C) The Europeans traded only at certain Chinese ports and paid tribute.

    (D) The Chinese merchants kept European trading companies weak by playing them off against each other.

    (E) The weaknesses of the Canton system required a new policy from the government.

292. The emperor who sent Zheng He on most of his exploratory voyages was

    (A) Yongle

    (B) Xuande

    (C) Jiangtai

    (D) Chenghua

    (E) Hongzhi

293. All of the following are reasons for the collapse of the Yuan dynasty EXCEPT

    (A) corruption in the court and in the army

    (B) the Four Class system

    (C) peasant rebellions

    (D) the military prowess of the Manchu in northeastern China

    (E) political instability

294. The Chinese Neo-Confucianist philosopher from the Ming dynasty whose interpretations affected Chinese thought for centuries was

(A) Zhu Xi
(B) Ouyang Xiu
(C) Wang Yangming
(D) Zhang Shi
(E) Ye Shi

295. What is the proper chronological order of the following Chinese dynasties from earliest to latest?

(A) Song, Tang, Yuan, Qing, Ming
(B) Song, Tang, Yuan, Ming, Qing
(C) Tang, Yuan, Song, Ming, Qing
(D) Tang, Song, Yuan, Qing, Ming
(E) Tang, Song, Yuan, Ming, Qing

296. All of the following were reasons for the collapse of the Ming dynasty EXCEPT

(A) famines
(B) economic problems resulting from fluctuations in the silver supply
(C) the aggression of the Manchu
(D) peasant rebellions
(E) the division of China into spheres of influence

297. All of the following are true regarding Emperor Kangxi EXCEPT that he

(A) was the longest-reigning Chinese emperor in history
(B) encouraged and rewarded people to reclaim wasteland
(C) failed to prevent Russian advances in Manchuria at the Treaty of Nerchinsk
(D) conquered Taiwan
(E) repeatedly reduced taxes

298. Europeans wanted to develop trade with China during the Qing dynasty because it was a source of all of the following EXCEPT

(A) slaves
(B) tea
(C) silk
(D) porcelain
(E) carved jades

299. During the Qing dynasty

(A) women had the right to divorce their husbands
(B) women rebelled against the patriarchal family
(C) female infanticide was supported by Confucian moralists
(D) most women were not provided an education
(E) the government encouraged wealthy families to extend the practice of foot binding

300. The results of the Chinese Rites controversy

(A) were a major cause of xenophobia in Ming China
(B) hampered the efforts of Catholics to convert the Chinese
(C) showed that the Pope knew more than the Jesuits regarding effective conversion strategies in China
(D) allowed the Chinese to continue to use Confucian rituals in Roman Catholic practice
(E) influenced the issuing of Emperor Kangxi's Edict of Toleration in 1692

301. At its greatest extent, Qing dynasty China directly ruled all of the following EXCEPT

(A) Manchuria
(B) Vietnam
(C) Inner Mongolia
(D) Tibet
(E) Taiwan

302. All of the following are true regarding the Qing dynasty EXCEPT that

(A) Manchu and Han Chinese were not permitted to intermarry
(B) the Manchu represented about one-third of China's population
(C) Neo-Confucian philosophy, emphasizing the obedience of subject to ruler, was enforced as the state creed
(D) the Manchu supported Chinese literary and historical projects
(E) the Manchu ended the Chinese civil service exams because they favored the Han Chinese

303. The Forbidden City

    (A) was constructed during the Qing dynasty

    (B) was burned by Nationalist forces after the deposition of the emperor in 1911

    (C) played a similar role for the Chinese as Topkapi Palace did for the Ottomans

    (D) was the residence of emperors but not their ceremonial center

    (E) has the distinction of never having been occupied by European powers

304. The Taipeng Rebellion

    (A) ended the Qing dynasty

    (B) demanded a return to traditional Chinese beliefs

    (C) was unrelated to European imperialism

    (D) was led by Hong Xiuquan, who claimed to be the younger brother of Jesus Christ

    (E) had a death toll of more than 65 million people

305. The Ming dynasty was most famous for its extraordinary innovation in

    (A) poetry

    (B) large statues

    (C) religion

    (D) ceramics

    (E) architecture

306. All of the following are true regarding the Hundred Days' Reform EXCEPT that it

    (A) slowed the growth of revolutionary forces against the Qing dynasty

    (B) was subverted by a coup led by Empress Dowager Cixi

    (C) was triggered by China's defeat in the First Sino-Japanese War

    (D) advocated changing the educational system

    (E) was supported by the emperor

307. The Four Great Classical Novels of Chinese literature include all of the following EXCEPT

    (A) *Journey to the West*

    (B) *Soul Mountain*

    (C) *Water Margin*

    (D) *Dream of the Red Chamber*

    (E) *Romance of the Three Kingdoms*

308. From about 1600 to 1999, Macao was controlled by

(A) China
(B) Portugal
(C) Great Britain
(D) Japan
(E) Russia

309. This rebellion against the Qing dynasty from 1796 to 1804 marked the end of their aura of military invincibility and the beginning of their downward slide.

(A) Du Wenxiu Rebellion
(B) Li Zicheng's Rebellion
(C) White Lotus Rebellion
(D) Triad Rebellion
(E) Taipeng Rebellion

310. All of the following are true regarding the Yongle Emperor EXCEPT that he

(A) was an emperor of the Ming dynasty
(B) was known for his despotism and cruelty
(C) repaired and reopened the Grand Canal
(D) moved the capital from Nanjing to Beijing
(E) conquered Taiwan

CHAPTER 12

Tokugawa Japan and the Meiji Restoration

311. All of the following are true of the Tokugawa shogunate EXCEPT that it

- (A) suppressed and persecuted Christians
- (B) did not permit its citizens to travel abroad
- (C) was a period of almost constant warfare dominated by roving bands of samurai
- (D) imposed costly requirements upon the daimyo
- (E) supported a strict hierarchical order in society

312. All of the following are true of the role of women in the Meiji Restoration EXCEPT that women

- (A) could own property
- (B) were subject to compulsory education
- (C) were the driving force in Japan's booming textile industry
- (D) were prohibited by law from joining political parties
- (E) received complete equality in divorce legislation

313. The Japanese master of the strict 17-syllable form of poetry known as haiku was

- (A) Ihara Saikaku
- (B) Matsuo Basho
- (C) Jippensha Ikku
- (D) Santō Kyōden
- (E) Ueda Akinari

314. All of the following are true of Japan in the 1500s EXCEPT that

(A) it was unified under the Tokugawa shogunate
(B) the power of feudal lords began to decline
(C) the Portuguese introduced European firearms
(D) Christian missionaries had success in converting the Japanese
(E) urban centers grew

315. The most famous Japanese woodblock artist, known for his print entitled *The Great Wave off Kanagawa*, was

(A) Katsukawa Shuncho
(B) Miyagawa Shunsui
(C) Suzuki Harunobu
(D) Katsushika Hokusai
(E) Utagawa Kunisada

316. In the term *Meiji Restoration*, the word *Meiji* refers to

(A) the city in which the new Japanese constitution was written
(B) the name for the prime minister who pushed for more representative government
(C) the Japanese word for "traditional," which the reformers tried to use to justify their revolt
(D) the name that Mutsuhito took when he was crowned emperor
(E) the name of the group of daimyo who organized the coup that overthrew the Tokugawa shogunate

317. All of the following are true of Oda Nobunaga EXCEPT that he

(A) attacked Buddhist monasteries
(B) embraced European innovations such as firearms
(C) invaded Korea and annexed it to Japan
(D) was the first of the three unifiers of Japan
(E) was followed by Toyotomi Hideyoshi

318. All of the following were reasons for discontent with the Tokugawa shogunate in the 1800s EXCEPT that

(A) daimyo were land rich but cash poor
(B) merchants resented their lack of social status
(C) government corruption was endemic
(D) many samurai had become economically dependent on merchants
(E) the Japanese need to respond to foreign intrusion was bankrupting the treasury

319. The Shimabara Rebellion led to

(A) the loosening of restrictions against Christians
(B) the fall of the Tokugawa shogunate
(C) the imposition of the *sakoku* policy
(D) an end to restriction on foreign travels by Japanese
(E) an elevation of the status and privileges of merchants in Japan despite their defeat at Shimabara

320. The Russo-Japanese War

(A) led to a comprehensive Russian defeat but did not affect domestic politics in Imperial Russia
(B) revealed the limitations of the military reforms of the Meiji Restoration
(C) surprised European observers with its relatively bloodless nature
(D) was caused by disagreements over the possession of Port Arthur
(E) was mediated by US President William Howard Taft

321. All of the following were results of the Meiji Restoration EXCEPT

(A) the creation of a highly centralized and bureaucratic government
(B) the development of a modern transport and communication system
(C) an educated population free of feudal class distinctions
(D) a deemphasis of the cult of the emperor in favor of Western democratic ideals
(E) the creation of a powerful army and navy

322. Geisha are Japanese

(A) single women of a marriageable age
(B) hostesses trained to entertain men with conversation, dance, and song
(C) prostitutes who worked in walled-in pleasure areas
(D) single girls who worked in the booming textile trades during the Meiji Restoration
(E) houses of prostitution

323. All of the following are true regarding kabuki EXCEPT that

(A) it is a classical Japanese dance-drama and more popular than Noh drama
(B) it was invented in 1603 by a woman
(C) the term is synonymous with bunraku
(D) it is known for its elaborate costumes and makeup
(E) men known as *onnagata* typically play female roles

324. The decisive battle that cleared the way for the creation of the Tokugawa shogunate was the

(A) Battle of Okehazama
(B) Battle of Nagashino
(C) Battle of Yamazaki
(D) Battle of Tsushima
(E) Battle of Sekigahara

325. For more than 200 years, Japan kept its ports closed to European trade except for the artificial harbor of Deshima at

(A) Nagoya
(B) Fukuoka
(C) Sendai
(D) Sapporo
(E) Nagasaki

326. Japan was successful at resisting imperialism because

(A) it created a unified government with a sound policy for modernization
(B) the samurai were the world's greatest warriors
(C) the Tokugawa shogunate effectively resisted European and American inroads
(D) it had abundant natural resources to begin an imperialist program of its own
(E) the United States was for more interested in Chinese markets than Japanese

327. Which event occurred last?

(A) the Russo-Japanese War
(B) Japan annexes Korea
(C) the First Sino-Japanese War
(D) the Treaty of Portsmouth
(E) the Gentleman's Agreement

328. Zaibatsu were

    (A) the inner circle of advisors to the emperor

    (B) factories created by the Japanese government and then sold to large investors

  ✓ (C) large Japanese business conglomerates

    (D) the persecuted opponents of the government who protested militarism and imperialism in Japan

    (E) conservative supporters of Buddhism who resented the inroads of Shintoism in the Meiji period

329. Japanese modernization during the Meiji Restoration

    (A) was governed by private individuals

    (B) produced an interest in the resources of Manchuria

    (C) was a gradual process because of lack of government support

    (D) diverted the country's attention from developing a military

    (E) was easily accomplished because of Japan's abundant natural resources

330. All of the following are true regarding Matthew Perry's expedition to Japan EXCEPT that

    (A) he used force to achieve the expedition's goal

    (B) he succeeded in opening the ports of Shimoda and Hakodate to American trade

    (C) his actions led to the Treaty of Kanagawa in 1854

    (D) he acted with the complete support of the United States government

    (E) he arrived in Japan directly after the First Opium War

CHAPTER 13

Colonial Africa

331. The Kingdom of Benin (in present-day Nigeria) is famous culturally for its

- (A) epic oral poetry
- (B) brass plaques
- (C) terra cotta sculptures
- (D) wood fetish figures
- (E) brass gold weights

332. All of the following were effects of the transatlantic slave trade on African societies EXCEPT

- (A) the collapse of all strong African kingdoms
- (B) the flooding of Africa with guns and an escalation of violence
- (C) an increase in polygamy
- (D) a legacy of racial prejudice
- (E) a decline in the economy of western Africa

333. The Zulu chief of the early 1800s who organized a huge army and dominated a large portion of southern Africa was

- (A) Dinuzulu
- (B) Shaka
- (C) Cetshwayo
- (D) Mpande
- (E) Dingane

334. The king of Kongo in the 16th century who established Catholicism in the country and wrote a long series of letters to the kings of Portugal was

(A) Manuel I
(B) João I
(C) Mpanzu a Nzinga
(D) Afonso I
(E) Henrique Kinu a Mvemba

335. Which of the following statements is true regarding Islam in eastern Africa?

(A) Eastern African societies tended to offer greater gender equality than traditional Islamic societies.
(B) In the 1600s, the lower classes were more eager to convert to Islam than the elite were.
(C) East African contact with Islam was generated by the transatlantic trade.
(D) African rulers feared that conversion to Islam would undermine their authority.
(E) Women who converted to Islam in eastern Africa generally abandoned tribal beliefs for traditional Islamic practices.

336. The famous trickster figure who features widely in tales in western Africa and the Caribbean is

(A) Iktomi the raven
(B) Mica the coyote
(C) Reynard the fox
(D) Br'er Rabbit
(E) Anansi the spider

337. The Great Trek

(A) describes the movement of more than 200,000 Boers to the north
(B) took place from 1885 to 1893
(C) defeated powerful African kingdoms through the skilled use of horses, guns, and defensive laagers
(D) was motivated by the discovery of diamonds and gold in northern South Africa
(E) led to the creation of the Cape Colony

338. Western African societies in 1500

(A) lacked any national states with governments and laws
(B) were isolated from the rest of the world
(C) exported iron products in exchange for cheap European cloth
(D) refused to participate in the slave trade
(E) viewed the Portuguese as just another trading partner

339. All of the following are true about the Kingdom of Dahomey EXCEPT that

(A) the abolition of slavery led to increased prosperity
(B) it reached the high point of its power and fame under Gezu
(C) it was organized for war
(D) it was a form of absolute monarchy almost unique in Africa
(E) it eventually became part of French West Africa

340. The Islamic scholar and preacher Usman dan Fodio is associated with the present-day nation of

(A) Mauritania
(B) Nigeria
(C) Algeria
(D) Ethiopia
(E) Kenya

341. The Suez Canal was completed in

(A) 1829
(B) 1849
(C) 1869
(D) 1889
(E) 1909

342. All of the following were negative effects of the colonial economy on African women EXCEPT that

(A) women lost access and control of a large percentage of fertile land
(B) migrant work for males removed them from their traditional labor responsibilities and led to a drop in cultivated acreage
(C) the cash economy favored the work of men over women
(D) male migration for economic reasons severely damaged the African family
(E) underpaid and mistreated women became the majority of workers on export-oriented plantations

343. Nzinga Mbande was

    (A) a queen who fought the Portuguese in present-day Angola

    (B) the leader of the movement to settle freed slaves in Liberia

    (C) a religious mystic and prophet who advocated a return to tradition and launched an anticolonial movement in western Africa

    (D) a Bamum king who learned German, converted to Christianity, and translated the Bible into Bamum

    (E) a Fulani queen who launched a jihad against the people living on the Bight of Benin

344. All of the following were merchandise imported into Africa EXCEPT

    (A) cotton textiles

    (B) weapons

    (C) cowry shells

    (D) cloves

    (E) alcoholic drinks

345. All of the following are true regarding Zanzibar EXCEPT that

    (A) the Omani Sultan Seyyid Said permanently moved his court there in 1841

    (B) the indigenous Bantu-speaking Hadimu wrested control of Zanzibar from the Omanis in 1890

    (C) in the 19th century, it became world famous for its spices, slaves, and ivory

    (D) the Arab elite in Zanzibar controlled much of the eastern African coast in the 1800s

    (E) the center of Zanzibar city contains a unique mixture of Moorish, Arab, Persian, and Indian architecture

346. The Tripolitan War

    (A) was entirely a naval war

    (B) was an example of Thomas Jefferson's belief in small government

    (C) was fought between the United States and the Barbary States of North Africa (Algiers, Morocco, Tripoli, and Tunis)

    (D) was the first war ever officially declared by the US Congress

    (E) ended piracy against American ships in the Mediterranean

347. All of the following is true of slave raiding in Africa EXCEPT that

(A) the business of slave raiding was left almost completely to the native Africans

(B) some West African kingdoms benefited from the slave trade

(C) groups of chained slaves marching to the coast were called *coffles*

(D) it increased warfare and destabilized Africa

(E) the Asante kings were the only major African rulers to oppose the slave trade

348. A barracoon was

(A) an African vessel used on shallow African rivers like the Gambia

(B) a type of cassava that led to increased caloric consumption by Africans in the 1800s

(C) an effigy figure that was the first African type of art item to be sold in large quantities in Europe

(D) a dungeon or a slave pen, usually found along the African coast

(E) a Cameroonian fetish figure that played an important role in court ceremony

349. Who was a noted African linguist as well as the first African Anglican bishop in Nigeria?

(A) Charles Lwanga

(B) Henry Townshend

(C) Herbert Macaulay

(D) Samuel Crowther

(E) James Hannington

350. Dona Beatriz Kimpa Vita was

(A) a female prophet who led a popular African movement in the Kongo

(B) the first black African Catholic saint

(C) a Portuguese nun who protested to no avail against the slave trade

(D) the wife of Governor Afonso Vita who drew the plans for the Cathédrale Notre-Dame des Victoires in Yaoundé

(E) an Angolan writer who rallied the people against the Portuguese

CHAPTER 14

The Era of the World Wars

351. About 15 million people were killed and 20 million wounded in World War I. This helps to explain

(A) the success of the Allied appeasement policy in the late 1930s
(B) the Munich Pact of 1938
(C) German contempt for the Treaty of Versailles
(D) the breakup of the British Empire in the 1930s
(E) the large number of American casualties in World War I

352. Which of the following best summarizes the contents of the Zimmermann Telegram?

(A) Germany offered Mexico a chance to regain the land taken by the United States in 1848 if Mexico attacked the United States.
(B) A British spy alerted the world to mass extermination camps in German-held territories.
(C) The United States assured the British that it would join the war in Europe if Germany continued unrestricted submarine warfare.
(D) German Foreign Secretary Arthur Zimmermann secretly admitted that German terror tactics in Belgium were intentional.
(E) The United States explicitly warned Germany that America would enter the war if unrestricted submarine warfare was reinstated.

353. All of the following are true regarding the Russian Provisional Government of 1917 EXCEPT that

(A) it was formed after Tsar Nicholas abdicated in March
(B) spontaneously elected soviets competed with the government for political support
(C) Aleksandr Kerensky lacked the political skills to create an effective wartime government
(D) it was threatened from the right in the Kornilov Affair
(E) it took control promising the people "Peace, land, and bread"

354. Experiments on dogs by Russian physiologist Ivan Pavlov seemed to demonstrate that

(A) humans were complete masters of their thoughts and behaviors
(B) dogs were smarter than humans because they were more rational
(C) dogs did not share the same phobias and anxieties that humans did
(D) behavior was reflexive and could be conditioned by stimuli over which individuals had no control
(E) the study of mental processes, rather than behavior, was a more insightful way of examining learning in humans

355. All of the following are true regarding the Nazi Party in Germany EXCEPT that it

(A) was the largest party in the Reichstag in 1932
(B) never received more than 40 percent of the vote in any election
(C) did not exist before the Great Depression
(D) promised to overturn the Treaty of Versailles
(E) campaigned against Jewish bankers and Bolshevik revolutionaries

356. The Treaty of Versailles contained all of the following provisions EXCEPT

(A) blaming Germany for starting World War I
(B) forcing Germany to pay reparations
(C) prohibiting Germany from having any army
(D) awarding Shandong to Japan
(E) returning Alsace-Lorraine to France

357. The turning point of World War II in Europe was

(A) the Battle of Kursk
(B) the Battle of Stalingrad
(C) D-Day
(D) the Battle of Rome
(E) the Battle of Dieppe

358. The immediate cause of World War I was

(A) the assassination of Austrian Archduke Francis Ferdinand
(B) the Second Balkan War in which Bulgaria attacked Serbia and Greece
(C) European rivalries over colonies and the size of military forces
(D) the "blank check" given the German government by Austria-Hungary
(E) the Second Moroccan Crisis

359. President Woodrow Wilson's Fourteen Points plan included all of the following EXCEPT

    (A) promotion of universal self-determination

    (B) lower tariffs to promote free trade

    (C) repayment of all Allied war expenses by Germany

    (D) arms reductions by all nations

    (E) the creation of an international peacekeeping organization

360. "We shall not flag or fail. We shall go on to the end. We shall fight in France, we shall fight on the seas and oceans . . . we shall fight on the beaches, we shall fight on the landing grounds, we shall fight in the fields and in the streets, we shall fight in the hills; we shall never surrender."

The author of this quotation was

    (A) Wilhelm II

    (B) Charles de Gaulle

    (C) Douglas Haig

    (D) Winston Churchill

    (E) Lloyd George

361. Pablo Picasso's painting entitled *Guernica* was a condemnation of

    (A) Japanese aggression in Asia

    (B) Nazi racial policy

    (C) German bombing of civilians in the Spanish Civil War

    (D) the murder of priests by Spanish nationalists

    (E) the refusal of England and France to defend democracy against fascism

362. All of the following are true regarding Japan in World War I EXCEPT that

    (A) Japan declared war against Germany

    (B) Japan invaded Shandong Province in China

    (C) Japan issued the Twenty-One Demands in 1915 to establish a Japanese protectorate over China

    (D) Great Britain believed Japanese diplomacy was overbearing and bullying

    (E) as a result of the Twenty-One Demands, Japan acquired control of mineral-rich northern Manchuria

363. The permanent members of the Security Council of the United Nations were chosen because they

(A) were the nations that had the greatest stake in keeping world peace
(B) were the main victorious nations in World War II
(C) had the same ideas about how best to preserve world peace
(D) represented a geographic balance of different continents and points of view
(E) were the countries most likely to use the veto power carefully

364. The Allies gave all of the following reasons for the Dardanelles (Gallipoli) Campaign EXCEPT that

(A) Turkish soldiers would be easier to defeat than German soldiers
(B) the Allies could open Russia's Black Sea ports to Allied supply ships
(C) control of the Balkans would help the Allies support Austria-Hungary against Germany
(D) the Allies could weaken Germany by knocking the Ottoman Empire out of the war
(E) the Allies could take some pressure off the Western Front

365. Buying *on margin* contributed to the American stock market crash of 1929 because it

(A) required investors to purchase only high-risk, volatile stocks
(B) imposed high interest rates that discouraged trading
(C) prevented buyers from learning the true state of the companies in which they invested
(D) allowed traders to pay for stock with projected future profits
(E) mandated that traders sell a stock as soon as it began to lose value

366. In World War II, Russian military and civilian casualties were how many times greater than American casualties?

(A) 2 times greater
(B) 5 times greater
(C) 10 times greater
(D) 25 times greater
(E) 50 times greater

367. The Nye Committee revealed all of the following EXCEPT
    (A) Dow Chemical had knowingly supplied Mussolini with materials to make poison gas to use against Ethiopia.
    (B) American bankers had pressed Woodrow Wilson to enter World War I to protect the value of their loans.
    (C) American munitions companies had regularly bribed foreign politicians to improve arms sales between 1920 and 1935.
    (D) Many American corporations were guilty of tax evasion and profiting from sales to Nazi Germany and Fascist Italy.
    (E) Franklin Roosevelt had conspired to involve the United States in World War II.

368. "With the October Revolution, the working class had hoped to achieve its emancipation. But there resulted an even greater enslavement of human personality. The power of the [czarist] police . . . fell into the hands of the Communists, who, instead of giving the people liberty, have instilled in them only the constant fear of the Cheka [Communist secret police]. It has now become clear that the Russian Communist Party is not the defender of the laboring masses, as it pretends to be. . . . Having gained power, it is now fearful only of losing it."

    This quotation was written by

    (A) Leon Trotsky
    (B) Kronstadt sailors
    (C) White Army officials
    (D) Joseph Stalin
    (E) Vladimir Lenin

369. All of the following occurred in the initial Japanese push between December 1941 and March 1942 EXCEPT that the Japanese
    (A) sank the HMS *Repulse* and HMS *Prince of Wales*, demonstrating that battleships are helpless against air power
    (B) destroyed most of the American planes in the Philippines on the ground
    (C) tried but failed to conquer the oil-rich Dutch East Indies
    (D) bombed Darwin, Australia
    (E) conquered Singapore in a brilliant land attack from Malaya

370. In *Korematsu v. United States*, the US Supreme Court
- (A) ruled that the wartime relocation of all West Coast Japanese Americans was constitutional
- (B) held that the Japanese government had no legitimate claim to reparations for the bombings of Hiroshima and Nagasaki
- (C) overturned the decision previously made in *Hirabayashi v. United States*
- (D) determined that the wartime relocation of the Japanese had been an unfortunate result of wartime hysteria
- (E) declared that German Americans and Italian Americans also must be placed in internment camps in order to make the relocation of Japanese Americans constitutional

371. "The Germans sentenced Louvain on Wednesday to become a wilderness, and . . . they left Louvain an empty blackened shell. The reason for this appeal to the torch and the execution of noncombatants [was that] 50 Germans were killed and wounded. For that, said Lutwitz, Louvain must be wiped out. . . . It was war upon the defenseless, war on churches, colleges, shops of milliners and lace makers, war brought to the bedside and the fireside; against women harvesting in the fields, against children in wooden shoes at play in the streets."

This account of the burning of Louvain in 1914 reveals
- (A) the horrors of Nazi German policy
- (B) an unusual case of 20th-century war against civilians
- (C) that Germany understood the value of propaganda in World War I
- (D) one reason for American support for France and England in World War I
- (E) the success of the German *Schrecklichkeit* policy

372. The United States during World War II can be characterized by all of the following EXCEPT
- (A) increased national debt
- (B) a large number of women in the workforce
- (C) racial riots in American cities
- (D) considerable opposition to the war effort
- (E) decrease in unemployment

373. "We are the hollow men
We are the stuffed men
Leaning together
Headpiece filled with straw. Alas!
Our dried voices, when
We whisper together
Are quiet and meaningless
As wind in dry grass
Or rats' feet over broken glass
In our dry cellar."

The author of this verse was

(A) James Farrell
(B) T. S. Eliot
(C) Robinson Jeffers
(D) John Dos Passos
(E) E. A. Robinson

374. Western European powers and the United States responded to Japanese aggression in China in the 1930s by

(A) declaring war on Japan
(B) enacting strict economic sanctions
(C) condemning the aggression
(D) calling for civil disobedience in China
(E) authorizing a League of Nations peacekeeping force to prevent further Japanese advances

375. The Long March was a name for

(A) a successful retreat by the Chinese Communists under Mao Zedong
(B) an astonishing offensive by the Kuomintang in Jiangxi province
(C) the Japanese attack down the Malaysian peninsula to take Singapore
(D) the march of American POWs after the fall of the Philippines
(E) the retreat by German soldiers after their defeat at Moscow

376. President Franklin Roosevelt invoked the Good Neighbor Policy when he

(A) supported the provision of England with munitions to allow it to protect itself against Germany

(B) authorized the creation of the Tennessee Valley Authority to provide power in the poor rural South

(C) banned the trade of war-related materials with Japan and then froze Japanese assets in the United States

(D) helped establish the Federal Deposit Insurance Corporation to stabilize bank savings

(E) recalled American troops from Nicaragua and Haiti

377. The Ukrainian famine of 1932–1933 was primarily caused by

(A) the deliberate policies of the government of the Soviet Union

(B) a shortage of rain and Dust Bowl–like conditions in the Ukraine

(C) civil war in the Ukraine between Communists and non-Communists

(D) Vladimir Lenin's tolerance of a Ukrainian national revival in the 1920s

(E) the refusal of the kulaks to grow food for the Communist government

378. All of the following are true of Marie Curie EXCEPT that she

(A) was the first person to win two Nobel Prizes

(B) died from aplastic anemia brought on by years of radiation exposure

(C) determined the characteristics of plutonium

(D) isolated radium and polonium

(E) was the first female professor at the Sorbonne (University of Paris)

379. "Fascism . . . believes neither in the possibility nor the utility of perpetual peace. . . . War alone brings up to its highest tension all human energy and puts the stamps of nobility upon the peoples who have the courage to meet it. All other trials are substitutes, which never really put men into the position where they have to make the great decision—the alternative of life and death."

This philosophy helps to explain all of the following EXCEPT

(A) the Belgian occupation of the Congo

(B) the German conquest of Poland in 1939

(C) the Italian invasion of Ethiopia

(D) Francisco Franco's victory in the Spanish Civil War

(E) Benito Mussolini's invasion of France

380. All of the following are true regarding the Lend-Lease Act EXCEPT that

    (A) it gave the president power to sell, transfer, lend, or lease materials without immediate cash payment

    (B) opponents argued that the act wiped out the last traces of American neutrality

    (C) by 1945, more than $40 billion of goods and services had been distributed to American allies

    (D) Congress refused to appropriate money for the Soviet Union because of anticommunist hysteria

    (E) despite some opposition, it passed Congress fairly easily

381. By *atonality*, composers referred to music that

    (A) used folk melodies for nationalistic purposes

    (B) ignored harmony

    (C) drew on jazz traditions of improvisation

    (D) disregarded key

    (E) tended to minimize elitism in music and encourage the middle classes to attend concerts

382. The vast majority of Jews killed in the Holocaust lived in

    (A) Poland

    (B) the Soviet Union

    (C) Hungary

    (D) Germany

    (E) France

383. "The policy of reducing Germany to servitude for a generation, of degrading the lives of millions of human beings, and of depriving a whole nation of happiness should be abhorrent and detestable—abhorrent and detestable, even if it were possible, even if it enriched ourselves, even if it did not sow the decay of the whole civilized life of Europe."

The author of this quotation was opposed to the

    (A) Fourteen Points

    (B) Treaty of Versailles

    (C) United States entry into World War I

    (D) aerial bombing of German civilians in World War I

    (E) trench warfare

384. The Schlieffen Plan called for Germany to

    (A) come to the immediate military aid of Serbia

    (B) wage a two-front war against France and Russia

    (C) fight a holding action in France while crushing the Russians at Tannenberg and Masurian Lakes

    (D) defeat France in six weeks and then redeploy Germany's western armies in the east

    (E) drive quickly through Alsace-Lorraine to Paris and avoid a long, drawn-out war of attrition

385. History is often affected by current events. After the slaughter of World War I, many American historians concluded all of the following EXCEPT

    (A) the US Civil War was caused by a "blundering generation" of politicians and could have been avoided

    (B) slavery really was not so bad as evidenced by the lack of slave revolts

    (C) the Civil War did not accomplish anything meaningful that was worth the casualties

    (D) Reconstruction was led by radical and self-serving northerners who wanted only to enrich themselves

    (E) President Andrew Johnson was a semialcoholic and racist obstructionist

386. All of the following are noteworthy British war poets associated with World War I EXCEPT

    (A) Wilfred Owen

    (B) Siegfried Sassoon

    (C) W. H. Auden

    (D) Isaac Rosenberg

    (E) Charles Sorley

387. As a result of the Dreyfus Affair

    (A) the French government banned anti-Semitism in political writings

    (B) many Jews lost their military commissions

    (C) Émile Zola's reputation fell as he attempted to defend the French government

    (D) the French government renewed its commitment to promoting the Catholic teaching orders

    (E) church and state were separated in France

388. All of the following are true regarding the Japanese cult of the emperor EXCEPT that it

(A) was used by militarists as a tool to encourage Japanese expansionism
(B) essentially ended after World War II
(C) was consciously encouraged by Meiji reformers
(D) was promoted by Buddhists as a way to hold back the revival of Shintoism
(E) depicted the emperor as a living god

389. All of the following are true regarding the German policy of *Lebensraum* EXCEPT that it was

(A) similar to the 19th-century American policy of Manifest Destiny
(B) outlined in *Mein Kampf*
(C) possible for Germany to achieve by negotiation
(D) based on depopulating eastern Europe
(E) inspired by social Darwinist racial ideology

390. All of the following were important women's suffrage leaders EXCEPT

(A) Alice Paul
(B) Emmeline Pankhurst
(C) Ichikawa Fusae
(D) Lida Gustava Heymann
(E) Mary Augusta Arnold (Mrs. Humphry Ward)

391. Sun Yat-sen

(A) battled Mao Zedong to a standstill in the 1920s
(B) refused aid from Chinese Communists in fighting Japan
(C) has a high reputation in both present-day mainland China and in Taiwan
(D) led the Northern Expedition against the warlords at Beijing
(E) rejected Western ideas as imperialist and advocated a return to traditional Chinese values

392. All of the following terms are associated with Sigmund Freud EXCEPT

(A) collective unconscious
(B) id
(C) free association
(D) anal stage
(E) superego

393. All of the following are true of the Fashoda Incident EXCEPT that it

(A) brought Great Britain and France to the brink of war in 1898

(B) took place in Egypt

(C) was caused by competing colonial ambitions

(D) led to a secret agreement in 1904 in which France guaranteed British claims to Egypt in return for French claims in Morocco

(E) ultimately led to the Entente Cordiale

394. All of the following were weaknesses of the League of Nations EXCEPT that

(A) it did not have armed forces to back up its decisions

(B) the United States was not a member nation

(C) when countries did not agree with the League's decisions, they simply quit

(D) the World Bank refused to provide it with the loans necessary to make its decisions stick

(E) it did not provide collective security

395. The modernist movement in the late 1800s and early 1900s

(A) emphasized nationalism over individualism

(B) was fascinated by new developments in metaphysics

(C) rejected psychological theories of the unconscious because they undermined the notions of rationalism and progress

(D) believed traditional cultural forms were outdated in the new industrial society

(E) rejected abstraction as inadequate for times of political upheaval

CHAPTER 15

The Cold War Era

396. All of the following were components of American Cold War foreign policy between 1952 and 1961 EXCEPT

(A) détente
(B) brinkmanship
(C) the domino theory
(D) massive retaliation
(E) covert operations

397. At the Potsdam Conference, Joseph Stalin, Harry Truman, and Clement Attlee agreed that

(A) the Soviet Union should be able to occupy all of Eastern Europe
(B) Germany would be divided into four zones
(C) European colonies would receive full independence
(D) the United States would occupy western Europe
(E) Poland would hold free elections

398. All of the following are true of the conflict between the Chinese Communists and Chinese Nationalists EXCEPT that it

(A) began after World War II
(B) involved massive American loans to the Nationalists, but no military support
(C) has never officially ended
(D) came to a partial halt during World War II in favor of national interests
(E) led to the creation of "two Chinas"

399. "Stalin acted not through persuasion, explanation, and patient cooperation with the people, but by imposing his concepts and demanding absolute submission to his opinion. Whoever opposed this concept . . . was doomed. . . . Arbitrary behavior by one person encouraged and permitted arbitrariness in others. Mass arrests and deportations of many thousands of people, execution without trial and without normal investigation created conditions of insecurity, fear, and even desperation."

The author of this quotation is

(A) Vladimir Lenin
(B) Franklin Roosevelt
(C) Georgy Malenkov
(D) Nikita Khrushchev
(E) Lavrentiy Beria

400. One version of Mao Zedong's "Three Main Rules of Discipline" for soldiers in the 1930s and 1940s reads

"1. Obey orders in all your actions.
2. Do not take a single needle or piece of thread from the masses.
3. Turn in everything captured."

These orders help explain the

(A) replacement of the Taiwan government by the Beijing government at the United Nations
(B) reason the United States supported Mao Zedong in World War II
(C) defeat of the Kuomintang in the Chinese Civil War
(D) popular support for Mao Zedong's Cultural Revolution
(E) success of Jiang Jieshi in mobilizing widespread support in China

401. "The truth of the matter is that Europe's requirements for the next three or four years of foreign food and other essential products—principally from America—are so much greater than her present ability to pay that she must have substantial additional help or face economic, social, and political deterioration. . . . It is logical that the United States should do whatever it is able to do to assist in the return of normal economic health in the world without which there can be no political stability and no assured peace."

The quotation above reflects the United States policy known as

(A) the Truman Doctrine
(B) the domino theory
(C) containment
(D) the Marshall Plan
(E) détente

402. The youth culture of the 1960s that revolved around rock music, liberal sexuality, and drugs

(A) succeeded in offering a viable alternative to capitalist consumer culture
(B) was largely embraced by mainstream culture after 1970
(C) lost its appeal among young people after 1970 because it had been coopted by the mainstream commercial culture
(D) rejected all forms of technology as hampering human development
(E) was unique to the United States

403. All of the following were obstacles to United States influence in the developing world in the 1950s EXCEPT that

(A) racism in America alienated the people of Asia and Africa
(B) US policy makers viewed neutralism as immoral and the first step toward Communism
(C) the US was hostile to revolution and often sided with European imperialists or conservative propertied classes
(D) US politicians tended to believe that all revolutions were Soviet-inspired rather than expressions of nationalism, anti-imperialism, or political instability
(E) capitalism had little appeal for the people of newly independent nations escaping colonial rule

404. All of the following are associated with the Red Scare in the United States from 1947 to 1957 EXCEPT

(A) Joseph McCarthy
(B) the McCarran Act
(C) the Palmer Raids
(D) Alger Hiss
(E) the Hollywood 10

405. As an alternative to "Western" abstract expressionism, the Soviet Union promoted

(A) neorealism
(B) socialist realism
(C) cubism
(D) social constructivism
(E) *samizdat*

406. All of the following are true regarding the Cuban Missile Crisis EXCEPT that

- (A) the United States was upset by the presence of Soviet medium-range missiles in Cuba
- (B) the Soviet Union wanted the United States to remove American missiles from Turkey
- (C) the United States sponsored an invasion by Cuban exiles to remove the missiles
- (D) the Cuban government wanted an American promise to respect Cuban sovereignty
- (E) for a few days, the world seemed poised on the brink of nuclear war

407. The Chinese invaded North Korea and attacked American troops because

- (A) the Americans bombed the bridges at Pusan
- (B) Douglas MacArthur's daring amphibious landing at Inchon had worked perfectly
- (C) they believed their army's performance had improved substantially since World War II
- (D) the Chinese wanted to spread Communism across all of southeastern Asia
- (E) the United States ignored Chinese warnings that United Nations forces should not threaten the Chinese border

408. The Soviet response to protests in Hungary in 1956 was to

- (A) send in Soviet troops and tanks
- (B) work out a compromise agreement similar to the one in Poland with Wladyslaw Gomulka
- (C) allow Hungary to govern in its own way
- (D) support the protests and call for change at home
- (E) encourage loyal Hungarians under Imre Nagy to roll back the reforms

409. The worst nuclear power plant accident as of 2012 occurred at

- (A) Fukushima Daiichi (Japan)
- (B) Three Mile Island (United States)
- (C) Chernobyl (Soviet Union)
- (D) SL-1 (Idaho Falls, United States)
- (E) Jaslovské Bohunice (Czechoslovakia)

410. "From Stettin in the Baltic to Trieste in the Adriatic, an iron curtain has descended across the continent. Behind that line lie all the capitals of the ancient states of central and eastern Europe."

The author of this quotation was

(A) Franklin Roosevelt
(B) Charles DeGaulle
(C) Joseph Stalin
(D) Winston Churchill
(E) Harry Truman

411. "In the councils of government, we must guard against the acquisition of unwarranted influence, whether sought or unsought, by the military-industrial complex. The potential for the disastrous rise of misplaced power exists and will persist."

The author of this quotation was

(A) John F. Kennedy
(B) Bill Clinton
(C) William F. Buckley
(D) Noam Chomsky
(E) Dwight Eisenhower

412. Television

(A) seduced people off the streets and moved them indoors
(B) had little effect on politics
(C) spread slowly in Europe
(D) was invented in 1951
(E) encouraged extreme opinions to attract viewers

413. The Antarctic Treaty, written in 1959,

(A) divided Antarctica into spheres of influence
(B) was the first arms control treaty of the Cold War
(C) prohibited the presence of military personnel on Antarctica
(D) was an agreement by the United States and its allies to prevent the Soviet Union from claiming any part of Antarctica
(E) specifically stated that the people of Antarctica had the right to vote to choose their own form of government

414. The "killing fields" refers to mass murder in the 1970s in
- (A) Rwanda
- (B) Cambodia
- (C) Yugoslavia
- (D) Uganda
- (E) Bolivia

415. The dropping of the atomic bomb on Nagasaki on August 9, 1945,
- (A) destroyed the city but resulted in relatively few casualties because of the early warning given by the United States
- (B) occurred a week after the bombing of Hiroshima in order to give the Japanese time to comprehend the new weapon
- (C) occurred after the Soviet attack on the Japanese in Manchuria
- (D) prevented the Soviet Union from entering the Pacific war
- (E) enabled the Allies to depose the emperor after Japan surrendered

416. "Section 1. Equality of rights under the law shall not be denied or abridged by the United States or by any State on account of sex."

This proposed amendment to the United States Constitution was
- (A) passed by Congress but not ratified by a sufficient number of state legislatures
- (B) passed by Congress and the states as the crowning achievement of the civil rights movement
- (C) always opposed by Republicans
- (D) originally written by A. Philip Randolph
- (E) rejected by Congress after nine years of debate

417. All of the following are true regarding the Chinese Cultural Revolution EXCEPT that it
- (A) was led by Mao Zedong
- (B) followed the failure of the Great Leap Forward
- (C) led to millions of deaths
- (D) was meant to eradicate the "Four Olds"
- (E) benefited the Chinese educational system

418. The development of new biological processes such as in vitro fertilization (IVF)

(A) led to a decrease in the marriage rate

(B) raised ethical questions regarding to what degree scientists should aid or interfere with reproduction

(C) was necessary as increasing numbers of women used birth control pills

(D) caused the Catholic Church to abandon its opposition to birth control and reproductive technologies

(E) led to a decrease in the birthrate

419. The US Central Intelligence Agency (CIA) helped overthrow democratically elected governments in all of the following countries between 1950 and 1975 EXCEPT

(A) Guatemala

(B) Iran

(C) Spain

(D) Chile

(E) Brazil

420. Joseph Stalin's approach to the governments of Eastern Europe between 1945 and 1948 was to

(A) allow people to elect the governments they wanted in order to show Communism's commitment to democracy

(B) immediately impose Communist governments in order to make sure Nazi sympathizers were punished

(C) establish military dictatorships led by Soviet generals

(D) gradually impose Communist rule

(E) order the Cominform to dictate to Communist Party members when to launch coups to take over the governments

421. All of the following called the Enlightenment faith in *progress* into question EXCEPT

(A) the Battle of the Somme

(B) Sigmund Freud's theories of the unconscious

(C) the Holocaust

(D) *Sputnik*

(E) the use of the atomic bombs on civilian populations

422. All of the following are considered feminist classics EXCEPT

(A) Phyllis Schlafly, *A Choice, Not an Echo* (1964)
(B) Betty Friedan, *The Feminine Mystique* (1963)
(C) Susan Brownmiller, *Against Our Will* (1975)
(D) Simone de Beauvoir, *The Second Sex* (1949)
(E) Alice Schwarzer, *The Little Difference and Its Huge Consequences* (1975)

423. All of the following are true regarding minimalism in music EXCEPT that it

(A) was associated with the early work of Steve Reich, John Adams, and Philip Glass
(B) attempted to simplify music by featuring repetition
(C) became the most popular classical music style for audiences in the late 1900s
(D) often stressed the use of modern technology in music
(E) was criticized for its emotional blankness

424. All of the following nations were part of the original Non-Aligned Movement (NAM) founded in 1961 EXCEPT

(A) Indonesia
(B) India
(C) Yugoslavia
(D) Ghana
(E) Australia

425. All of the following are related to the Angolan Civil War EXCEPT

(A) *musseques*
(B) MPLA
(C) GIA
(D) UNITA
(E) Jonas Savimbi

426. The main goals of Ronald Reagan's presidency included

(A) eliminating all social programs and balancing the federal budget
(B) reducing the size of the federal government and increasing defense spending
(C) using the federal government to enforce civil rights legislation and reducing American influence in Latin America
(D) increasing income tax rates to boost revenue and strengthening environmental regulations to protect the environment
(E) promoting nuclear energy and destroying Al Qaeda

427. The leader of Yugoslavia from 1943 to 1980 who advocated *national communism* was

(A) Slobodan Miloševic

(B) Josip Broz Tito

(C) Ivan Šubašić

(D) Dragoljub Mihailović

(E) Ante Pavelić

428. All of the following represent positive steps toward the achievement of gay (homosexual) rights EXCEPT

(A) the Mattachine Society

(B) the 1973 revision of the Diagnostic and Statistical Manual of Psychiatric Disorders (DSM) by the American Psychiatric Association

(C) the model penal code drafted by the American Bar Association in 1961

(D) *Bowers v. Hardwick* (1986)

(E) the Stonewall riots

429. The Vietnamese victory that sealed the French defeat in Vietnam was the battle of

(A) Khe Sanh

(B) Binh Gia

(C) Dien Bien Phu

(D) Tet

(E) Dong Xoai

430. All of the following occurred in 1968 EXCEPT

(A) the first human landing on the moon

(B) the Tet Offensive

(C) the Soviet defeat of Prague Spring

(D) the assassination of Martin Luther King

(E) a large general strike and riots in France

CHAPTER 16

Global Liberation and Independence Movements

431. The Polish movement that heralded the collapse of Communism across Eastern Europe was called

(A) A Good Sword
(B) For Our Freedom and Yours
(C) the National Liberation Front
(D) Freedom Now!
(E) Solidarity

432. All of the following are related to the Kenyan independence movement EXCEPT

(A) Jomo Kenyatta
(B) the Mau Mau
(C) Harry Thuku
(D) Idi Amin
(E) Daniel arap Moi

433. Muhammad Ali Jinnah was the

(A) president of the Muslim League and the founder of Pakistan
(B) chief of Afghani nationalists who fought against the Soviet invasion
(C) leader of the Tunisian independence movement against France
(D) head of the secessionist Islamic movement in northern Nigeria
(E) promoter of a pan–North African Islamic state in the 1960s

434. Which of the following statements best describes the relations between Tibet and the People's Republic of China (PRC)?

(A) Tibetans acknowledge that Tibet has been part of China since the 1200s.

(B) The PRC encourages traditional Buddhist practices in order to prevent riots and resistance.

(C) The PRC has destroyed most of Tibet's more than 6,000 monasteries and broken up the monastic estates.

(D) The PRC's failure to modernize Tibet has provoked rebellions by native Tibetans.

(E) As of 2012, most nations recognize the Government of Tibet in Exile in India.

435. Muslim women who became active participants in Algeria's war for independence (1954–1962)

(A) lived primarily in cities

(B) supported the National Liberation Front (FLN)

(C) nursed soldiers but did not actively participate in the fighting

(D) were disparaged by anticolonial Algerian propaganda for fulfilling an un-Islamic role

(E) made great strides towards female emancipation after the Algerian War

436. All of the following are true regarding the Tamil people EXCEPT that

(A) they live mostly in southern India and Sri Lanka

(B) the Sri Lankan Civil War cost almost 100,000 lives

(C) they are primarily Buddhist

(D) the Tamil Tigers (LTTE) carried out numerous attacks on civilians

(E) the Tamil Tigers were defeated by the Sri Lankan armed forces in 2009

437. The leader of the Indonesian independence movement who became the first president of Indonesia and was deposed in a coup in 1966 was

(A) Sukarno

(B) Mohammad Hatta

(C) Suharto

(D) Tunku Abdul Rahman

(E) Yusof bin Ishak

438. All of the following statements are true regarding the Sikhs EXCEPT that

(A) despite Sikh protests, the 1947 partition of the Indian subcontinent divided their homeland in the Punjab

(B) many Sikhs believed that the Indian government desecrated the Golden Temple at Amritsar

(C) religious violence led to Hindu attacks on Sikhs with the collusion of the Indian government

(D) the Sikh bodyguards of Indira Gandhi assassinated her in 1984

(E) Sikh militancy eventually led to the creation of the Sikh-majority state of Khalistan

439. All of the following are true of the literary movement known as Negritude EXCEPT that

(A) it was influenced by the Harlem Renaissance

(B) it was dominated by French-speaking African and Caribbean writers in Paris

(C) it began in the 1960s as part of a movement against French colonialism

(D) Senegalese poet Léopold Senghor was one of the most important adherents

(E) it decried the lack of humane qualities in European culture compared to African culture

440. Patrice Lumumba

(A) was placed in power in the Congo by a CIA-backed coup

(B) supported the secession of the oil-rich province of Katanga

(C) won the Nobel Peace Prize for nonviolently settling the so-called Congo Crisis

(D) was assassinated with the support of the United States and Belgium

(E) was a US-backed dictator who ruled the Congo from 1965 to 1997

441. The first sub-Saharan nation to achieve independence after World War II was

(A) Ghana

(B) Sierra Leone

(C) Uganda

(D) Kenya

(E) Zambia

442. All of the following national states became independent nations after the breakup of Yugoslavia in 1991–1992 EXCEPT

(A) Croatia
(B) Albania
(C) Bosnia
(D) Macedonia
(E) Slovenia

443. All of the following are closely related to the struggle against apartheid in South Africa EXCEPT

(A) Stephen Biko
(B) the Sharpeville Massacre
(C) the African National Congress
(D) the South West Africa People's Organization (SWAPO)
(E) the Soweto riots

444. The discovery of oil in the Niger Delta led to

(A) the Nigerian government nationalizing the oil industry in 1995
(B) the execution of environmental activists with the collusion of multinational oil companies
(C) a rise in the production of both cash and food crops in Nigeria
(D) an increase in the standard of living for most Nigerians
(E) the decline of Islamic fundamentalism in Nigeria

445. Which nation was the last to grant women the right to vote?

(A) India
(B) Malaysia
(C) Ecuador
(D) Portugal
(E) Saudi Arabia

446. The US Congress voted to return the Panama Canal and the Panama Canal Zone to Panama during the administration of President

(A) Lyndon Johnson
(B) Richard Nixon
(C) Jimmy Carter
(D) Ronald Reagan
(E) George H. W. Bush

447. Robert Mugabe

- (A) initiated a controversial fast-track land reform program to redistribute farmland
- (B) was the leader of Swaziland's independence movement
- (C) headed the opposition party of Zimbabwe that attempted to create a multiparty democracy
- (D) invaded Zambia from Botswana to prevent the flow of economic refugees
- (E) organized the Front for the Liberation of Mozambique (FRELIMO) that fought a guerrilla war against Portuguese rule

448. Václav Havel was

- (A) the main inspiration for an independent Slovakia
- (B) the last Communist ruler of Czechoslovakia
- (C) a writer who became the first and last democratically elected president of Czechoslovakia
- (D) an opponent of the Velvet Revolution because it was not sufficiently confrontational
- (E) a Czech nationalist who argued for the breakup of Czechoslovakia into two nations

449. The sub-Saharan African nation with the longest history of uninterrupted free elections (as of 2012) is

- (A) Mauritania
- (B) Guinea
- (C) Madagascar
- (D) Botswana
- (E) Niger

450. The first African writer to win the Nobel Prize in literature was

- (A) Ben Okri
- (B) Chinua Achebe
- (C) Nadine Gordimer
- (D) J. M. Coetzee
- (E) Akinwande "Wole" Soyinka

451. Biafra was

(A) a mineral-rich province that attempted to secede from the Republic of the Congo

(B) a territory on the Red Sea that attempted to secede from Ethiopia

(C) the home of the Igbo people that attempted to secede from Nigeria

(D) the southern half of Sudan that attempted to secede from the northern half of Sudan

(E) a small Spanish territory across from the Canary Islands that was annexed by Morocco

452. All of the following have used violent attacks against civilians EXCEPT

(A) the Euskadi Ta Askatasuna (ETA) in Spain

(B) the Cluster Munition Coalition

(C) Chechen separatists in Russia

(D) the Armed Islamic Group (GIA) in Algeria

(E) the Irish Republican Army (IRA)

453. The revolution that overthrew Fernando Marcos in the Philippines is popularly known as

(A) the Singing Revolution

(B) the Velvet Revolution

(C) the Rose Revolution

(D) the Orange Revolution

(E) the People Power Revolution

454. The end of the Cold War and German reunification are often dated to the fall of the Berlin Wall. This occurred in

(A) 1984–1985

(B) 1989–1990

(C) 1994–1995

(D) 1999–2000

(E) 2004–2005

455. All of following were female heads of states EXCEPT

(A) Benazir Bhutto

(B) Corazon Aquino

(C) Ellen Johnson Sirleaf

(D) Toni Morrison

(E) Michelle Bachelet

CHAPTER 17

The Middle East Since 1900

456. The development of Jewish nationalism in the 1800s that centered on Palestine was

    (A) a response to growing anti-Semitism in Europe
    (B) not supported by eastern European Jews
    (C) encouraged by Christians as a way to further Jewish assimilation
    (D) discouraged as an insane idea by rich Jews such as Walter Rothschild
    (E) first proposed by Theodor Herzl

457. Thomas Edward Lawrence, also known as Lawrence of Arabia,

    (A) captured Damascus and installed himself as de facto ruler
    (B) believed only a military revolution could lead to an independent Arabia
    (C) checked Faisal I's nationalistic revolution in order to extend the British Empire
    (D) led Arab forces to victories over Ottoman Turks in World War I
    (E) worked closely with the British to establish an independent Syria

458. All of the following experienced major unrest in the Arab Spring of 2011 EXCEPT

    (A) the United Arab Emirates
    (B) Egypt
    (C) Syria
    (D) Tunisia
    (E) Libya

459. All of the following were reforms instituted by Mustafa Kemal Atatürk EXCEPT

(A) instituting equal rights for women
(B) encouraging the wearing of traditional Turkish clothing such as the veil, fez, and turban
(C) separating Islamic law from secular law
(D) creating an entirely new Turkish alphabet
(E) disestablishing Islam as the state religion

460. All of the following are true regarding the Iranian Revolution of 1979 EXCEPT that it

(A) indirectly led to the election of Ronald Reagan as United States president
(B) severely restricted the rights of women
(C) was led by Ayatollah Khomeini
(D) established a theocratic constitution
(E) was instituted by a minority of Islamic intellectuals against the will of the majority of Iranians

461. As a result of the Six-Day War, Israel acquired all of the following territories EXCEPT

(A) Gaza
(B) the Sinai Peninsula
(C) the Golan Heights
(D) eastern Jerusalem
(E) the Negev

462. Religious issues played a major role in all of the following conflicts EXCEPT

(A) the Intifada
(B) the Yom Kippur War
(C) the Six-Day War
(D) the Persian Gulf War
(E) the Iranian Revolution

463. The famous modern Arabic writer who won the Nobel Prize in Literature in 1988 was

(A) Tawfiq al-Hakim
(B) Naguib Mahfouz
(C) Son'allah Ibrahim
(D) Badr Shakir al-Sayyab
(E) Ali Ahmad Said Asbar (Adonis)

464. The Young Turks

 (A) instigated a revolution in 1908 that replaced Sultan Abdülhamid II with Mustafa Kemal Atatürk
 (B) rejected secular nationalism in favor of a multinational pan-Islamic vision
 (C) tried to suppress nationalist uprisings in Egypt, Syria, and the Balkans
 (D) opposed Turkish entry into World War I
 (E) overthrew the Ottoman Empire

465. The Lebanese Civil War

 (A) began with the Israeli invasion of southern Lebanon
 (B) lasted 16 years but involved relatively few casualties
 (C) ended after Syria conquered Beirut and annexed Lebanon in 1990
 (D) was the direct cause of the expulsion of the Palestine Liberation Organization from Jordan
 (E) was partially caused by problems with the Lebanese constitution

466. All of the following are positions attributed to al-Qaeda EXCEPT

 (A) opposition to American military bases in the holy land of Saudi Arabia
 (B) support for secular Middle Eastern governments that oppose the United States
 (C) the establishment of an Islamic Caliphate from Spain to Indonesia
 (D) anger over continued support of Israel by the United States
 (E) the use of violence against civilians to achieve their goals

467. Gamal Abdul Nasser

 (A) exemplified Pan-Arab leadership in the post–World War II era
 (B) supported pro-British cooperation in the Arab world
 (C) worked to reconcile Arabs and Israelis
 (D) repelled a United States–backed invasion of Egypt to take the Suez Canal
 (E) was president of Egypt during the Yom Kippur War

468. All of the following reasons were given by Jews to explain the establishment of the State of Israel in 1948 EXCEPT the

 (A) historical ties of the Jewish people to the land of Israel
 (B) murder of six million Jews in World War II
 (C) precarious position of minority ethnic groups without a nation of their own
 (D) need to provide homes for poor Jews
 (E) Balfour Declaration

469. All of the following nations contain large petroleum reserves EXCEPT
- (A) Iraq
- (B) Libya
- (C) the United Arab Emirates
- (D) Egypt
- (E) Kuwait

470. Black September refers to
- (A) King Hussein's war on the Palestinian Liberation Organization leading to its expulsion from Jordan
- (B) the defeat of Israel in the Yom Kippur War
- (C) the murder of Israeli athletes at the Seoul Summer Olympics
- (D) the name given by Arabs to the events leading to the creation of the State of Israel
- (E) the use of poison gas against the Kurds in the 1980s

471. The Second Intifada
- (A) began after the assassination of Yasser Arafat
- (B) ended by the early 1990s
- (C) led to more than 50,000 deaths
- (D) is an example of how facts have one meaning regardless of political orientation
- (E) is also called the Al-Aqsa Intifada after a mosque on the Temple Mount of Jerusalem

472. The Iran-Iraq War
- (A) confirmed the weakness of the shah and encouraged revolution in Iran
- (B) exposed Saddam Hussein's ruthlessness when it came to the use of chemical weapons
- (C) demonstrated the principled opposition of the United States to chemical warfare
- (D) ended quickly as Iran used its much larger population to great advantage
- (E) ultimately resulted in large Iranian territorial gains around the Persian Gulf

473. The Balfour Declaration of 1917

    (A) declared that all nations in the British Commonwealth of Nations are of equal status

    (B) promised that Egypt would be given its independence if the Allies won World War I

    (C) committed the British government to establish Palestine as a national home for the Jewish people

    (D) announced that the Suez Canal would henceforth be demilitarized

    (E) threatened T. E. Lawrence with dire consequences if he continued to support Arab nationalism

474. The Yom Kippur War

    (A) led to the annexation of the Sinai Peninsula by Israel

    (B) was a decisive Israeli victory

    (C) resulted in 20 years of hostility and on-and-off conflict between Israel and Egypt

    (D) began with a two-pronged attack on Israel by Egypt and Syria

    (E) completely reversed the territorial results of the Six-Day War

475. All of the following are true of the Kurds EXCEPT that

    (A) the Kurds joined with Saddam Hussein in the Iran-Iraq War to gain leverage for a state of their own

    (B) there are more than 30 million Kurds

    (C) the PKK, a Kurdish independence group, uses violence to try to achieve an independent Kurdistan

    (D) the Turks, fearing the loss of their eastern provinces, have often violently suppressed Kurdish nationalism

    (E) the Kurds make up about 15 percent of the Iraqi population

CHAPTER 18

Global Interdependence Since 1990

476. Which of the following statements is true regarding acquired immune deficiency syndrome (AIDS)?

(A) AIDS is not a problem in North Africa.
(B) More than one-third of South Africans have contracted AIDS.
(C) AIDS is a severe problem in Botswana and Zimbabwe.
(D) Sub-Saharan Africa has 90 percent of the world's AIDS cases.
(E) The highest percentage of people with AIDS live in central Africa.

477. Global warming in the late 20th and early 21st century is caused by the

(A) decrease in the amount of carbon dioxide in the atmosphere
(B) improper storage of nuclear waste
(C) overcutting of forests and the increased use of fossil fuels
(D) dumping of inorganic material into lakes and rivers
(E) use of herbicides and toxic substances such as asbestos and DDT

478. Al-Qaeda has claimed responsibility for all of the following EXCEPT the

(A) 1999 bombing of a shopping arcade and apartment building in Moscow
(B) 1998 bombing of the US embassies in Nairobi, Kenya, and Dar es Salaam, Tanzania
(C) 2005 bombing of the London public transportation system
(D) 2002 bombing of a synagogue in Tunisia
(E) 2004 bombing of a Madrid commuter train

479. All of the following are well-known authors who write in the style known as magical realism EXCEPT

(A) Miguel Ángel Asturias
(B) Gabriel García Márquez
(C) Salman Rushdie
(D) Jorge Amado
(E) Isabel Allende

480. "The time for the healing of the wounds has come. The moment to bridge the chasms that divide us has come. The time to build is upon us."
    —Nelson Mandela

These words led to

(A) the establishment of homelands for black South Africans
(B) the murder of Stephen Biko
(C) the lifting of economic sanctions against South Africa
(D) the creation of the Truth and Reconciliation Commission
(E) the conviction of apartheid President P. W. Botha for crimes against humanity

481. Desertification is a major problem in all of the following African nations EXCEPT

(A) Mali
(B) São Tomé and Príncipe
(C) Mauritania
(D) Nigeria
(E) Chad

482. All of the following are usually considered elements of postmodernism EXCEPT

(A) irony
(B) the mixing of influences from different styles and historical periods
(C) the importance of interpretation vis-à-vis subjective facts
(D) skepticism toward explanations claiming to be valid for all groups, cultures, or traditions
(E) emphasizing the distinction between the "low" culture of the masses and the "high" culture of postmodernism

483. All of the following are true regarding the US invasion of Afghanistan in 2002 EXCEPT that

(A) the direct cause of the invasion was al-Qaeda's attack on the United States in 2001

(B) it led to the fall of the Taliban government of Afghanistan

(C) it led directly to the death of Osama bin Laden

(D) the war cost more than $400 billion dollars over 10 years

(E) it was the longest war in US history

484. Which nation is NOT linked with a mineral or raw material that it produced in large quantities in the early 2000s?

(A) Congo—rubber

(B) South Africa—gold

(C) Botswana—diamonds

(D) Zambia—copper

(E) Namibia—uranium

485. Foreign workers in western Europe were

(A) appreciated by Europeans for contributing to economic recovery

(B) celebrated as the living embodiment of globalization

(C) deported unilaterally

(D) attacked by right-wing parties reacting to high unemployment

(E) refused admission to right-wing parties because of discrimination and fear of crime

486. As of 2012, about how many people lived on the planet Earth?

(A) 5 billion

(B) 7 billion

(C) 9 billion

(D) 11 billion

(E) 13 billion

487. The Tiananmen Square protests of 1989

(A) were caused by an outpouring of mourning on the death of Deng Xioaping

(B) revealed the effectiveness of nonviolent civil disobedience

(C) were put down without any casualties

(D) were restricted to Beijing

(E) demanded both economic and political reform

488. The predecessor to the Internet was

(A) the World Wide Web
(B) MS-DOS
(C) ARPANET
(D) the information superhighway
(E) mainframes

489. This Burmese politician led the opposition to the military dictatorship in Burma and was awarded the Nobel Peace Prize in 1991.

(A) Tawakel Karman
(B) Aung San Suu Kyi
(C) Liu Xiaobo
(D) Ellen Johnson Sirleaf
(E) Kim Dae Jung

490. NAFTA

(A) eliminated tariffs on many American imports from Mexico
(B) reduced the number of ICBMs positioned in Europe
(C) set cap-and-trade restrictions to prevent global warming
(D) restricted the export of American nuclear technology or fuels anywhere outside of North America
(E) established the mechanism to bail out large banks affected by the fiscal crisis of 2008

491. One example of a problem resulting from internal migration would be

(A) the rise of the National Front Party under Jean-Marie Le Pen
(B) the growth of favelas surrounding Rio de Janeiro
(C) the control of disease in UN-sponsored Breidjing Camp for Sudanese refugees in Chad
(D) the extinction of Cayuse, a Native American language
(E) the passage of an Arizona law requiring that local police check the immigration status of anyone whom they suspected of being undocumented

492. In these attacks, commonly considered attempted genocide, more than half a million people were murdered in four months in 1994 in

(A) Rwanda
(B) Darfur, in the Sudan
(C) Srebrenica, in Bosnia
(D) Ethiopia
(E) East Timor

493. Under Chinese leader Deng Xiaoping,

(A) the productivity of communal farms was increased
(B) all Western influences were discouraged
(C) foreign investment was discouraged
(D) small private businesses were allowed
(E) the Cultural Revolution began

494. The election of Vicente Fox as president of Mexico in 2000

(A) marked the first time presidential elections had ever been held in Mexico
(B) resulted in major drug-related riots in almost every large Mexican city
(C) allowed the Institutional Revolutionary Party (PRI) to take power for the first time since the Mexican Revolution
(D) led to the dissolution of the Institutional Revolutionary Party (PRI)
(E) was the first time a president was elected from an opposition party in almost a century

495. According to a 2008 survey, all of the following were among the largest multinational corporations in the world (in the top 20) EXCEPT

(A) United States Steel
(B) Wal-Mart Stores
(C) Royal Dutch Shell
(D) Toyota Motor
(E) General Electric

496. Which of the following nations is not a member of the EU (as of 2012)?

(A) Bulgaria
(B) Portugal
(C) Slovenia
(D) Switzerland
(E) Spain

497. The biggest cause of deforestation in Brazil is

(A) global warming
(B) population pressure leading to subsistence farming
(C) unchecked wildfires
(D) conversion of forest into pastureland by commercial and speculative interests
(E) a shortage of roads in Brazil

498. All of the following are recent demographic trends in South America EXCEPT the

    (A) transition of South America from a rural to an urban society over the last half century

    (B) increase in the number of cities over five million people from 1 in 1950 to 20 in 2010

    (C) creation of large urban slums on the outskirts of major cities to house migrants

    (D) stagnation of the total rural population

    (E) tremendous growth in urban population

499. In 2010, the number of cell (mobile) phones in use worldwide totaled about

    (A) 50 million

    (B) 100 million

    (C) 1 billion

    (D) 3 billion

    (E) 5 billion

500. The European debt crisis of 2009 to 2012 led to all of the following EXCEPT

    (A) increased faith in the euro as a European-wide currency

    (B) riots against austerity measures in Greece

    (C) rage in Ireland that the majority of people should suffer for the mistakes of bankers

    (D) anger in Germany about having to bail out other indebted European countries

    (E) arguments between economists over whether national spending cuts were the best way to solve the problem

ANSWERS

Chapter 1: European Renaissance

1. (B) Printing with movable type was invented in the 1440s by Johannes Gutenberg (c. 1400–1468). This invention was an enormous technological breakthrough that took bookmaking out of the hands of human copyists. The mass production of identical books and pamphlets made the world of ideas more available to an increasingly literate audience. Two preconditions were probably necessary for the advent of printing: the industrial production of paper (not parchment and vellum) and the existence of a commercial market for manuscripts. By the 1400s, that commercial market flourished in Europe's university towns and major cities. Stationers organized workshops known as scriptoria where the manuscripts were copied. In 1467, two German printers established the first press in Rome and produced 12,000 volumes in five years.

2. (E) The term *Renaissance* originated with the Italian painter and architect Giorgio Vasari (1511–1574) in his *Lives of the Most Excellent Italian Architects, Painters, and Sculptors* (1550). Vasari argued that classical art declined into barbarism after the collapse of the Roman Empire. Only in the past generation, argued Vasari, had Italian artists begun to return to the purity and perfection of Greco-Roman art. He called this development *rinascita*, the Italian word for rebirth, but it was the French translation—*renaissance*—that became popular. The term originally referred to a rebirth in arts and literature but over time has been applied to a set of changes that define an awareness of modernity. The term *renaissance* acquired widespread recognition with the publication of Jacob Burckhardt's *The Civilization of the Renaissance in Italy* in 1860. Burckhardt considered the thousand-year period between the Roman Empire and the Renaissance to be essentially without any artistic or intellectual accomplishments. Historians revised this concept in the 20th century, pointing out the continuities between the Middle Ages and the Renaissance; some historians now deny a period of renaissance ever existed.

3. (E) Humanism developed during the 1300s and 1400s as a response to medieval scholastic education's emphasis on practical, preprofessional studies. Humanists disparaged training professionals in jargon and practice, and they instead advocated the creation of citizens (sometimes even including women) able to speak and write with eloquence and clarity. Humanists believed that this could be accomplished through the study of the humanities: grammar, rhetoric, history, poetry, and moral philosophy. Citizens educated in this way could engage in the civic life of their communities and persuade others to virtuous actions, a concept sometimes known as *civic humanism*. Humanists believed the purest lifestyle was one of service to humankind in this world, and not a retreat into monastic life. Petrarch (1304–1374), a famous poet, is known as the "Father of Humanism." Enea Silvio Piccolomini (1405–1464), later Pope Pius II, was a prolific author; his works include a treatise titled "The Education of Boys." With the adoption of printing after 1500, humanism spread northward to France, Germany, Holland, and England, where it became associated with the Protestant Reformation.

4. (A) The Italian Wars (1494–1559) were caused by the attempts of the larger nation-states of Europe to control the small independent states of Italy. This struggle affected Italian history for more than three centuries. The Italian city-states brought problems on themselves by making foreign alliances with France and Spain. The Italian Wars began in 1494 when Charles VIII of France invaded Italy and seized Naples (1495), only to be driven back by a coalition of Spain, the Holy Roman Emperor, the Pope, Venice, and Milan. The wars became increasingly confusing from there, as alliances constantly shifted over the next half-century. In the Treaty of Cateau-Cambrésis in 1559, Hapsburg Spain achieved temporary supremacy on the peninsula and became the premier power of Europe. The states of Italy, which had wielded influence disproportionate to their size in the Middle Ages, were reduced to second-rate powers or destroyed entirely. Militarily, the Italian Wars symbolized the end of medieval notions of warfare and chivalry.

5. (C) The late Middle Ages and the Renaissance were extremely popular periods for the use of fresco (painting on wet plaster), particularly in Italy. Perhaps the most distinctive feature of Renaissance art was the use of a technique known as linear perspective, developed by Tommaso Masaccio (1401–1428) and Filippo Brunelleschi (1377–1446). In linear perspective, nearby objects were drawn bigger while far objects were drawn smaller. As a result, the painting had a three-dimensional quality where the lines of perspective merged into a distant focal point. This use of perspective gave a huge impetus toward realism. Artists such as Leonardo da Vinci and Michelangelo studied anatomy so that the individuals portrayed in the art seemed more lifelike. Noted Renaissance portraitists included Albrecht Dürer, Hans Holbein the Younger, Raphael, and Jan van Eyck. Renaissance art was famous for its portrait painting, but the use of themes from nature was characteristic of Romanticism, and not of Renaissance art.

6. (D) The movement known as the Renaissance has numerous possible causes. Feudalism was on the decline in the 1400s because of the increasing use of money rather than land as a medium of exchange. Nation-states formed with monarchies intent on reducing the power of feudal lords. Feudal armies became useless because of new technology such as artillery. The Black Death (1349) and subsequent recurrences of plague weakened the feudal structure and gave agricultural laborers more bargaining power and mobility. The decline of feudalism opened the way for the changes associated with the Renaissance in western Europe. The Renaissance has also been attributed to the decline of the prestige of the Roman Catholic Church, weakened by the Western Schism (1378–1417) when two men simultaneously claimed to be pope. The quarrel, driven by politics rather than theology, hurt the reputation of the office of the pope. The invention of the movable-type printing press sped the transmission of the scientific and political ideas of the Renaissance throughout Europe. The printing press increased the availability of books written in vernacular languages, and the Bible became available in translation.

7. (C) The Renaissance in northern Europe developed from the ideas of the Italian Renaissance. The invention of the movable-type printing press spread humanism around Europe. The new thinking was evident in the prevalence of portrait painting in northern Europe. However, the Northern Renaissance was generally more religious than in Italy. While highly realistic in style, even secular northern paintings were filled with religiously symbolic objects. Northern humanists such as Desiderius Erasmus and Thomas More were more concerned with religious issues than their Italian counterparts were. The religious emphasis of the Northern Renaissance would later influence the Protestant Reformation. Another difference was in the centralization of political power: while Italy and Germany were dominated by independent city-states, many parts of central and western Europe (France, Spain, England, and Portugal) began emerging as nation-states.

8. (E) About 1430, composers in the Low Countries began to reject writing pieces with one major melodic line; instead, they began composing for three or four instrumental or human voices. In this new style, known as polyphony, each melodic line was equally important in expressing a melody in harmony with the others. Polyphony grew out of the practice of organum, a plainchant melody with at least one added voice to enhance the harmony. Organum was first used in the Middle Ages but developed into much freer forms of counter-melody in the 1400s and 1500s. The leader of the polyphonic movement was Guillaume Dufay (1400–1474), whose successful career took him to all the cultural centers of the Renaissance.

9. (A) In Italian Renaissance culture, children born out of wedlock were known as *illegitimate*. Illegitimacy in itself did not necessarily carry a social stigma in 15th-century Europe. Most upper-class men acknowledged and supported their illegitimate children as a sign of their virility. Illegitimate children of noble lineage often rose to prominence, such as Leon Battista Alberti, Leonardo da Vinci, and Erasmus. Any social stigma was borne primarily by the woman, whose ability to marry became compromised.

10. (D) Matthias Corvinus (c. 1443–1490) was the King of Hungary who briefly united the Bohemian and Hungarian crowns. Matthias achieved great renown as a crusader against the Ottomans. Pope Pius II encouraged him to attack Bohemia, and Matthias had himself crowned king of Bohemia in 1469. He repeatedly defeated the encroaching Hapsburgs and even occupied Vienna in 1485. His military successes were aided by his creation of a standing army. Matthias promoted the Italian Renaissance in central Europe; many artists and humanists from Italy and western Europe lived at his court. His library at Buda, the Corvina, contained Europe's greatest collections of secular books, including historical chronicles and philosophic and scientific works. However, Matthias's central-eastern European empire collapsed after his death. In the 1520s, the Ottomans conquered most of Hungary (the Battle of Mohács took place in 1526).

11. (A) During the Renaissance, unwed mothers or poor families in cities sometimes could not afford to raise their children. In some cases, they abandoned their children to strangers or to a public charity. In 1445, Florence opened the Ospidale degli Innocenti, a foundling hospital, to deal with the large numbers of abandoned children and offer an alternative to infanticide. Unwed mothers were often domestic servants who had been impregnated by their masters; one-third of the first 100 foundlings were children of these unequal liaisons. More than two-thirds of the hospital's abandoned children were female, revealing the cultural value of males and females in the Renaissance. Although the hospital employed wet nurses, the high number of foundlings overtaxed its resources and resulted in a high rate of infant mortality. The building, originally designed by Filippo Brunelleschi in 1419, still stands in Florence.

12. (D) Dante's *Divine Comedy* was written in Italian, Geoffrey Chaucer wrote *The Canterbury Tales* in Middle English, François Rabelais wrote *Gargantua and Pantagruel* in French, and Luís de Camões wrote *The Lusiads* in Portuguese. Leonardo Bruni (1370–1444) was an Italian humanist and politician, sometimes called the first modern historian. Bruni's most famous work is *History of the Florentine People*, written in Latin. In this book, Bruni was one of the first historians to use the three-period view of history: Antiquity, Middle Ages, and Modern. Bruni also rejected the medieval-style chronicle, instead using Livy (the Roman historian) as a model for language, format, and style. He based his writing on specific information provided by the city archives.

13. (A) Before the Renaissance, artists were often thought of as simply skilled artisans. However, in the 1400s, especially in Italy, artists began to acquire a more prominent social status. The Renaissance boosted the idea that artists possessed individual talent and/or genius, and there was a tremendous increase in the number of artworks individually signed by artists. Renaissance artists worked under three possible types of employment: long-term service in princely courts, commissioned piecework, and production for the market. Although many artists continued to rely on wealthy patrons, a market did emerge for visual arts in the Low Countries. At first, this market was limited to smaller altarpieces, woodcuts, engravings, sculpture, and pottery. Gradually, the art market began to extend to larger panel paintings. This urban, commercialized art market developed into a major force for creativity in the Renaissance because the artists controlled their creations as opposed to commissioned pieces by wealthy patrons.

14. (D) The origins of modern diplomacy are often attributed to the northern Italian states in the early Renaissance. The first embassies were established in the 13th century, but the concept was expanded by Milan under Francesco Sforza (1401–1466), who established permanent embassies in other city-states of northern Italy. Many traditions of modern diplomacy began in Italy, such as the presentation of an ambassador's credentials to the head of state. However, because Rome was the center of Christian Europe in the 1400s, it became the continent's diplomatic hub. In the 1490s, more than 200 diplomats were stationed in Rome. The papacy regularly sent out far fewer envoys (nuncios) than it received until the end of the 15th century.

15. (C) The War of the Roses (c. 1455–1485) was a series of civil wars fought for the English crown between supporters of two rival noble families: the houses of Lancaster and York (whose emblems were the red and the white rose, respectively). The final victory went to a remote Lancastrian claimant, Henry Tudor, who defeated the last Yorkist king, Richard III, at Bosworth in 1485. The House of Tudor then ruled England and Wales for the next century. The War of the Roses caused heavy casualties among the nobility and so weakened the feudal power of nobles, strengthened the merchant classes, and led to the growth of a centralized monarchy under the Tudors. Yet despite the wars, the English economy grew during the 15th century. The cloth industry expanded as the English took the wool they had been exporting to the Low Countries and used it to manufacture goods at home. London merchants assumed greater political prominence, but wool merchants constituted only a small minority in the House of Commons, which was dominated by the country gentry.

16. (A) To many of his Renaissance contemporaries, Giovanni Pico della Mirandola (1463–1494) was the ideal man, whose physical beauty reflected his inner harmony. He was a precocious child, avidly studied Latin and Greek philosophy, and became friends with Marsilio Ficino, Florence's leading neo-Platonic philosopher. Pico enjoyed the patronage of Lorenzo de Medici, who provided him with a villa after the Papacy condemned some of his writings. Pico is most famous for the events of 1486, when at the age of 23, he proposed to defend 900 theses on religion, philosophy, and magic against any opponent. To support his theses, Pico published *Oration on the Dignity of Man* (*Oratio de hominis dignitate*), which embodied the optimism of Renaissance philosophy. In it, Pico proclaimed that individuals face no limits to their development except those that are self-imposed. Pico placed humans at the center of the universe as the measure of all things and the "molder and maker" of their destiny. Yet before his death, he became a follower of the book-burning friar Girolamo Savonarola.

17. (C) Leon Battista Alberti (1404–1472) began the trend of constructing urban palaces for the Florentine ruling elite when he designed the Rucellai Palace (c. 1446). Alberti was the first architect to argue for the "correct" use of the classical orders during the Renaissance. Some of his commissions include the exteriors of the churches of San Francesco in Rimini and Sant' Andrea in Mantua. However, Alberti is more important for his theoretical works. His *On Architecture* (c. 1450), modeled after the work of the Roman author Vetruvius, became the first printed book on architecture (1485). In it, Alberti argued for large-scale urban planning, with monumental buildings set on open squares that would be harmonious and beautiful in their proportions. His ideas were enacted by Pope Sixtus IV (reigned 1471–1484) and his successors, who completely transformed Rome.

18. (B) In 1469, decades of civil war in Spain ended with the marriage of Isabella of Castile and Ferdinand of Aragon. The united strength of Aragon and Castile brought the *reconquista* to a close with the fall of Granada, the last Muslim Iberian state, in 1492. The triumph of Catholicism in Spain ended the relative religious tolerance of the Middle Ages, in which Iberian Muslims, Jews, and Christians had lived side by side. In 1480, Ferdinand and Isabella introduced the Inquisition to Spain, primarily as a means to control the *conversos* (Jewish converts to Christianity). Many "Old Christians" suspected *conversos* of practicing their ancestral religion in secret while pretending to follow the Christian faith. As a result, the Spanish clergy, serving as *inquisitors*, set up courts to investigate people accused of religious deviancy. The Inquisition often arrested people on the basis of anonymous accusations, and the accused could not confront their accusers. As with all European tribunals of the time, torture was employed, although the degree is disputed. The Inquisition rarely acquitted people, and punishments ranged from small monetary fines to burning at the stake. In 1492, Ferdinand and Isabella ordered all Jews in Spain to choose between exile and conversion. Estimates vary widely; perhaps 100,000 Jews chose exile, many fleeing to the Ottoman Empire or the Low Countries. In 1501, Muslims in Spain were likewise ordered to convert or leave their country.

19. (C) Raphael (1483–1520) was known for his Madonnas and painted frescoes in papal chambers. Titian (1477–1576), a Venetian painter, was known as the greatest colorist of the Renaissance. Michelangelo (1475–1564) is primarily considered a sculptor but is noteworthy for his fresco painting of the Sistine Chapel in the Vatican. The multitalented Leonard da Vinci (1452–1519) was an artist, architect, musician, mathematician, and scientist. As a painter, he is noted for the *Mona Lisa* and *The Last Supper*. Diego Velázquez (1599–1660) was a Spanish baroque painter at the court of King Philip IV.

20. (A) This is probably the most famous quotation from *The Prince* (written c. 1505) by the Italian author Niccolò Machiavelli (1469–1527). In 1498, he began working for the Florentine republic and rose rapidly in importance. As defense secretary, he substituted (1506) a citizens' militia for the mercenary system prevailing in Italy. This reform sprang from his belief, explained in *The Art of War*, that the use of mercenaries caused the political weakness of Italy. When the Medicis returned to power (1512), he was briefly imprisoned and tortured for his alleged complicity in a plot against them. Machiavelli retired to his country estate; he never regained authority and died embittered. In *The Prince*, Machiavelli describes how a ruler may gain and maintain power. His ideal prince (apparently modeled on Cesare Borgia) often seems to be an amoral and calculating tyrant who could establish a unified Italian state. The last chapter pleads for the eventual liberation of Italy from foreign rule. The adjective *Machiavellian* has come to be a synonym for amoral cunning and for justification by power.

Chapter 2: European Reformation and Wars over Religion

21. (A) Desiderius Erasmus (1466–1536) of the Netherlands was the greatest humanist of northern Europe. He knew most of the scholars of Europe and was friends with Thomas More and Henry VIII. Erasmus's editions of Greek and Latin classics and of the Fathers of the Church (especially Jerome and Athanasius) were influential, as was his Latin edition of the New Testament based on the original Greek text. *In Praise of Folly* was written in 1509 in Latin. In this long essay, Folly is personified and gives a number of humorous speeches praising self-deception and madness. Folly then satirizes the corruption and pious but superstitious abuses of doctrine in parts of the Catholic Church. The attack on the theologians and widely practiced religious observances shocked many people. However, the book was a major success; by Erasmus's death, 36 Latin editions had been printed. Although Erasmus criticized the church, he refused to join the Reformation and remained committed to reforming the church from within.

22. (B) Martin Luther (1483–1546) was a German priest and professor of theology who began the Protestant Reformation. He taught that the Bible is the only source of divinely revealed knowledge, a belief that challenged the authority of the Pope and the Roman Catholic Church. In 1520, Luther composed three treatises, the last of which was *On the Freedom of a Christian*. This work was composed in Latin and addressed to Pope Leo X. In it, Luther argued that the Roman Catholic Church's numerous rules and stress on good works were useless. He taught that salvation from damnation was not earned by good deeds but received only as a free gift of God's grace through faith in Jesus Christ as redeemer from sin. Luther sharply distinguished between supposedly true Bible teachings and invented church doctrines. He argued that Christ, by his suffering on the cross, had freed humanity from sin and that only God's justice and mercy could save believers. Luther also suggested that there should be a priesthood of all believers instead of a caste of clerics. *Freedom of a Christian* was immediately translated into German and circulated widely. Its principles—by faith alone, by Scripture alone, and the priesthood of believers—became central features of Protestantism.

23. (C) Protestant reformers tended to glorify the patriarchal family as opposed to the Catholic emphasis on celibacy. Protestant judges established marital courts, closed brothels, and sometimes inflicted harsh punishments for sexual deviance. Women both gained and lost by this new attitude toward sex and marriage. Most reformers removed marriage from the list of sacraments, turning it into a civil rite that opened the way for the possibility of divorce. Protestant laws stipulated that a woman could seek divorce for desertion, impotence, and flagrant abuse. However, a woman's role took on a more limited definition as obedient wife, helpful companion, and loving mother. Unlike Catherine of Siena, Teresa of Ávila, and other Catholic women, Protestant women could not renounce family, marriage, and sexuality to gain recognition and power in the church.

24. (A) John Calvin (1509–1564) was a French Protestant theologian; in about 1533, he experienced a sudden conversion and turned all his attention to the cause of the Reformation. Between 1534 and 1536, he wrote *Institutes of the Christian Religion*, one of the most influential theological works of all time. The work rejected papal authority and accepted justification by faith alone. Calvin's doctrine of predestination stated that God had already chosen every human for salvation or damnation, even before the creation of the world. In 1536, Calvin moved to Geneva and tried to construct a government based on the subordination of the state to the church. The Genevan laws and constitution were recodified, regulation of conduct was extended to all areas of life, and magistrates enforced the religious teachings of the church as set forth by the synod. Calvin tolerated no dissenters; when the Spanish physician Michael Servetus passed through Geneva in 1553, Calvin had him burned at the stake for anti-Trinitarian views.

25. (E) Gustavus Adolphus (1594–1632) was King of Sweden and founder of the Swedish Empire. He led his nation, with a population of only one million, to military supremacy in northern Europe during the Thirty Years' War. He is regarded as one of the greatest military commanders of all time, especially for his victory at the First Battle of Breitenfeld (1631). Johann Tserclaes, Count of Tilly (1559–1632), and Duke Albrecht von Wallenstein (1583–1624) were the two chief commanders of the Holy Roman Empire's forces. Wallenstein, a Bohemian Protestant by birth, offered to raise an army for the Catholic Holy Roman Emperor Ferdinand II and soon became the supreme commander of the armies of the Hapsburg monarchy. Louis de Bourbon, Prince of Condé (1621–1686), was an admired French general. At age of 22, he defeated the Spanish army in northern France in the Battle of Rocroi that began the long period of French military superiority. Prince Eugene of Savoy (1663–1736) was one of the most successful military commanders in history, but he was born after the Thirty Years' War ended.

26. (E) The Thirty Years' War left much of central Europe in shambles; an estimated 3 million to 12 million people were killed. Peasants fled their villages, which were often burned down. Sometimes, desperate peasants revolted and attacked nearby castles and monasteries. In 1618, Magdeburg had a population of 25,000 with 35,000 more in the surrounding rural area. In 1635, there were only 400 homes left standing in the city, and by 1644, its population had fallen to 2,464. Much of the destruction of civilian lives and property was caused by the cruelty and greed of marauding mercenaries. By the end of the Thirty Years' War, the population in the German states was reduced by 15 to 30 percent and the male population reduced by almost half. Bohemia's population declined by about a third because of war, disease, famine, and the expulsion of Protestant Czechs.

27. (C) The Peace of Westphalia (1648) was a series of treaties that ended the Thirty Years' War (1618–1648) in the Holy Roman Empire and the Eighty Years' War (1568–1648) between Spain and the Dutch Republic. France and Sweden gained the most from the Peace of Westphalia; France gained Alsace and emerged as the dominant power in Europe. Sweden took several territories from the Holy Roman Empire, which ceased to exist as an effective institution. The Hapsburgs lost the most in the Peace of Westphalia, ceding control over the German states and recognizing the Swiss Confederation and an independent Netherlands. Most of the territorial changes in Europe lasted until the 1800s. Territorial rulers could determine the religion of their subjects, but it was stipulated that subjects could worship as they had in 1624. This meant Lutheranism would dominate northern Europe, Calvinism in the area of the Rhine River, and Catholicism in the south.

28. (A) The Peasants' War (1524–1526) refers to the rising of the German poorer classes in southern and central Germany, particularly in Franconia, Swabia, and Thuringia. It was the climax of a series of local revolts that dated from the 1400s. The Catholic Church was the largest landowner in the Holy Roman Empire; about one-seventh of the empire's territory was controlled by bishops or abbots. Although most of the peasants' demands were economic, Reformation attacks on the church sparked the explosion. The *Twelve Articles of the Peasantry* listed some of their demands: liberty to choose their own pastors, relief from lesser tithes, abolition of serfdom, and impartiality of the courts. The war was marked by atrocities on both sides, and the revolt split the reform movement. Swiss reformer Huldrych Zwingli supported it, and in Thuringia, it was led by the radical Anabaptist leader Thomas Müntzer. However, Martin Luther condemned the revolt. Luther believed that rulers were ordained by God and so must be obeyed even if they were tyrants. The Swabian League destroyed the peasant forces, who lacked unity and firm leadership. An estimated 100,000 peasants were killed in the revolt, the largest popular uprising in Europe before the French Revolution of 1789.

29. (B) The Battle of Lepanto (1571) was a naval battle fought between the Christians (under John of Austria) and Ottomans (commanded by Uluç Ali Pasha) in a strait off Lepanto, Greece. The allied fleet (about 200 galleys) consisted mainly of Spanish, Venetian, and Papal ships and carried about 40,000 fighting men. Although the Ottoman fleet was about the same size, the five-hour battle ended with the virtual destruction of the Ottoman navy. About 15,000 Turks were killed or captured, and 10,000 Christian galley slaves were liberated; the victors lost about 8,000 men. Miguel de Cervantes (later to write *Don Quixote*) lost the use of his left arm in the battle. The victory at Lepanto boosted European morale; Lepanto was the first major Ottoman defeat by Christian powers and prevented the Mediterranean from becoming a highway for Muslim forces. It did not, however, affect Ottoman supremacy on the land. Lepanto was the last major naval battle fought almost entirely between the oar-powered galleys that had ruled the seas since before the Roman Empire. The future would belong to sailing ships, which had more speed in the long haul than did galleys (although less for short distances).

30. (A) Rembrandt (1606–1669) of the Netherlands is considered the greatest painter of northern Europe. His evocative portraits are well known for their contrasts between light and shadows. Albrecht Dürer (1471–1528) became famous for his copper engravings and woodcuts. Little is known of Jan van Eyck (c. 1390–c. 1441), but his *Adoration of the Lamb* in Ghent is considered one of Europe's first landscape paintings. His painting is distinguished by an amazing precision of draftsmanship. Pieter Bruegel (c. 1525–1569) used paintings of the countryside and peasants to criticize the intolerance of society. His vivid depiction of the rituals of village life—agriculture, hunts, meals, festivals, dances, and games—are a prime source of pictorial evidence about aspects of 16th-century life. Thomas Gainsborough (1727–1788) was an 18th-century English painter.

31. (E) In Roman Catholic theology, an indulgence alleviates suffering after death in purgatory. It provides the full or partial remission of temporal punishment caused by sins that have already been forgiven. The indulgence is granted by the Catholic Church only after the sinner has confessed and received absolution. Catholics believe that indulgences draw on the so-called Treasury of Merit accumulated by Jesus Christ's sacrifice on the cross and the good deeds of Christian saints. Indulgences are supposed to be granted for specific prayers and good works such as going on pilgrimage. In the early 1500s, the practice of selling indulgences suggested that the church was more interested in making money than in saving souls. In 1516, the Archbishop of Mainz, Albrecht of Brandenburg, sold indulgences to cover the cost of constructing St. Peter's Basilica in Rome and also to pay for Albrecht's expenses in pursuing his election. Such blatant profiteering outraged many people, including Martin Luther, and triggered Luther's posting of the *Ninety-Five Theses on the Power and Efficacy of Indulgences*. Luther argued that the sale of indulgences violated the original intention of confession and penance, and that Christians could not find absolution through the purchase of indulgences. Protestants eventually rejected the concept of indulgences (and purgatory) altogether, while since the Council of Trent (1562), the buying and selling of indulgences has been unlawful.

32. (C) In 1545, Pope Paul III called a general church council at Trent to meet the crisis of the Protestant Reformation. The Council of Trent met sporadically for the next 17 years and shaped the Catholic Church until Vatican II in the 1960s. At Trent, the council affirmed the importance of good works as well as faith in providing salvation for individuals. The council also reasserted the importance of the seven sacraments to Christian theology as opposed to Luther's claim that there were only two sacraments (baptism and communion). On the tricky issue of the sacrament of the Eucharist, the Council of Trent specifically declared that the bread actually *becomes* Christ's body. This rejected all Protestant positions (the position on the Eucharist in the question is that of Huldrych Zwingli). The council called for the establishment of seminaries in every diocese to ensure that the clergy was fluent in Latin and understood Catholic theology. Bishops were required to live in their dioceses and charged with overseeing the education of the clergy. All weddings were to take place in churches and be registered by the parish clergy, and all marriages remain valid, explicitly rejecting the Protestant allowance for divorce. The Jesuits, founded by Ignatius of Loyola (1491–1556) in 1540, were inspired by the Council of Trent but not a direct result of its decrees.

33. (A) The actual degree of corruption within the Catholic Church in the 1500s is disputed. However, many people in the 1500s perceived that abuses (such as sale of indulgences and clerical ignorance) were rampant and that the church could no longer provide for the spiritual needs of its people. Renaissance Popes did not set a good example: Alexander VI (reigned 1492–1503) owed his position to bribery and had a string of mistresses and illegitimate children. Julius II (reigned 1503–1513), known as the Warrior Pope, was more concerned with power politics than spirituality. Leo X (reigned 1513–1521) was obsessed with rebuilding St. Peter's Basilica. In addition, Renaissance thinking encouraged questioning of the Bible and stimulated a search to uncover uncorrupted texts from the original languages. Nationalism was increasing in northern Europe, and Italians were extremely unpopular in Germany because of Papal taxes leaving Germany to rebuild St. Peter's. German peasants and lesser nobles blamed their depressed position on church greed. The decentralized Holy Roman Empire (which had no imperial army or regular taxation) lacked the ability to resist papal demands for more money and offered little check on the Reformation once it began. Yet unlike Jan Hus, who was burned at the stake a century earlier, Martin Luther received support from Elector Frederick the Wise.

34. (D) Huldrych Zwingli (1484–1531) was a Protestant reformer who worked independently of Martin Luther. Zwingli is associated with the city of Zurich, where he attacked the corruption of the Catholic Church as well as the ritual of fasting and clerical celibacy. Although he often agreed with Luther, Zwingli wanted to create a theocratic society that would unite religion, politics, and morality—an idea radically different from Luther's. Luther and Zwingli also differed on the role of the Eucharist: Luther insisted that Christ was both truly and symbolically present in this central Catholic sacrament, while Zwingli, influenced by Erasmus, insisted that the Eucharist was simply a ceremony symbolizing Christ's union with believers. In 1529, Protestant reformers met at Marburg in central Germany; they resolved many doctrinal differences but could not decide on the precise meaning of the Eucharist. The Swiss and German reform movements continued on separate paths. The issue of the Eucharist would later divide Lutherans and Calvinists.

35. (D) The Edict of Nantes (1598) was issued by Henry IV of France and marked the end of France's Wars of Religion (1562–1598). The Edict of Nantes determined the rights of French Protestants (Huguenots) in Catholic France. Henry IV had been a Protestant but converted to Catholicism in order to become King of France. His Edict of Nantes granted Huguenots substantial concessions such as the right to hold public worship in many parts of France, with the major exception of Paris. The Huguenots were granted full civil rights, as well as several universities and schools and numerous fortified cities. Henry's decree also offered Protestants the right to work in any field, to work for the state, and to bring grievances directly to the king. The Edict of Nantes was a revolutionary document; it was one of the first long-lasting decrees of religious toleration in modern Europe. However, Pope Clement VIII and many French Catholics resented the edict. In 1629, Cardinal de Richelieu, chief minister of King Louis XII, annulled the edict's political clauses. In 1685, Louis XIV revoked the entire edict, depriving French Protestants of all religious and civil liberties. Within a few years, thousands of French Huguenots left France; the effect devastated France's economy. The Huguenots who remained in France did not regain their civil rights until after the French Revolution.

36. (C) Catherine of Aragon (1485–1536) was the first wife of Henry VIII. Catherine was pregnant six times, but only one child survived the first year, a daughter, Mary (later Queen of England from 1553–1558 and remembered as "Bloody Mary"). Henry wanted a male child to inherit the throne, and he simultaneously became infatuated with Anne Boleyn. The Catholic Pope Clement VII refused to allow Henry to dissolve his marriage. As a result, Henry abandoned the Roman Catholic religion and asked Parliament to declare him head of the independent Anglican Church. The formal break with the Papacy was masterminded by Thomas Cromwell (1485–1540), the king's chief minister. Under Cromwell's direction, Parliament passed the Act of Supremacy (1534) that defined the king's leadership over the church. As Archbishop of Canterbury, Thomas Cranmer (1489–1556) annulled Henry's marriage to Catherine, allowing the king to marry Anne Boleyn. Although Henry was reluctant to make doctrinal changes, Cromwell and Cranmer authorized the translation of the Bible into English. In this way, the English Reformation occurred as a direct result of Henry VIII's efforts to divorce Catherine of Aragon. This is not to say that England would have remained Catholic without this incident. However, while large trends may be determined by technology, economics, and climate, major historical changes are also sometimes triggered by chance events.

37. (B) Belief in witches was not new in the 16th century, but the persecution was greater than anything in the Middle Ages. Trials of witches peaked between 1560 and 1640, and witchcraft trials were common in the Holy Roman Empire. The victims of the persecution were overwhelmingly female; women accounted for about 80 percent of the accused witches in about 10,000 trials in Europe and North America during the 1500s and 1600s. About one-third of these women were sentenced to death. Yet before 1400, when witchcraft trials were

Zwingli = Eucharist is purely symbolic

much rarer, nearly half of those accused had been men. Explanations for this gender difference are disputed. Some historians speculate that the trials expressed a hatred of women that peaked during conflicts over the Reformation; both Catholics and Protestants attacked the supposedly undisciplined sexuality of women as a manifestation of popular unruliness and heresy. Other historians see the witchcraft trials as an economic or social class problem, with the accused usually being the poorest and most socially marginal people in most communities (such as older never-married women and widows). Some believe witchcraft accusations were invented by elites for political or material gain. Others contend witchcraft actually existed as a survival of pre-Christian folk religion. Historians estimate about 40,000 to 100,000 Europeans were executed for witchcraft.

38. (A) Baroque was the most important new style in 17th-century art, although the word was not coined until the 18th century. Baroque rejected the Renaissance emphasis on line, harmony, design, unity, and clarity. Instead it emphasized curves, exaggerated lighting, intense emotions, and a kind of artistic sensationalism. As opposed to Renaissance art, which usually showed the moment before an event took place, baroque artists chose the dramatic moment when the action was occurring. Baroque painting and architecture were closely identified with Catholicism. They reaffirmed the expression of religious feeling through art; the emotional impact helped strengthen the ties between believers and the Catholic Church. Baroque was also an urban and spectacular style that was well suited to public festivities and display. Baroque portraits, such as the numerous ones of Philip IV by Diego Velázquez, celebrated authority. The baroque style spread from Rome to other Italian states and then to Hapsburg Europe and Spanish America.

39. (A) This quotation, revealing the persistence of anti-Semitism in Europe, is from the diary of Glückel of Hameln (1646–1724). Glückel was a German Jewish woman who raised 14 children, engaged in trade, and ran her own factory. She was married at age 14 to Chaim Hameln. They were married for 30 years; Chaim traveled throughout Europe trading gold, silver, and jewels while Glückel advised him on business dealings, drew up partnership contracts, and kept accounts. After her husband died accidentally in 1689, she began keeping a diary (at age 44) as a sort of therapy. As a widow, she auctioned her husband's possessions and paid off his creditors. She resumed the trade of pearls, manufactured and sold stockings, sold imports and local wares, and lent money. Her diary, written in Yiddish, provides an intimate picture of German Jewish communal life in the late 17th and early 18th centuries. (Mary Wollstonecraft was an 18th-century advocate of women's rights; the other choices are medieval Christian writers.)

40. (B) An obvious result of the Reformation was the division of European Christianity into Protestant and Catholic areas. Initially, this led to a century of religious wars that culminated in the Thirty Years' War. Protestants encouraged everyone to read the Bible and promoted widespread literacy and the popularization of vernacular languages. The development of national churches strengthened the growth of modern national states. Although the Reformation weakened the claim to universal power by the Papacy, the Catholic Counter-Reformation, epitomized by the Council of Trent and the formation of the Jesuits, breathed new life into Catholicism and was a direct result of the Reformation.

41. (C) European historians now accept that there was a Medieval Warm Period from around 800 to 1300 CE followed by a Little Ice Age from about 1300 to 1850. In the Little Ice Age, glaciers advanced, average temperatures fell, and winters were more severe. This climatic shift happened gradually. The 1300s were an era of unpredictable weather and famine that helped end the prosperity of the late Middle Ages. In some years, snowfall reached the highest levels in recorded history. Many springs and summers were extremely chilly and wet and the growing season may have been shortened by as much as four weeks. The causes of the Little Ice Age are not clear. Some scientists propose decreased sunspot activity, while others suggest increased volcanic activity. Whatever the reason, the Medieval Warm Period had many cold periods and the Little Ice Age had at least three warming intervals. European glaciers began retreating only after 1850.

42. (A) Katharina Schütz Zell (c. 1497–1562) was an outspoken German Protestant writer during the Reformation. She was wife of Matthias Zell, one of the first priests to marry. After his death, she continued to defend Protestantism. In her *Letter to the Entire Citizenry of the Town of Strasbourg* (1557), she campaigned for the right of clergy to marry and the responsibility of laypeople—women as well as men—to preach the Gospel. When a critic cited Saint Paul to argue that women should remain silent in church, Katharina Zell responded, "I would remind you of the word of this same apostle that in Christ there is neither male nor female." In 1525, she helped feed thousands of refugees, regardless of denomination, who flooded Strasbourg after their defeat in the Peasants' War. She consistently opposed Protestant persecution of dissenters such as Anabaptists.

43. (E) The Fuggers were a famous family of wealthy merchant princes and European bankers in the 1400s and 1500s. Their wealth began with Hans Fugger, supposedly a weaver, who moved to Augsburg in 1367. His descendants built up the family fortune by trade and banking. The family reached its zenith with Jakob Fugger II (1459–1525), nicknamed Jakob the Rich. The Fuggers owned palaces, extensive real estate, and merchant fleets; their bank was the largest in the 16th century, with branches in the Netherlands, Italy, and Spain. Jakob's fortune was built on a monopoly granted him by the Hapsburgs for the mining and trading of silver, copper, and mercury. He lent immense sums to Holy Roman Emperor Maximilian I and helped win the election (1519) of Charles V as Holy Roman Emperor by bribing the electors. This alliance between Europe's largest bank and largest empire lasted for the next three decades. The house declined with the fortunes of the Hapsburgs.

44. (E) Anabaptists are Protestant sects that believe that infant baptism is not authorized in the Bible and that baptismal candidates must make their own confession of faith. A convert, if baptized in infancy, must be baptized again as an adult. Anabaptists were prominent in Germany, Switzerland, Moravia, and the Netherlands in the 16th century, when they were part of the so-called radical wing of the Reformation. Many Anabaptists also rejected wearing wedding rings, taking oaths, and participating in civil government. Their pacifism and their desire to separate church and state earned them persecution from Catholics and Protestants alike. The followers of Jakob Hutter (c. 1500–1536), founder of the Hutterite Brethren, stressed the common ownership of goods modeled on the primitive church. There are about 40,000 Hutterites in North America today. Menno Simons (1469–1561) was the founder of the Mennonites, a group with more than a million members worldwide as of 2012. The Amish, a subgroup of the Mennonites, total about 250,000 in North America. The Schwarzenau Brethren originated in 1708 in Germany; they were strongly influenced by Anabaptist theology. In the United States, they have also been called Dunkers.

45. (D) Elizabeth I (1533–1603) was queen of England from 1558 until her death. She was the daughter of Anne Boleyn and Henry VIII, and the last monarch of the Tudor dynasty. In the mid-1580s, Spain attempted to conquer England, overthrow the Protestant Elizabeth, and establish the Catholic Philip on the English throne. The defeat of the Spanish Armada by Charles Howard in 1588 marked the beginning of the decline of the Spanish Empire and made England the world's preeminent naval power.

Chapter 3: Islamic Gunpowder Empires: Ottoman, Safavid, and Mughal

46. (D) Historians sometimes use the term *gunpowder empire* to describe the Ottoman, Safavid, and Mughal Empires. These empires existed from about 1300 to 1800, often reaching their greatest extent in the 1500s and 1600s. Each used newly developed firearms, especially cannon, to create their empires. Each state developed a highly centralized administration that could mobilize the men, money, and natural resources necessary to purchase weapons and train soldiers. Although the term *gunpowder* focuses attention on military exploits, these empires were also centers of impressive cultural achievements. However, the Safavids, although Muslim, spoke Persian (Farsi).

47. (B) The Safavids are named after their first ruler, Safi al-Din (1252–1334), and were originally from northwestern Persia. Because they were Shiites, the Safavids were archrivals of the Ottomans, who were Sunni Muslims. The Safavids ruled from 1501 to 1722 (and a brief return from 1729 to 1736). At its height, the Safavid Empire included present-day Iran, Azerbaijan, Armenia, and most of Iraq, Georgia, Afghanistan, and the Caucasus. They also controlled parts of Pakistan, Turkmenistan, and Turkey.

48. (C) Shah Abbas I (1571–1629) tried to form trade and political relationships with European powers to fight against the Ottoman Empire. In 1599, Abbas sent his first diplomatic mission to Europe; it was received by Rudolph II in Germany, Pope Clement VIII in Rome, and finally by Philip III in Madrid. Although Iranian attempts to make alliances with most Europeans powers did not work out, Abbas's contacts with the English were more fruitful. The Shirley brothers came from England to Iran in 1598 as envoys from the Earl of Essex and helped Abbas reorganize and train the Safavid army. The English East India Company also took an interest in Iran; in 1622, four of its ships helped Abbas take Hormuz from the Portuguese.

49. (C) The Battle of Chaldiran (1514) took place in present-day northwestern Iran and resulted in a victory for the Ottomans over the Safavid Empire. The Ottomans, under Selim I, had a larger army as well as more advanced weaponry. As a result, the Ottomans gained control over eastern Anatolia and northern Iraq. The battle began 41 years of almost constant warfare between the two Islamic empires that only ended in 1555 with the Treaty of Amasya. Some Safavid losses, such as Azerbaijan, were temporary, but the loss of Iraq, as well as parts of eastern Anatolia, became permanent. The defeat defined the Ottoman-Safavid borders, and this line essentially remains the border between Turkey and Iran today. With the new border, Tabriz became a frontier city and uncomfortably close to the Ottoman enemy. That led to the decision to move the Safavid capital to Qazvin, in the 1500s, and to Isfahan, in central Persia, in 1598.

50. (E) In spite of the animosity between the Ottomans and Safavids, Shah Abbas I (reigned 1587–1629) created a culture that blended Persian, Ottoman, and Arab traditions. Abbas moved the Safavid capital from Qazvin to the more central and more Persian Isfahan in 1598, and it became a great cultural center. Royal patronage inspired the creation of paintings, metalwork, textiles, and carpets. Some of Iran's finest painters worked under Abbas's rule, including Reza Abbasi and Muhammad Qasim. Isfahan was embellished by magnificent parks, gardens, baths, colleges, and caravanserais; it is famous for its Safavid Islamic architecture, with many beautiful boulevards, covered bridges, palaces, and mosques. At its height, Isfahan was one of the world's largest cities (with about one million people) and also a place where many cultures and nationalities mingled. Naghsh-e Jahan Square is situated at the center of Isfahan. It was constructed between 1598 and 1629 and surrounded by buildings from the Safavid era. It is now one of UNESCO's World Heritage Sites. Isfahan eventually fell to the Afghans in 1722.

51. (C) The Mughal Empire ruled much of the subcontinent of India from 1526 to 1827. The dynasty was founded by Babur (1483–1530), a Turkish chief descended from Timur (Tamerlane). In 1504, Babur captured Kabul and established a kingdom in Afghanistan. After the failure of his final attempt (1512) on Samarkand, Babur began raids southward into India. In 1525, he invaded India and defeated the sultan of Delhi at a crucial battle at Panipat in 1526. He then captured Agra and Delhi and conquered nearly all of northern India. At its height from about 1650 to 1725, the Mughal Empire extended from Bengal in the east to Baluchistan in the west, Kashmir in the north to the Kaveri basin in the south.

52. (A) Urdu is an Indo-European language identified with Muslims on the Indian subcontinent. It is the national language of Pakistan and spoken by more than 50 million people in parts of India, where it is an official language of five states. Urdu developed from local Persian, Arabic, and Turkic influence over about 900 years. It took shape during the Delhi Sultanate (1206–1526) and continued to develop under the Mughal Empire (1526–1858). Standard Urdu is mutually intelligible with Standard Hindi; the combined population of Hindi and Urdu speakers constitutes the world's fourth-largest language group.

53. (E) *Delhi Sultanate* is a general term to cover five short-lived Islamic kingdoms (sultanates) in India between 1206 and 1526, when the last was replaced by the Mughal dynasty. The five dynasties were the Mamluks (c. 1206–1290), the Khilji (c. 1290–1320), the Tughluq (c. 1320–1414), the Sayyid (c. 1414–1451), and the Lodio (c. 1451–1526). The Delhi Sultanate was founded after Muhammad of Ghor captured Delhi in 1192. The loosely organized sultanate reached its greatest extent in the early 1300s, when Delhi's authority reached to the extreme south of India. The sultanate repeatedly turned back Mongol invaders, but Timur sacked Delhi in 1398 and the sultanate disintegrated. However, local rulers lingered on until the invasion of Babur and the Mughal conquest (1526). The Delhi Sultanate began a period of an Indo-Muslim fusion of cultures leaving lasting changes in architecture, music, literature, and clothing.

54. (A) Akbar (1556–1605), Babur's grandson, was the third Mughal emperor. Through force of arms, Akbar regained the family's territory in northern India that had been lost by Babur's son. Because the Mughal Empire represented foreign rule in India, Akbar tried to reconcile Muslims and Hindus (who made up 80 percent of the empire). Akbar abolished the hated jizya tax on Hindus, extended opportunities in government to some Hindu subjects, and allowed Hindus to rebuild temples. He rejected forced conversions and encouraged intermarriage between the two groups. Akbar himself used marriage alliances with various royal Hindu houses to expand his empire. He also outlawed suttee and discouraged child marriage. These policies helped maintain the power and stability of the empire; they were eventually discarded by Aurangzeb (reigned 1658–1707).

55. (C) The Mughal Empire reached its greatest extent under Aurangzeb (reigned 1658–1707). Under his rule, the empire included the entire subcontinent except for a small area at the southern tip. Aurangzeb was a scholar and devoted to Islam; he made two copies of the Qur'an using his own calligraphy. However, he persecuted the Hindus and executed the guru of the Sikhs when he refused to convert. By taxing Hindus and destroying their temples (and rebuilding them as mosques), he earned the hatred of Hindus for generations. His religious intolerance led Hindus and Sikhs to revolt and hastened the decline of the empire. From 1682, Aurangzeb concentrated his energies on crushing the Marathas in the Deccan, but his expensive wars were only temporarily successful and weakened his authority in the north. The Mughal Empire fell apart soon after his death.

56. (B) After the death of Aurangzeb in 1707, the Mughal Empire experienced several succession crises. Peasant revolts and religious violence threatened stability, while nobles and warlords tried to control the weak emperors. Around the borders, powerful new kingdoms began to chip away at Mughal lands. Most of the empire's territories in India passed to the Marathas, Nawabs, and Nizams. By about 1760 the Mughal Empire ceased to be a political force. Although several regional kingdoms experienced economic growth and political stability (e.g., Bengal, Hyderabad, and Punjab), in general, the 1700s in India are known as a Dark Age or the Great Anarchy. In 1804, the blind and powerless Shah Alam II formally accepted the protection of the British East India Company, which had gained in power as the Mughals became weaker. The British disbanded the once-powerful Mughal army in 1805, and the Mughal Empire officially ended in 1857.

57. (B) Mehmed II the Conqueror (1432–1481) was sultan of the Ottoman Empire from 1444 to 1446 and again from 1451 to 1481. He is sometimes considered the founder of the Ottoman Empire. At the age of 21, he conquered Constantinople after a 53-day siege and ended the Byzantine Empire. In Asia, he unified all of Anatolia under Ottoman control, and in Europe, he advanced as far as Belgrade before being checked by John Hunyadi in 1456. The Knights Hospitaller also turned back Mehmed's forces at Rhodes in 1480 (Belgrade fell to Suleiman the Great in 1521 and Rhodes fell in 1522).

58. (C) The Ottoman Empire reached the height of its power under Sultan Suleiman I (the Magnificent), who reigned from 1520 to 1566. At this time, Francis I (1494–1547), the Valois ruler of France, had been humiliated at the Battle of Pavia in 1525 by Spanish Hapsburg forces. Francis was desperate to overcome the superior military of King Charles V, ruler of both Austria and Spain. So he forged an alliance (1536) with the Turkish sultan. For the next several decades, Suleiman and Francis worked together to prevent Charles V from conquering France. For example, the Turkish fleet besieged Nice when it was occupied by Hapsburg troops. Francis even ordered (1543–1544) all inhabitants of nearby Toulon to vacate their town so that he could use it as a Muslim colony for the wintering of the fleet. Toulon Cathedral was transformed into a mosque, the call to prayer occurred five times a day, and Ottoman coinage was widely used. The French would remain on-and-off allies of the Ottomans for the next two centuries.

59. (B) In the second half of the 1600s, the Ottomans consolidated their far-flung empire using different techniques from those of the European states. Instead of suppressing mercenary armies, the Ottoman state negotiated with them and incorporated them into the state army. To avoid a revolt, Ottoman leaders played elites off against each other and even absorbed some into the bureaucracy. The constantly shifting social and political alliances help explain how the coup-ridden Ottoman state could appear weak in European eyes and yet still pose a military threat on Europe's southeastern borders. In the end, the Ottoman state far outlasted Louis XIV's absolute monarchy.

60. (B) The Ottoman Empire lasted from about 1300 to 1923. It reached its greatest extent in the 16th and 17th centuries, when it controlled territory in southeastern Europe, southwestern Asia, and northern Africa. However, the Ottomans never occupied Sicily, although Arabs did conquer the island in the ninth century after raiding it for two centuries. The Arabs were displaced by the Norman conquest of Sicily (led by Roger I) in the 11th century, and Sicily remained under Christian control after that time.

61. (E) The Valide Sultan was the mother of a ruling sultan in the Ottoman Empire. Through her influence over their sons, the Valide Sultan could control the affairs of the empire. In the late 1500s and early 1600s, a series of incompetent or child sultans led to a period known as the Sultanate of Women. The Valide Sultans influenced the appointment and dismissal of ministers and built mosques, hammams (bathhouses), and palaces. These women could not sit publicly at the Divan (council of state); instead, they sat behind a decorative screen and communicated with the sultan. In the Topkapi Palace harem, the Valide Sultan's quarters were centrally located so she could supervise the family apartments as well as those of the servants and administrators. One famous Valide Sultan was Nurbanu Sultan (1525–1583), either a Venetian of noble birth or a Spanish Jew. She was the wife of Selim II, the mother of Sultan Murad III, and the first Valide Sultan to act as coregent. Safiye Sultan (c. 1550–1603) was the consort of Murad III and coregent of her son, Mehmed III. She began the construction of the New Mosque in Istanbul in 1598. The most powerful of all was Kosem Sultan (1589–1651), one of only two women to rule the Ottoman Empire officially and alone.

62. (B) The Ottoman Empire had abundant agricultural resources to support its population. However, the expenses of the large empire constantly drained the treasury. High taxes caused unrest in the provinces. The problem of the Janissaries made it difficult or impossible to modernize the army. The initial Ottoman advantage over Europe in technology was reversed by 1700. Ineffective leaders could not rival the sultans of the early years, and Ottoman Islam became more focused on maintaining tradition and spirituality. New trade routes led Europeans to dominate commerce with India and China. The millet system was less effective as nationalism swept over eastern Europe in the 1800s. In addition, the aggressiveness of the new European powers meant that the Ottomans would seem to be declining even if they were remaining static. Ultimately, the Ottoman Empire collapsed at the end of World War I.

63. (D) Much of the Ottoman Empire's economy was based on textile production and trade in carpets, silks, cottons, and other luxury goods. Women played an extremely important role in this economy. Although both men and women embroidered, most embroidery came from the harems of high officials, from workshops and factories, and from women working independently in the *haremliks* (women's quarters) of their homes. Ottoman women in cities, confined to their homes by social convention, used embroidery as an outlet to socialize, gossip, and take tea. However, the pieces they produced became a source of income and independence. Most women were hired by the putting-out merchants to produce in their homes; few guilds accepted women until the late 1800s.

64. (D) In the Ottoman Empire, non-Muslim communities were organized according to the millet system. The word *millet* comes from the Arabic word *millah* and literally means "nation." The Ottoman millet system gave minority religious, ethnic, and geographical communities a limited amount of power to regulate their own affairs. Sultan Mehmed II instituted an Orthodox Christian millet after he conquered Constantinople in 1453; in this way, he tried to reorganize the Ottoman Empire as the heir of the Eastern Roman Empire. Armenian, Syriac, Jewish, and other millets followed. Millets set their own laws and collected and distributed their own taxes. The Ottomans only required that they remain loyal to the Empire. Millets created a direct and usually harmonious relationship between individual ethnic groups and the sultan. However, they tended to promote discord between ethnic groups because they depended on a relationship with the sultan rather than with other member groups of the Ottoman Empire.

65. (C) Janissaries were elite infantry soldiers in the Ottoman Empire. The corps was formed in the 14th century and became distinctive because the soldiers wore unique uniforms, received salaries, marched to music, and lived in barracks. They were the backbone of the Ottoman army and soon acquired the power to make and unmake sultans. Any sultan who attempted to modernize the Ottoman army and replace the Janissaries was killed or deposed. In 1622, the teenage sultan Osman II (1604–1622) attempted to disband the Janissary corps, blaming them for defeats in Poland. The Janissaries revolted, imprisoned the sultan, and had him murdered. In 1807 a Janissary revolt deposed Sultan Selim II, who had tried to remake the army along western European lines. In 1826, Sultan Mahmud II rid himself of the useless Janissaries by having them massacred in their barracks by his loyal cavalry (Spahis). About 4,000 Janissaries were killed, and the survivors were imprisoned or executed.

Chapter 4: The Rise and Expansion of European Nation-States

66. (B) The location of the Netherlands was perfect for maritime commerce, and the Dutch developed a thriving shipping and shipbuilding industry in the 1500s. In other European countries, elites put their effort and money into their landholdings, whereas the wealthy Dutch looked for investments in trade. After the Dutch gained unofficial independence from Spain in about 1598 (officially in 1648), Amsterdam became the chief commodities market and main European center for banking for two centuries. By 1670, the Dutch commercial fleet was bigger than the English, French, Spanish, Portuguese, and Austrian fleets combined. Because of the Dutch Republic's cosmopolitan nature, it tolerated more religious diversity than other European states. About one-third of the Dutch Republic remained Catholic, and the secular authorities allowed them to worship as they chose as long as it was in private.

67. (E) The European invasion of the Western Hemisphere that began in 1492 resulted in the exchange of previously isolated plants, animals, and organisms. This is known as the Columbian Exchange. Before the Columbian Exchange, there were no tomato products in Italy, oranges in Florida, sugarcane in Jamaica, coffee in Colombia, rubber trees in Africa, burros in Mexico, cattle or horses in Texas, bananas in Honduras, or chocolate in Switzerland. The Columbian Exchange completely changed the world's ecosystems.

national interest

68. (A) *Raison d'état* is a French phrase meaning "reason of state," although it is often translated as "national interest" in English. Niccolò Machiavelli was the first major thinker to support the primacy of the national interest. However, the policy is associated with Cardinal Richelieu (1585–1642), chief minister to French King Louis XIII. According to Richelieu's interpretation, the interests of the French state were more important than all other concerns, including religion. His ideas of a strong nation-state and aggressive foreign policy helped create the modern system of international politics.

69. (C) Philip II (reigned 1556–1598) of Spain was the most powerful monarch in Europe. He inherited the western Hapsburg lands of Spain and the Netherlands from his father (Charles V), and he also benefited from his own personal tragedies. All four of his wives died, but through them he became part of four royal families (Portuguese, English, French, and Austrian) and felt he had legitimate reasons to intervene everywhere in Europe. Although Philip was unable to defeat the Calvinist rebels who established an independent Dutch Republic in the Netherlands, he controlled all the Spanish colonies in the Americas. However, by the time he died, the debilitating effects of colonial overexpansion and the influx of gold and silver (and resulting inflation) became apparent. Philip was a devout Catholic who longed to restore Europe's religious unity, but tax increases could not finance all of his wars and had to be supplemented with loans. The king repudiated his debts four different times during his reign. The overburdened peasantry could not pay the taxes to meet rising expenses and grew resentful. Philip II was succeeded by Philip III, his son by his fourth wife, Anne of Austria.

70. (A) The origins and early history of nation-states are the subject of much dispute. It is not clear whether "nations" predate and create the nation-state, or vice-versa. The national states of Spain, Portugal, England, and France already existed by 1700, while Italy and Germany would not unify into their modern form until the late 1800s. The causes of the failure of the Holy Roman Empire to turn into Germany are controversial, but the fact is indisputable. From the end of the Thirty Years' War in 1648, the Holy Roman Empire basically existed in name only. In the 18th century, the Holy Roman Empire consisted of more than 1,500 separate territories governed by distinct authorities.

71. (A) Capitalism is an economic system based on private ownership of the means of production. In a capitalist system, personal profit can be acquired through the investment of capital and the employment of labor. Capitalism is grounded in the concept of free enterprise and the restriction of government intervention in the economy. Capitalists believe that a free market, based on supply and demand, will ultimately maximize consumer and social welfare; risk is inherent in the system. Profit, and not social good, is the defining motive in capitalism.

72. (D) In 1415, the Portuguese captured Ceuta (surrounded by present-day Morocco) during the reign of John I. After that, Portuguese ships sailed down the western African coast looking for gold and slaves. By the late 1400s, the Portuguese chain of forts had reached Guinea. The islands of São Tomé and Príncipe (now independent) in the Gulf of Guinea were uninhabited before the arrival of the Portuguese around 1470. Elmina Castle was erected by Portugal in 1482 as São Jorge da Mina Castle in present-day Ghana. It was the first trading post on the Gulf of Guinea. The Portuguese built Fort Santo Antônio in 1515 near Axim, in present-day Ghana. Goa was a Portuguese outpost in India.

slaves

73. (A) This statement is attributed to Louis XIV (1638–1715), who supposedly declared it to the Paris high court of justice in 1651. Louis XIV epitomized the absolutist model of government; he claimed uncontestable power and shared it with no one. Louis built up Europe's largest army, manipulated the ambitions of his nobles and courtiers, chose middle-class men who owed him everything as his ministers, and eliminated religious or political opposition. He continued the nobility's exemption from taxes but forced its members into financial dependence on the crown. The court nobility became preoccupied with ceremonial etiquette and petty intrigues, while provincial nobles lost power. Louis also tried to impose religious uniformity, culminating in the revocation of the Edict of Nantes.

74. (E) A salon was an informal gathering held regularly in a private home and usually presided over by a socially eminent woman. Salons are commonly associated with French literary and philosophical movements of the 17th and 18th centuries. The salon became a way that courtly manners and Enlightenment ideas reached the upper classes. Hostesses of salons encouraged lively conversations about love, literature, and philosophy. This gave authors such as Corneille and Racine a forum to share their work. The first renowned salon in France was the Hôtel de Rambouillet in Paris. Its hostess, Roman-born Catherine de Vivonne (1588–1665), ran it from 1607 until her death. She later faced competition in 1652 from the rival salon of Madeleine de Scuéry in the Marais section of Paris. French-style salon sociability spread through Europe; in the 18th and 19th centuries, many large cities in Europe had salons copied from the Parisian model.

75. (D) Sweden had become a major force in European politics because of the military genius of Gustavus Adolphus (1594–1632). It retained this position until the reign of Charles XII (1682–1718). In 1700, a triple alliance of Denmark-Norway, Poland-Lithuania, and Russia (under Peter the Great) launched an attack on Swedish-controlled territory in northern Europe. The following two decades of fighting were known as the Great Northern War. In 1700, at the Battle of Narva (in present-day Estonia), the army of Charles XII defeated a Russian force three times larger; 10,000 Russians were killed while the Swedes lost less than 1,000. Charles later invaded Russia in 1708 with Moscow as his goal, but the Russians slowed the Swedish advance with a scorched-earth policy. Charles, with about 17,000 men, unwisely decided to fight the Russians (with about 44,000 men) at Poltava (1709) on the Vorskla River. He was decisively defeated, and Russia replaced Sweden as the major power in the Baltic region.

76. (D) The Levellers were a Puritan group that challenged England's social and religious structure during the English Civil War. The name was applied to them in 1647 to make fun of their belief in equality. Many Levellers were disgruntled soldiers from Oliver Cromwell's New Army who argued that farmers, shopkeepers, and artisans should have access to Parliament. The leader of the movement was John Lilburne. The Levellers wanted Parliament to meet regularly and its members to be paid so that common people could serve. They also advocated widening suffrage so that every male head of a household could vote, and they skillfully used petitions and pamphleteering to popularize their positions. Cromwell suppressed the Levellers as a threat to property owners.

77. (C) Before Louis XIV (reigned 1643–1715), French nobles exercised local authority by retaining their own private armies, administering law on their estates, providing jobs for subordinates, and resolving their conflicts through dueling. Louis XIV domesticated the quarrelsome French nobles by replacing violence with court ritual. He convinced the nobles to cooperate with him by giving them pensions, offices, honors, and gifts; noncooperating nobles faced disfavor or punishment. In 1682, Louis XIV moved his court to Versailles. At this elaborate court, the nobles attended ballets and theatricals and learned the rules of etiquette he supervised. Access to the king was the most valuable commodity at the court, and the nobles essentially became Louis's clients, dependent on him for their advancement.

78. (B) The mercantilist Navigation Act of 1651 reinforced the idea that English commerce should be carried in English vessels. The Navigation Act banned foreign ships from transporting goods from outside Europe to England or its colonies. It also banned third-party country's ships from transporting goods from another European country to England. These rules specifically targeted the Dutch, who controlled most of Europe's international trade at the time. Oliver Cromwell tried to carry this policy even further by waging naval war on the Dutch from 1652 to 1654. As a result of the First (of four) Anglo-Dutch naval wars, the English navy gained control of the seas around England and forced the Dutch to accept an English monopoly on trade with English colonies.

79. (A) In the Middle Ages, the upper classes had often participated in the entertainments of the common people. This changed in the 1600s and 1700s, when the social elites attempted to widen the distinction between their own "superior" culture and the "inferior" culture of the common people. More important, they tried to instill new forms of discipline in their social inferiors by eliminating parts of popular culture. Both Protestants and Catholics campaigned against popular religious practices, nature worship, indecent images of saints, and the profusion of feast days. They also tried to root out maypole dances, Sunday village fairs, gambling, taverns, and bawdy ballads. Clergy, officials, and local police worked together to regulate pilgrimages to shrines and suppress cockfighting and bearbaiting. The emphasis on discipline cleared the way for the creation of a more efficient capitalist workforce in the 1800s.

80. (C) Rococo (sometimes known as late baroque) describes a popular style in painting and architecture in the 1700s. Rococo originated in France and spread across Europe, especially Germany, Austria, and Venice. In general, rococo was less symmetrical and more linear and understated than earlier baroque styles. Parisian tapestry weavers, cabinetmakers, and bronze workers arranged motifs such as shells, scrolls, leaves, flowers, and bamboo stems into ingenious and engaging compositions. An enthusiasm for Chinese art also added to the new style. In France, the major architects associated with the style were Robert de Cotte and Gilles Marie Oppenord. Rococo painters such as Antoine Watteau and François Boucher captured scenes of everyday life among the aristocracy and the upper middle classes. Thomas Chippendale transformed British furniture design through his adaptation and refinement of the rococo style.

81. (D) The Thirty Years' War forced nation-states to field ever-larger armies. Governments needed more revenue and officials to supervise the troops, collect taxes, and then repress resistance to higher taxes. After the war ended, most European states did not return to the status quo. Instead, they justified the growth of state authority and bureaucracy by cultivating their royal images. One way to do this was by building huge palaces with extensive parks, formal gardens, grottoes, areas for exotic animals, and rooms filled with expensive or exotic artwork. In the 1630s, Philip IV (reigned 1621–1665) built an enormous palace near Madrid. Louis XIV's famous palace at Versailles was begun in the 1660s. The construction of Sweden's Drottningholm Palace began in 1662.

82. (C) Inflation in Spain in the early 1500s was primarily caused by the vast amounts of silver and gold imported into Spain. In the decade of the 1520s, Spain imported 149,000 grams of silver. That number increased in the next three decades: 86.2 million in the 1530s, 178 million in the 1540s, and 303 million in the 1550s. Likewise, the amount of gold imported into Spain increased from 5 million grams in the 1520s to 14 million grams in the 1530s, 25 million grams in the 1540s, and 43 million grams in the 1550s.

83. (D) About half of all slaves went to Dutch, French, Danish, or British sugar plantations in the Caribbean. Approximately 40 percent went to Portuguese Brazil, and about one-tenth to Spanish America. Only about one in twenty slaves were sent from Africa to the British colonies of North America.

84. (B) The movement of Africans across the Atlantic to the Americas was the largest forced migration in world history. Historians estimate that between 10 and 13 million Africans were kidnapped and transported like cattle to the Americas between 1400 and 1900. Africans made up the largest group of people to come to the Western Hemisphere. Less than 5 percent of the total number of slaves were sent before 1600, and only about 14 percent arrived between 1600 and 1700. Nearly three-quarters of all African slaves (about 7 million) arrived between 1701 and 1810.

85. (E) During the Thirty Years' War (1618–1648), armies grew much larger. Most armies in the 1550s had fewer than 50,000 men, but Gustavus Adolphus commanded 100,000 men in 1631. By 1700, France under Louis XIV had Europe's largest army of about 400,000 soldiers. Rulers now recruited more of their own subjects to replace foreign mercenaries. To produce more firepower, commanders began spreading out the soldiers firing the guns; they set up long, thin lines of three to five ranks firing in turn to produce a continual hail of lead. Maintaining discipline in huge armies required new methods; drill and a clear chain of command became essential. Governments introduced uniforms during the Thirty Years' War to improve discipline and create standardization. The cost of the larger armies and weapons strained the resources of every state in the late 1600s. (The pike square was abandoned because of the musket's deadly firepower.)

86. (B) In the four centuries of the slave trade, historians estimate there were about 40,000 slaving voyages. With so many voyages, it is unsurprising that slaves on different ships had very different experiences. The crew of slave ships generally tried to feed and treat the slaves decently according to the standards of the time, not because they cared about the slaves as people but because only a living (and healthy-looking) slave would fetch a good profit when the ship landed. There were, of course, many exceptions. Slaves died on the Middle Passage at a much higher rate than did criminals, soldiers, and free immigrants who took similar ocean voyages. Probably about 12 percent of slaves died on the Middle Passage. In general, the mortality rate declined over time, but it remained high for a specially selected young adult population. Although the Middle Passage was horrible, more slaves died in slave raiding in Africa, the march to the coast, and waiting in barracoons for slave ships; it is impossible to accurately estimate these numbers.

87. (C) This statement was made by Jacques-Bénigne Bossuet (1627–1704), a French bishop who served as court preacher to Louis XIV. Bossuet was famous for his sermons, and some consider him one of the best French orators of all time. Bossuet was an advocate of political absolutism and the divine right of kings. He argued that government was divine and kings like Louis XIV receive their power from God. François Ravaillac (1578–1610) was a Catholic zealot who murdered King Henry IV of France in 1610.

88. (C) Under a patent granted by Henry VII of England, John Cabot sailed from Bristol in 1497 and landed on the North American coast, touching at Cape Breton Island or Newfoundland. His voyage gave the English claim to Canada. Amerigo Vespucci explored the eastern coast of South America between 1499 and 1502. In 1500, Pedro Álvares Cabral landed in Brazil while on his way to the Cape of Good Hope and India. Jacques Cartier sailed up the St. Lawrence River on his second voyage of 1535 to 1536. The last chronologically (by almost a century) was Henry Hudson's third voyage (1609). He became the first European to sail up the Hudson River (named for him), nearly to present-day Albany.

89. (E) In France, constitutionalism was originally a doctrine that stated that a government's legitimacy rested upon its upholding the contract between ruler and ruled. The doctrine was developed by Huguenot pamphleteers after the St. Bartholomew's Day Massacre (1572). The Huguenot constitutionalists believed that they could lawfully resist a Catholic monarch because upholding the true religion was a legitimate part of the contract. Constitutionalist ideas appeared in François Hotman's *Franco-Gallia* (1573) and Theodore Beza's *De jure magistratum* (1574).

90. (B) Bartolomeu Dias (c. 1451–1500) was the first European to round (1488) the Cape of Good Hope, which he called Cabo Tormentoso (Cape of Storms). That voyage opened the road to India. For the first time, Europeans could envision trading directly with Asia and bypassing the dangerous and expensive overland routes through the Middle East. The cape was later renamed by John II (of Portugal) to the Cape of Good Hope (Cabo da Boa Esperança) because it represented the opening of a route to the east.

91. (E) Unlike most eastern European powers, Poland-Lithuania did not develop a strong monarchy. Decades of war weakened the Polish kingship and made the great nobles into autonomous warlords. They constantly used the Sejm (parliament) and demands for constitutionalism to reduce monarchical power. The result was virtual anarchy. In 1648, Ukrainian Cossacks under Bohdan Chmielnicki revolted against the king of Poland, beginning a 20-year period known as "The Deluge." Many towns were destroyed in the fighting, and as much as a third of the Polish population may have perished. Chmielnicki declared the elimination of Jews from Ukraine as one of his goals; somewhere between 20,000 and 100,000 Jews were killed by Cossacks, Polish peasants, or Russian troops. The Polish version of constitutionalism fatally weakened the state.

92. (C) The Treaty of Utrecht (1713) was a series of individual peace treaties between several European states, including Spain, Great Britain, France, Portugal, Savoy, and the Dutch Republic. The treaty ended the War of the Spanish Succession, confirmed the defeat of France's ambitions from the wars of Louis XIV, and attempted to preserve a European peace based on a theory known as the balance of power. The term was first mentioned in 1701 by Charles Davenant in *Essays on the Balance of Power*; the concept promoted the idea of maintaining a balance of power in Europe guided by diplomatic and military leagues, maneuvering, and negotiations.

93. (A) Peter the Great (1672–1725) expanded the power of the Russian state and the office of the tsar. He personally cut off the beards of his nobles and ordered them to replace their long robes and conical hats with European dress. He introduced conscription, enlarged and modernized the army, founded the navy, and established technical schools to train men for military service. He placed taxes on every conceivable item and created a rudimentary civil service. Peter subsidized private industry and also established state mines and factories to provide war materials. During Peter's reign, the Russian Orthodox Church was reformed and the Patriarch of Moscow eliminated. The transfer of the capital from Moscow to St. Petersburg, built on the northern swamps at tremendous human cost, dramatically symbolized Peter's reforms. Russia was almost continuously at war during Peter's reign; his greatest military achievement was the defeat of Charles XII of Sweden at the Battle of Poltava (1709). Peter's reign transformed Russia, and he remains one of the most controversial figures in Russian history.

94. (E) Bernard Mandeville (1670–1733) was an English author who settled permanently in Holland. His most important work, *The Fable of the Bees*, was written in 1714 and enlarged in 1723 and 1728. In *The Fable of the Bees*, Mandeville declared that the self-seeking effort of individuals drives commercial and industrial society. He claimed that pride, self-interest, and the desire for material goods—all Christian vices—actually promoted economic prosperity. Mandeville's attitude was attacked by many contemporaries as false, cynical, and degrading. However, Mandeville captured the emerging spirit of consumption that would form the basis of modern capitalism.

95. (D) The transatlantic slave trade disturbed some Europeans who noted the questionable ethics of the entire enterprise. However, in the 1700s, slaveholders retaliated by demeaning the mental and spiritual qualities of the enslaved Africans. White Europeans and colonists sometimes described black slaves as animal-like. One of the peculiarities of the time was that the constant talk of liberty and self-evident rights, especially in Britain and North America, coexisted with the belief that some people were either born or meant to be slaves. Although Christians theoretically believed in the spiritual equality of all people, the churches often defended, or at best did not oppose, the slave trade. The transatlantic slave trade to North America did not peak until the 1780s.

96. (B) The Atlantic system was an informal economic structure from about 1600 to 1800 that connected regions on both sides of the Atlantic Ocean based on the slave trade. Europeans bought slaves in western Africa and transported and sold them to colonists in North America, South America, and the Caribbean. These slaves worked the plantations that produced sugarcane and tobacco, which were exported to European markets. The Atlantic system destabilized Africa and produced tremendous misery for Africans. However, it generated enormous wealth for traders, planters, and merchants and for the states that sponsored and protected those enterprises. The Atlantic system hindered economic and population growth in Africa but had the opposite effect on Europe, where it resulted in optimism about the future and the development of new consumer tastes.

97. (B) Afonso de Albuquerque (1453–1515) was a Portuguese admiral who established the Portuguese colonial empire in the Indian Ocean. In 1510, Albuquerque captured Goa, which he turned into the center of Portuguese power in India for four centuries. He also conquered Malacca (1511), extending Portuguese domination to southeastern Asia. As an administrator, Albuquerque built numerous fortresses, such as Goa, Calicut, Malacca, and Hormuz. Albuquerque achieved nearly complete control of the spice sources and trade routes during his brief lifetime. He successfully closed all Indian Ocean naval passages to the Atlantic Ocean, Red Sea, Persian Gulf, and Pacific Ocean, transforming the Indian Ocean into a Portuguese sphere of influence.

98. (B) Tea, chocolate, and especially coffee became virtual necessities in the consumer revolution of the late 1600s and early 1700s. Around 1700, the Dutch East India Company introduced coffee plants to Java and other Indonesian islands. Coffee production then spread to the French Caribbean, where African slaves provided the labor. In Europe, imported coffee led to the development of a new kind of meeting place—the coffeehouse. The first coffeehouse opened in London in 1652. In 1700, England had 2,000 coffeehouses, and the idea quickly spread to other European cities. The first cafés in Paris date from the end of the 1600s. Berlin opened its first coffeehouse in 1714; Bach's Leipzig boasted eight coffeehouses by 1725. The coffeehouse became a place where men gathered to drink, read newspapers, and talk politics. Jürgen Habermas, in *The Structural Transformation of the Public Sphere* (1962), argued that coffeehouses played a crucial role in the emergence of the *public sphere*, which emerged in contrast to court society.

99. (A) Great Britain was the name given to the territories of England, Scotland, and Ireland after the English monarchy incorporated Scotland and subjugated Ireland. Wales had been annexed by England under the Laws in Wales Acts (1535–1542). In the Acts of Union of 1707, Scotland agreed to abolish the Scottish Parliament and send representatives to the British Parliament. In 1801, under a new Act of Union, Great Britain merged with the Kingdom of Ireland to create the United Kingdom of Great Britain and Ireland (southern Ireland became independent in 1921). The Faroe Islands are a Danish territory.

100. (D) Pietism was a form of Protestant revival that occurred during the late 1600s and early 1700s in parts of northern Europe and North America. Pietism emphasized emotion, mysticism, ethical purity, heartfelt religious devotion, and intense Bible study; it downplayed the importance of theology. The Baal Shem Tov (1698–1760) was a mystical Jewish rabbi who founded the movement known as modern Hasidism. He taught that Jews must worship and follow God not only in the traditional acts of specific religious observance but also in everyday affairs. The Baal Shem Tov believed that Jews must worship God in joy and not in sorrow, and that repentance was always possible. His view of Jewish religious life allowed the uneducated as well as the scholar to experience a sense of redemption. The Baal Shem Tov gained a large circle of followers that later developed into the several communities of modern Hasidim.

Chapter 5: The Scientific Revolution and the Enlightenment

101. (A) Galileo Galilei (1564–1642) was an Italian astronomer and mathematician who provided evidence to support Copernicus's heliocentric theory. Galileo developed a better telescope and observed the earth's moon, four moons of Jupiter, the phases of Venus, and sunspots. His observations seemed to show that the heavens were not perfect and unchanging and that the earth was simply a moving part of a much larger system. In 1616, the Catholic church forbade Galileo to teach that the earth moves. However, in 1632, he published a work written in Italian for the nonspecialist called *Dialogue on the Two Chief Systems of the World*. That work supported the Copernican system and marked a turning point in scientific and philosophical thought. The next year, the Catholic Church forced him to appear before the Inquisition and publicly recant his assertion in order to save himself from torture. Since 1761, accounts of the trial have related that Galileo, as he arose from his knees before the Inquisition, murmured in a whisper, *"E pur si muove"* ("Nevertheless it does move"). That statement was considered legendary, but it was discovered written on a portrait of Galileo completed about 1640.

102. (C) The quotation is from the final chapter of *Candide*, a work written in 1759 by the French philosopher Voltaire (1694–1778). Voltaire was the most influential writer of the early Enlightenment. He was a deist, well known for his epigram "If God did not exist, he would have to be invented." Through his immense popularity in the 1750s and 1760s, Voltaire helped popularize the scientific worldview. In *Candide*, he attacked the philosophical optimism made popular by Gottfried Leibniz. In this quotation, he mocks the problem of theodicy (the question of why there is evil in the world). The book ends a few pages later with a discussion of the proper role of human existence and the famous conclusion, "we must cultivate our garden."

103. (A) Michel de Montaigne (1533–1592) was a French magistrate who resigned his office during the wars of religion to write about the need for tolerance. He is known for reviving the ancient doctrine of skepticism, which held that total certainty is never attainable. This worldview is embodied in his remark, *"Que sais-je?"* ("What do I know?"). This doctrine was repugnant to Catholics and Protestants alike, both of whom were sure they possessed the only truth. Montaigne invented the essay as a short form of expression, and he remains one of its greatest practitioners. Montaigne's essays are written in a familiar style, full of concrete images and humorous tangents. He was famous for his effortless ability to merge serious intellectual speculation with casual anecdotes.

104. (B) Isaac Newton (1642–1727) was an English mathematician and physicist who made fundamental contributions to mathematics, astronomy, optics, and physics. In the 1660s, Newton discovered the law of universal gravitation, began to develop calculus, and discovered that white light is composed of all colors of the spectrum. Newton summarized his discoveries in his *Principia Mathematica* (1687), perhaps the greatest milestone in the history of science. In the *Principia*, he showed how universal gravitation explained both falling bodies on the earth and the motions of planets in the heavens. Once set in motion, the universe operated like clockwork with no need for God's intervention. Although gravity was a mysterious force, it could still be expressed mathematically. The first part of the *Principia* also includes Newton's three famous laws of motion. Newton's system remained the basis of all physics until the discovery of the theory of relativity and quantum mechanics in the 20th century.

105. (A) In 1543, Flemish scientist Andreas Vesalius (1514–1564) published *On the Construction of the Human Body* based on public dissections in the medical faculties of European universities. Paracelsus (1493–1541), a professor at the University of Basel, helped establish the modern science of pharmacology; he also pursued other interests in magic, alchemy, and astronomy. William Harvey (1578–1657) used dissection to examine the circulation of blood within the body and demonstrated that the heart worked like a pump. Jean Fernel (1497–1588) wrote *A Universal Medicine* (1567), which divided the study of medicine into the now-standard disciplines of physiology (the normal functioning of the body), pathology (the abnormal functioning of the body), and therapeutics (those things that might resolve abnormalities). Galen (c. 130–c. 200 CE) was a Greek physician during the Roman Empire.

106. (C) Ironically, trials of witches peaked in Europe between 1560 and 1640, the time of the celebrated breakthroughs of "modern" science. They declined in the late 1600s after the end of the wars of religion in Europe. Scientific thinking about cause and effect gradually raised questions about the evidence used in court to convict witches. Lawyers, physicians, judges, and clergy came to suspect that accusations were based on popular superstition. In 1682, a French royal decree treated witchcraft as fraud, meaning that the law did not recognize anyone as a witch. In 1693, the jurors who had convicted 20 witches in Salem, Massachusetts, recanted. The last executions for witchcraft in England took place in 1682; Janet Horne was executed for witchcraft in Scotland in 1727. The last execution of a witch in the Dutch Republic was probably in 1613; in Denmark in 1693; in France in 1745; in Germany in 1775; in Switzerland in 1782; and in Poland in 1793.

107. (B) The scientific revolution contributed to a belief system known as deism, which became popular among the intellectual elite in the 1700s. Deists believed in a powerful god who created and presided over an orderly realm but did not interfere in its workings. The deists often compared God to a cosmic watchmaker—one who set up the world, gave it natural laws by which to operate, and then let it run by itself under natural laws that could be proved mathematically. Deism also helped explain the problem of evil—if a person found a broken watch in the desert, that did not discount the existence of a watchmaker (although, as David Hume pointed out, it did discredit God's omnipotence and possibly good intentions). Deism was popular among elite Christians who found they could not believe in supernatural miracles or that every word of the Bible was literally true. The founders of the United States were heavily influenced by deism, including Alexander Hamilton, James Madison, Ethan Allen, Thomas Paine, Thomas Jefferson, Benjamin Franklin, and Gouverneur Morris.

108. (D) John Locke (1632–1704) used the notion of a social contract to provide the logic for constitutionalism. In *Two Treatises of Government* (1690), Locke justified the Glorious Revolution of 1688. The book denied the divine right of kings and ridiculed the royalist idea that political power in the state mirrored the father's authority in the family. Locke insisted that government's only purpose was to protect life, liberty, and property; ultimate authority should rest in the will of a majority of men who own property, and government should be limited to its basic task of protection. A ruler who failed to uphold his (or her) part of this social contract between the ruler and the people could be justifiably resisted; this idea would become essential to the American Revolution. Ironically, Locke was also a major investor in the Royal Africa Company, justified a master's absolute power over his or her slaves, and unsuccessfully attempted to establish a feudal aristocracy in North and South Carolina.

109. (E) Montesquieu (1689–1755) was a French judge and political philosopher. In his bestselling *Persian Letters* (1721), he satirized French institutions. His greatest work, *The Spirit of Laws* (1748), is a comparative study of three types of government: republic, monarchy, and despotism. It concluded that climate and circumstance play a major role in determining the form of government. More important, Montesquieu advocated that the powers of government should be separated and balanced in order to guarantee the freedom of the individual. His ideas influenced the United States Constitution.

110. (D) René Descartes (1596–1650) was a French philosopher and mathematician who spent most of his life in the Dutch Republic. He is often considered the founder of modern philosophy, and his *Meditations on First Philosophy* (1641) is still studied. Descartes had an enormous influence on mathematics, most obviously in the Cartesian coordinate system (allowing algebraic equations to be expressed as geometric shapes) that was named after him. In his *Discourse on Method* (1637), he argued that mathematical and mechanical principles provide the key to understanding all of nature. He suggested that even if all prior assumptions were repudiated, a person was left with one elementary principle: "I think, therefore I am." That doubt showed the certain existence of someone thinking. From that one certainty, Descartes created an entire philosophical system. He insisted that human reason could not only unravel the secrets of nature but also logically prove the existence of God. Through his work in mathematics and philosophy, Descartes helped spread the prestige of the scientific method.

111. (E) Blaise Pascal (1623–1662) was a brilliant French mathematician and Jansenist who wrote his *Provincial Letters* (1656–1657) to defend Jansenism against charges of heresy. (Jansenists emphasized the importance of original sin.) Pascal made numerous contributions to mathematics and physics, including the invention of a calculating machine and the development of probability theory. He is best known for his *Pensées* (*Thoughts*), written in 1660, in which he examined several philosophical paradoxes: infinity and nothing, faith and reason, soul and matter, death and life, and yet could not arrive at a definitive conclusion beyond ignorance, humility, and grace. On this basis, he constructed the concept now known as *Pascal's wager*—that if the existence of God could not be determined through reason, a rational person should wager as if God exists, because a life lived on that basis has everything to gain and nothing to lose. This application of probability theory to the question of God's existence has raised controversy from the moment he first proposed it.

112. (C) In *An Essay Concerning Human Understanding* (1690), John Locke (1632–1704) concluded that the human mind at birth was a *tabula rasa*—a blank slate (although he did not use precisely those words). As opposed to the Catholic emphasis on original sin, Locke believed humans had no nature at all at birth other than animal needs and appetites. He particularly rejected the concept of innate ideas (associated with René Descartes). For Locke, everything that a person becomes is the result of things written on that "slate," including education, culture, feelings, and attitudes acquired from one's family, community, society, or environment. Locke's essay was a founding document of the philosophical school known as empiricism, and it influenced many Enlightenment philosophers such as David Hume and George Berkeley.

113. (A) The English politician Francis Bacon (1561–1626) had a long and erratic government career under Elizabeth I and James I. He rose to great political heights as lord chancellor, but his career ended in disgrace in 1621. His reputation rests on his works as a philosopher and a writer. In *The Advancement of Learning* (1605), Bacon attacked intellectuals' reliance on ancient writers and optimistically predicted that the scientific method would lead to social progress. He advocated the collection, comparison, and analysis of information gained primarily through careful observation. For this reason, Francis Bacon has sometimes been called the founder of empiricism. Bacon looked to the Protestant English state for leadership on the road to scientific progress. He wrote numerous essays as well as *The New Atlantis* (1627), a description of a scientific utopia.

114. (D) Because of their exclusion from most universities, women rarely participated in the new scientific discoveries of the 1600s. In 1667, the English Royal Society invited Margaret Cavendish (1623–1673), a writer of philosophical treatises, to attend a meeting to watch experiments. Cavendish later urged the formal education of women, complaining, "Many of our sex may have as much wit, and be capable of learning as well as men but since they want [lack] instruction, it is not possible that they should attain it." However, some women scientists did contribute to the scientific revolution of the 1600s. Maria Sibylla Merian (1647–1717) was a naturalist who studied plants and insects and made meticulous paintings of them. Her detailed observations and documentation of the metamorphosis of the butterfly made a significant contribution to entomology. Maria Cunitz (1610–1664) was an accomplished Silesian astronomer; she wrote *Urania Propitia*, in which she provided new tables and solutions to problems in mechanics. Elisabeth Catherina Koopmann Hevelius (1647–1693) is considered one of the first female astronomers and sometimes called "the mother of moon charts." Elena Cornaro Piscopia (1646–1684) was the first woman to receive a PhD degree (1678).

115. (A) Hugo Grotius (1583–1645) became a lawyer when he was 15 years old. Maurice of Nassau condemned Grotius to prison for life (1619), but Grotius made a daring escape in 1621 (his wife hid him in a chest of books). He fled to Paris, and in 1625, he wrote *The Laws of War and Peace*, considered the first definitive text on international law. Grotius argued that natural law stood beyond the reach of either secular or divine authority; it would be valid even if God did not exist. He contended that natural law prescribes rules of conduct for nations as well as for private individuals, and he directly challenged the use of torture in judicial procedures. Grotius believed natural law should govern politics and downgraded the Bible, religious authority, or tradition. Natural law and natural rights would play an important role in the founding of constitutional governments after 1640.

116. (E) A caravel is a small, highly maneuverable sailing ship developed about 1450 by the Portuguese. The lateen sails gave caravels speed and the capacity to sail in any direction regardless of the wind. The Portuguese used caravels for the oceanic exploration voyages during the 15th and 16th centuries. Astrolabes date to the Hellenistic era, but the first metal astrolabes, more accurate than their wooden precursors, did not appear in western Europe until the 15th century. The dry mariner's compass was invented in Europe around 1300; this compass had a needle that no longer floated in water to stay in horizontal equilibrium. The sextant was invented around 1730 virtually simultaneously by an English mathematician, John Hadley (1682–1744), and an American inventor, Thomas Godfrey (1704–1749). The sextant provided mariners with a more accurate means of calculating latitude.

117. (D) In 1543, the Polish clergyman Nicolaus Copernicus (1473–1543) revolutionized astronomy by publishing *On the Revolution of the Celestial Spheres*. Copernicus attacked the geocentric Ptolemaic account. Instead, he proposed that the earth and planets revolved around the sun, a view known as heliocentrism. The placement of the sun at the center of the system of spheres greatly simplified all calculations. Copernicus died soon after publishing his theories, but when the Italian monk Giordano Bruno (1548–1600) taught heliocentrism, the Catholic Inquisition arrested him and burned him at the stake.

118. (C) The basic ideas of the Enlightenment stated that humans were essentially good and could be improved through education. Reason, not faith, was the key to truth. Enlightenment thinkers supported science and tried to rationally analyze the nature of society and government. Criminologists came to believe that cruel punishments failed to deter crime. Thomas Hobbes and John Locke disputed the idea that laws existed to avenge crimes; instead, they emphasized a version of the social contract that traded individual freedoms for social security.

119. (C) The *Encyclopédie* championed the skepticism and rationalism of the French Enlightenment. It was the work of the French *Encyclopedists*, also known as *philosophes*. The work was originally planned as a translation of an older work, but the publisher agreed to let Denis Diderot and Jean Le Rond d'Alembert edit an entirely new work. With the aid of François Quesnay, Montesquieu, Voltaire, Jean-Jacques Rousseau, and others, the first volume appeared in 1751. The secular emphasis of the volume infuriated the Jesuits, who attacked the work as irreligious and convinced the government to withdraw the official permit (1759). Alembert resigned, but Diderot persevered, with the help of the Chevalier de Jaucourt (1704–1779), who wrote 18,000 articles, almost 25 percent of the entire work. Diderot had the *Encyclopédie* secretly printed in 1772. Through its stress on scientific determinism and its attacks on legal, juridical, and clerical abuses, the *Encyclopédie* helped cause the French Revolution.

120. (E) This is probably the most famous quotation from Thomas Hobbes (1588–1679), the English philosopher who wrote *Leviathan* (1671). In this book, Hobbes argued that humans are by nature selfishly individualistic and at constant war with all other humans. In a state of nature, men would live lives that were "nasty, brutish, and short." Fear of violent death was the principal motive that caused people to create a government, contracting to surrender their natural rights and submit to the absolute authority of a sovereign. For Hobbes, government should only preserve the peace and stability of society. Yet although Hobbes favored a monarchy as the best form of government, his theory could apply equally well (and was applied) to a parliamentary form of government. Hobbes's writings led to investigations by other political theorists such as John Locke, Baruch Spinoza, and Jean-Jacques Rousseau, who created their own very different theories of the social contract.

Chapter 6: Colonial North and South America

121. (D) Before 1500, Europeans had only honey and fruit juice for sweetness. Growing sugarcane in Brazil and the Caribbean was difficult and expensive, but a planter could become rich if he or she grew enough of it. By 1750, sugar made up a fifth of all European imports, and by 1800, almost four-fifths of the sugar came from the British and French colonies in the West Indies. The production of sugar was the driving force behind the slave trade; the Spanish, British, Dutch, and French began pouring enslaved Africans into their Caribbean colonies. By the mid-1700s, about 1.4 million slaves worked to produce sugar; the slaves' misery supplied Europeans with the sugar for their tea and cakes. Average consumption continued to climb even after the end of slavery; the British consumed 36 pounds of sugar per person in 1850, and more than 100 pounds per person in the 20th century.

122. (B) The Treaty of Tordesillas (1494) was an agreement signed at Tordesillas, Spain, in which Spain and Portugal divided the non-Christian world into two zones of influence, one for each country. The treaty followed the papal bull issued in 1493 by Pope Alexander VI, which fixed the dividing line along a circle passing 100 leagues west of the Cape Verde Islands (already Portuguese) and through the two poles. This division gave the entire New World to Spain while Portugal received Africa and India. However, the actual Treaty of Tordesillas shifted the demarcation line to a circle passing 370 leagues west of the Cape Verde Islands, and therefore gave Portugal a claim to Brazil. Almost none of the newly divided area had been seen by Europeans as of 1494; Pedro Cabral did not land in Brazil until 1500, and it is disputed whether the Portuguese knew of its existence in 1494. The Tordesillas line was never strictly enforced, and with the decline of Spanish and Portuguese power, it was completely ignored.

123. (E) The Battle of Cajamarca was a surprise attack on the Inca royal party orchestrated by Francisco Pizarro in 1532. The ambush took place in the great plaza of Cajamarca and captured the Inca king, Atahuallpa, while killing thousands of his followers. Pizarro collected a huge ransom for Atahuallpa and then had him strangled anyway. Pizarro's victory at Cajamarca established the Spanish in power in Peru; the Incan people were conquered, their culture destroyed, their wealth shipped to Spain, and their religion suppressed.

124. (C) The *encomienda* was a system used by Spain in the early 1500s to regulate Native behavior in Spanish America. In 1503 the Spanish crown began to legally grant *encomiendas* (grants of land) to soldiers and officials. In the *encomienda*, a person was granted a specific number of Natives whom they were supposed to protect from warring tribes and instruct in the Spanish language and the Catholic faith. In return, they could extract tribute from the Natives in the form of labor, gold, or other products. However, in practice, the Spanish landowners forced the Natives to do hard labor and subjected them to torture and death if they resisted. The New Laws of 1542 attempted to prevent the exploitation of the Natives by the *encomenderos* (large landowners), but these laws were ineffective. By the late 1500s, the *encomienda* system was being replaced by the *repartimiento* system.

125. (A) In 1638, there were 6,000 Europeans and 200 Africans living on Barbados. Then the British began raising sugarcane. In 1660, there were 26,000 Europeans and 27,000 Africans on Barbados. In a single year, between August 1664 and August 1665, Barbados exported 28 million pounds of raw sugar. By 1680, Barbados was the wealthiest of England's American colonies. The island averaged 265 slaves per square mile compared to 2 slaves per square mile in recently captured Jamaica. Many planters in Barbados worked their slaves to death and then imported more Africans. From 1708 to 1735, about 85,000 Africans were imported into Barbados, but the total black population only increased from 42,000 to 46,000. However, the slave trade was slow to develop in British North America where sugar would not grow. These colonies were relatively poor compared to the sugar colonies of the Caribbean.

126. (C) Bartolomé de Las Casas (1484–1566) was a high-ranking Christian churchman in South America who worked to end the enslavement of Natives in the Spanish colonies. His extensive writings, such as *Brief Report on the Destruction of the Indians*, chronicle the first decades of Spanish colonization focusing on the atrocities committed by the colonizers against the Natives. In 1542, he wrote to the king of Spain to complain about the brutal treatment of the Natives. Las Casas's efforts led to laws protecting the Natives of the Spanish colonies. Unfortunately, his desire to protect Natives led him to support the use of Africans as slaves, a position he later regretted.

127. (C) The *repartimiento* system was a colonial forced-labor system imposed upon the Native population of Spanish America and the Philippines. Between 1550 and 1600, the *repartimiento* system was supposed to reform the *encomiendas*. The *repartimiento* was similar to other tribute-labor systems, such as the *mita* of the Inca Empire or the *corvée* in early modern France. The natives had to perform low-paid or unpaid labor for a certain number of weeks or months each year on Spanish-owned farms, mines, workshops, and public projects. This was not officially slavery because the worker was not owned outright and the work was intermittent. However, it created slavery-like conditions in certain areas, especially in the mines of 16th-century Peru.

128. (A) Instead of African slaves, Chesapeake planters in the 1600s used indentured servants to work on the tobacco plantations. Indentured servants were a kind of temporary slaves; they agreed to work for a master, usually for four to seven years, before receiving their full freedom. In many cases, the master had paid the money that allowed the indentured servant to come to America in the first place. Between 1640 and 1700, more than 80,000 English indentured servants moved to Virginia and Maryland, making up about three out of every four English migrants to the Chesapeake. Most of them were males under 25 years of age, and half died before receiving their freedom. Because people died so quickly in the Chesapeake, it did not make economic sense for a planter to buy a slave for life; it was better to hire an indentured servant for seven years since that might be the servant's entire life. An indentured servant could produce as much as five times his or her purchase price in a single year. Indentured servants were the main labor source in the Chesapeake until about 1680.

129. (E) Spanish colonial society was hierarchical. At the top were the *peninsulares*, the select group of Spanish officials sent to govern the colonies. Below them were the *criollos*, people born in the colonies to Spanish parents. Because they were not born in Spain, they were barred from high positions, yet because they were children of Spaniards, the criollos were often educated and wealthy. Below the criollos were the *mestizos*, those with European and Native ancestry. Mestizos were almost always the children of Spanish men and Indian women. By 1800, the children of those unions formed more than a quarter of the population of the Spanish colonies. On the next step down were the *mulattos*, those with European and African ancestry. Finally, there were slaves and Natives (*indios*), who had little or no freedom and worked on estates or in mines. A person's legal racial classification in colonial Spanish America was closely tied to social status, wealth, culture, and language.

130. (D) Before the Puritans landed in Massachusetts in 1630, John Winthrop (1587–1649) gave a famous sermon entitled "A Modell of Christian Charity" aboard ship. This quotation is an excerpt from that sermon. Winthrop was a wealthy English Puritan lawyer and a founder of the Massachusetts Bay Colony. He led the first large wave of migrants from England in 1630 and served as governor for 12 of the colony's first 20 years. His vision of the Massachusetts Bay Colony as a "city upon the hill" dominated New England colonial development, influenced the government and religion of neighboring colonies, and affected the worldview and self-concept of the United States as a whole. The phrase is a quotation from a parable in Jesus's Sermon on the Mount (Matthew 5:14). Winthrop's usage conveys the responsibility entailed when "the eyes of all people are upon us." However, implicit in the idea is condescension for those in a less exalted position. "A city on a hill" is a core text that makes up the concept of American exceptionalism.

131. (E) Maroons were runaway slaves in the Western Hemisphere who escaped from plantations and tried to form independent settlements in remote areas. In Brazil, maroons founded free communities in the deep forest and jungle where attempts to conquer them were unsuccessful. One of the best-known maroon settlements (*quilombos*) in Brazil was Palmares (the Palm Nation), founded in the early 17th century. It remained independent for almost a century; at its height around 1680, it contained more than 20,000 free people. Palmares was eventually conquered by the Portuguese in 1694. The most successful maroon community in North America was the Black Seminoles, made up of escaped slaves from Georgia and Florida who joined the Seminole Indians in the swamps of Florida. Escaped slaves in Jamaica fled to the rugged interior and joined with the Tainos living there. Maroon communities also existed in Spanish America; the walled Palenque de San Basilio in northern Colombia is considered the first free town in America.

132. (D) Settlers in the Chesapeake colonies tended to be young men in search of economic opportunity. Very few women made the voyage to settle in the colonial South. English Puritans tended to immigrate to New England in search of religious freedom and also for economic gain. Many of these settlers were nonseparatists; they intended to remain associated with the Church of England to purify it from within. Chesapeake residents tended to be tolerant of religious differences, as evidenced by the Maryland Act of Toleration in 1649. About 10 percent of Africans coming to America entered northern port towns such as New York and Newport, Rhode Island. In 1710, almost 2,000 African slaves lived in New England, about 2 percent of the population.

133. (C) The Revolt of the Comuneros (1717–1735) was caused by discontent with the Spanish colonial administration in present-day Paraguay. The revolt's leader was José de Antequera y Castro (1689–1731), a Panamanian lawyer and judge in Peru. He was sent to Asunción to examine accusations of misgovernment against Diego de los Reves Blamaceda, who had been named governor at the request of the Jesuits. After investigating, Antequera sided with the settlers, who then elected him temporary governor. Many poor Paraguayan settlers sided with him and against Jesuit privileges and the government that protected them. In 1724, the viceroy sent in troops, including 6,000 Indians from the Jesuit missions, who defeated the Comuneros. Antequera was captured, imprisoned for five years at Lima, and shot on his way to his execution. Ferdinand Mompox (also Fernando Mompó y Zayas) led further revolts in Asunción in 1730 and 1732, but these also failed. This was not the only revolt of the 18th century. For example, Juan Santos Atahualpa led a revolt between 1742 and 1756 in the central jungle of Peru. In 1780, the Viceroyalty of Peru faced the insurrection of Tupac Amaru II.

134. (D) James II, who came to the British throne in 1665, was a firm believer in the divine right of kings. In 1686, the British Lords of Trade revoked the charters of Connecticut and Rhode Island and merged these colonies with the Massachusetts Bay and Plymouth Colonies to form the Dominion of New England. In 1688, the Lords added New York and New Jersey to create a massive province extending from the Delaware River in the south to Penobscot Bay in the north. James II appointed Edmund Andros (1637–1714) as governor and empowered him to abolish the existing legislative assemblies and town meetings and rule by decree. Andros's actions were very unpopular, and following the Glorious Revolution of 1688, Puritan leaders in Boston arrested Andros and sent him back to England. The colonies then reverted essentially to their former governments. However, new charters were eventually issued by William and Mary that essentially ended the old system of Puritan rule and gave Massachusetts (now a combination of the Massachusetts Bay and Plymouth Colonies) a more representative system of government.

135. (A) José Celestino Mutis (1732–1808) was a Spanish-Colombian naturalist, physician, and mathematician. Mutis spent the last 48 years of his life in New Granada, primarily in Bogotá, where he taught and researched in botany, entomology, medicine, mineralogy, mathematics, and astronomy. Mutis introduced the concept of vaccination into Spanish America and also extensively studied the species and varieties of cinchona (quinine). His most remarkable accomplishment was creating and heading the Royal Botanical Mission (Expedition) in 1783, a center for collecting and mapping the flora and fauna of Colombia. The Mission explored thousands of square miles and produced paintings, maps, letters, notes, and manuscripts. Mutis's collection included an estimated 24,000 dried plants, 5,000 drawings of plants, and a collection of woods, shells, resins, minerals, and skins. The botanical collection was admired by the great German scientist Alexander von Humboldt (1769–1859), who stayed with Mutis for two months in 1801.

136. (E) Hernán Cortés (1485–1547) was a Spanish conquistador who led the expedition that defeated the Aztec Empire and brought most of Mexico under Spanish control in the early 1500s. Montezuma II (1466–1520) was the Aztec emperor of Tenochtitlán, reigning from 1502 to 1520. During his reign the Aztec Empire reached its maximum size. He was killed in the first stages of the conquest. Bernal Díaz del Castillo (1492–1585) served under Cortés and later wrote a famous and detailed eyewitness account of the conquest entitled *The Conquest of New Spain*. La Malinche (c. 1496–c. 1529) was a Nahua woman from the Mexican Gulf Coast who acted as interpreter, advisor, lover, and intermediary for Cortés. She and Cortés had a son—Martin—who is sometimes considered the first mestizo. La Malinche knew both the Aztec and Maya languages and became a valuable interpreter and counselor. She remains a controversial historical figure in Mexico, sometimes portrayed as a traitor, but also as the symbolic mother of the new Mexican people. Juan de Betanzos wrote one of the most important sources on the conquest of Peru, *Narrative of the Incans*.

137. (C) From 1630 to 1654, the Dutch Republic ruled the northern portion of Brazil. The Dutch West India Company set up headquarters in Mauritsstad (Recife), which became the capital of Dutch Brazil and an extremely cosmopolitan city. The first Jewish community and the first synagogue in the Americas were founded in this city. However, at the Second Battle of Guararapes in 1649, the Portuguese essentially ended the Dutch occupation of northern Brazil. The Jewish community was unwilling to exchange the relative religious tolerance of Dutch rule for the Portuguese Inquisition. In September 1654, 23 Jews of Dutch ancestry from Recife arrived in the Dutch colony of New Amsterdam (New York City). Governor Peter Stuyvesant tried to discriminate against the Jews, but his superiors at the Dutch West India Company in Amsterdam overruled him. This was the first Jewish community in North America.

138. (B) The Pilgrims were separatists; they believed they had to leave the Church of England to escape a life that was morally corrupt and theologically incorrect. First they went to Holland, but in 1620, they sailed to the New World in the *Mayflower*. The Pilgrims settled in Massachusetts and established the settlement of Plymouth. On the other hand, the Puritans believed that they needed to remain in the Church of England to stand as examples and purify it from within. From 1629 to 1642, the so-called Great Puritan Migration helped found the Massachusetts Bay Colony, a much larger colony than Plymouth. Neither Separatists nor Congregationalists tolerated religious freedom in their colonies, even though both had fled religious persecution in England. The two colonies merged in 1692 after the collapse of the Dominion of New England.

139. (C) The Spanish invasion and European diseases changed life forever throughout the Western Hemisphere. In 1500, probably 45 million Indians lived in Mesoamerica; by 1650 that region had only three million Native Americans. Within a single generation, virtually all the Indian residents of Hispaniola—an estimated one million people—were wiped out by disease and warfare. The population of Peru collapsed from nine million in 1530 to less than 500,000 a century later.

140. (B) John Rolfe, the man who married Pocahontas, reported that "a Dutch man of war that sold us twenty Negars" came to Jamestown, Virginia, in 1619. Ironically, this was the same year that the House of Burgesses met in Virginia, the first democratic assembly to meet in America. Still, in 1649, only about 400 Africans lived in the Chesapeake colonies and they made up only about 2 percent of the population of those colonies.

141. (D) Britain's American colonies, unlike the West Indies, did not have the climate or the soil to raise sugar. However, American planters in the Chesapeake colonies of Virginia, Maryland, and Delaware discovered tobacco would grow very well there. In 1616, American planters exported 2,500 pounds of tobacco to England. In the 1660s, they were exporting 20 million pounds. By 1771, American planters exported 105 million pounds. Rice was also produced by slave labor in South Carolina and Georgia, but at a later date than tobacco. Cotton did not become an important crop until after 1800. American exports of rice increased from 10,000 pounds in 1698 to 84 million pounds in 1770. Indigo is a purple dye that was grown by slaves in Georgia and South Carolina; exports of indigo rose from 138,000 pounds in 1747 to one million pounds in 1774.

142. (B) Mercantilism was an economic doctrine followed by most European countries from about 1500 to 1800. According to mercantilist ideas, governments should actively support policies to increase trade, commerce, and manufacturing if they wanted to increase the national wealth. Mercantilist nations worked to increase exports and collect gold and silver in return; they always favored foreign trade over domestic trade because it meant an inflow of gold and silver. European governments followed mercantilist policy when they chartered joint-stock trading companies and established colonies in North America and the Caribbean. They created treaties that would give their nation exclusive trading privileges in Asia and Africa and exploited the commerce of colonies for the benefit of the mother country. In England, the mercantilist Navigation Acts helped to weaken the commerce of Holland, England's chief rival.

143. (C) Because 90 percent of Spanish settlers were men, they often took Native women or slaves as wives or mistresses. As a result, the Spanish colonies developed a large *mestizo* population with a culture that combined Spanish and Indian values and practices. The population of Spanish America was about 17 million people at the end of the colonial era. Historians estimate that about 7.5 million were Indians, 3.2 million were Europeans, 1 million were enslaved Africans, and 5.5 million were of mixed race.

144. (C) The Great Awakening was a series of religious revivals that swept over the American colonies in the middle of the 1700s. In New England, it began with the preaching of Congregationalist minister Jonathan Edwards, famous for his graphic descriptions of hell in the sermon "Sinners in the Hands of an Angry God." The Methodist George Whitefield preached an emotional Christianity that was the forerunner of modern southern Christian evangelism. The appeal to hearts over minds was a direct response to the rationalism of the Enlightenment. Preachers of the Great Awakening ignored theology, instead emphasizing moral behavior, emotional church services, and mystical union with God. The Great Awakening also stimulated missionary activity among Native Americans and led to the founding of a number of American colleges such as Princeton, Brown, Rutgers, and Dartmouth. It indirectly built up intercolonial interests, increased opposition to the Anglican Church, and encouraged a democratic spirit in religion. People began to question religious taxes, the idea of an established church, the morality of economic competition, and the authority of ministry.

145. (E) Trade with the Caribbean created the first American merchant fortunes and urban industries. Traders in Boston, Philadelphia, and New York built fine townhouses and invested in new ships and factories (e.g., to distill Caribbean molasses into rum). Merchants in cities such as Salem and Marblehead established a fishing industry to feed the slaves of the sugar islands and to export to southern Europe. By 1750, Newport (RI) and Charleston (SC) had nearly 10,000 residents, Boston had 15,000, New York almost 18,000, and Philadelphia 30,000. Religious and ethnic diversity was greater in colonial cities than the countryside, but the wealth of merchants grew much more rapidly than that of everyone else. By the 1770s, the poorest 60 percent of the taxable inhabitants of New York, Boston, and Philadelphia owned less than 5 percent of the taxable wealth, while the top 10 percent controlled 65 percent of the wealth. Colonial cities served as the cultural centers of America, although less than 10 percent of Americans lived in them; it is no surprise that the American Revolution began in Philadelphia and Boston.

Chapter 7: An Age of Revolutions

146. (A) The Grito de Dolores ("Cry of Dolores") was uttered by Miguel Hidalgo from the small town of Dolores, near Guanajuato, on September 16, 1810. Hidalgo's speech represents the beginning of the Mexican War of Independence (1810–1821); the date is the most important national holiday in Mexico. Hidalgo was a Mexican priest who led a group of peasants in a revolt against the dominant *peninsulares* under the banner of the Virgin of Guadalupe. Hidalgo was captured in March 1811 and executed in July. Because Hidalgo's efforts eventually led to the downfall of the colonial government of Spain in Mexico, he is often considered the "Father of the Nation." Ironically, there is no precise text of exactly what Hidalgo said at the time.

147. (B) Without the benefit of hindsight, many historians have difficulty seeing impending signs of a political and social revolution in France in 1787. The Enlightenment had spread into most elite circles in western Europe without affecting the social prominence of aristocrats or the political control of royalty. European monarchies, especially the French, appeared firmly established. Montesquieu and Rousseau, the leading political theorists of the Enlightenment, both taught that republics only worked in small countries. France had been humiliated in the Seven Years' War (1756–1763) but regained international prestige by supporting the winning side in the American Revolution. Louis XVI, an intelligent if indecisive ruler, was not particularly despotic. The French national debt was high, but not for the first time. In general, the French people were wealthier, healthier, more numerous, and better educated than ever before, perhaps leading to expectations that were frustrated by economic conditions in the 1780s.

148. (A) The Thermidorian Reaction was a revolt within the French Revolution against the excesses of the so-called Reign of Terror. It was triggered by a vote of the Committee of Public Safety to execute Maximilien Robespierre and several other leaders on July 27, 1794 (9 Thermidor, Year II). Robespierre was guillotined the next day, and within the year, the new leaders abolished the Revolutionary Tribunal, closed the Jacobin Club in Paris, and reversed most of

Robespierre's policies. Popular demonstrations met severe repression, and a White Terror replaced the Jacobins' Red Terror. The events of 9 Thermidor ended the most revolutionary, the most democratic, and the most repressive phases of the French Revolution. The term *Thermidor* now refers to the phase in some revolutions when a radical regime is replaced by a more conservative regime, sometimes even creating a government resembling the prerevolutionary state. Leon Trotsky popularized the term by referring to the rise of Joseph Stalin as the Soviet Thermidor.

149. (E) In 1777, the British concocted a plan to end the American Revolution by splitting the colonies along the Hudson River and isolating the New England colonies. John Burgoyne was to advance south from Canada along Lake Champlain to Albany, where he would join William Howe, advancing north from New York City, and also Barry St. Leger, coming east along the Mohawk River. Howe, however, became distracted in fighting around Philadelphia, and that army never reached Albany. Burgoyne took Fort Ticonderoga, but the Hessians (German mercenaries) he sent to raid Bennington were badly beaten by soldiers under John Stark and Seth Warner. Despite a bloody victory at Oriskany (in western New York), St. Leger decided to retreat to Canada. This left Burgoyne on his own marching southward through the forests of upstate New York. Burgoyne halted near present-day Schuylerville, where, with supplies running low, he tried to break through the American position at Freeman's Farm and Bemis Heights. Both attempts were stopped by American soldiers under Benedict Arnold and Daniel Morgan. The British, outnumbered and surrounded, surrendered on October 17, 1777. The Battle of Saratoga is the turning point of the Revolution because the American victory virtually ensured that the French would join an alliance with the Americans against the British. The ultimate American triumph would have been impossible without French money, weapons, and military support.

150. (C) Louis XVI, faced with a mounting deficit in 1789, called the Estates-General (which had last met 175 years before) to propose solutions to his government's financial problems. The Estates General was divided into three estates: the clergy, the nobility, and everyone else. Nobles insisted on voting by estates as a whole, as had been done previously. However, the deputies of the Third Estate, who represented about 95 percent of France's population, refused to proceed. Led by the comte de Mirabeau, they declared themselves and whoever would join them the National Assembly in which each deputy would vote as an individual. The new group was barred from the meeting hall (for reasons that remain disputed), but on June 20, 1789, they met on a nearby indoor tennis court. At that meeting, 576 of the 577 members of the Third Estate swore an oath not to disband until they had given France a constitution. The Tennis Court Oath was a statement that political authority derived from the people and their representatives rather than from the monarch himself. Three weeks later (July 14, 1789), an armed crowd marched on the Bastille.

151. (B) The *ancien régime* refers to the aristocratic, social, and political system in France from about 1500 to 1789, especially under the Bourbon dynasty. Although the nobility fought to maintain their privileges, France was probably the most centralized state in Europe in the late 1700s. For example, the *intendants*—representatives of royal power in the provinces—undermined local control by regional nobles. The French Revolution did not reverse this tendency; the Montagnards under Maximilien Robespierre especially pushed for the centralization of power in Paris. The Republican government imposed a new social and legal system, a new system of weights and measures (which became the metric system), a new calendar, and centralized educational standards. Napoleon continued this trend when he established the University of France and essentially placed French education under state control. Power continued to flow away from the countryside to the government in Paris, where ministers of the Council of State supervised a vast bureaucracy based on talent, not birth.

152. (A) The *Declaration of the Rights of Man and Citizen* (1789) is the fundamental document of the French Revolution. It is a stirring statement of Enlightenment principles that defines the individual and collective rights of all the French estates as universal. The *Declaration*, whose first draft was written by the marquis de Lafayette, states, "Men are born and remain free and equal in rights." The *Declaration* granted freedom of religion, freedom of the press, equality of taxation, and equality before the law. It also established the principle of national sovereignty. Because "all sovereignty rests essentially in the nation," the king would from now on derive his authority from the nation rather than tradition or divine right. The *Declaration* recognized many rights as belonging to citizens, who could only be male. Women never received the right to vote during the French Revolution, though Protestant and Jewish men did. The *Declaration* also did not discuss the status of slaves in France's overseas colonies. However, it did declare the ownership of property an inviolable and sacred natural right.

153. (D) Mary Wollstonecraft (1759–1797) was one of the first supporters of educational equality between men and women, expressing this radical opinion in *Thoughts on the Education of Daughters* (1786). Her most important book, *A Vindication of the Rights of Women* (1792; the quotation is from Chapter 3), was one of the first modern feminist documents. Wollstonecraft called for equality of the sexes in public life as well as legal rights. She also wrote several novels. Wollstonecraft lived in Paris for most of the French Revolution and was close to many of the Revolution's leading political figures. She died as a result of childbirth; her daughter, also named Mary, married the famous Romantic poet Percy Bysshe Shelley and wrote the novel *Frankenstein* (1818).

154. (D) The First Amendment to the US Constitution states, "Congress shall make no law respecting an establishment of religion, or prohibiting the free exercise thereof; or abridging the freedom of speech, or of the press; or the right of the people peaceably to assemble, and to petition the Government for a redress of grievances." It is part of the Bill of Rights, the first 10 amendments to the US Constitution ratified in 1789 and adopted in 1791. The amendment specifically restricted the US Congress and *not* the individual states. However, since *Gitlow v. New York* (1925), the US Supreme Court has held that the due process clause of the Fourteenth Amendment (1868) applies the First Amendment to each individual state and any local government.

155. (A) Napoleon was indirectly responsible for spreading many of the ideals of the French Revolution throughout Europe. For example, Protestants and Jews were allowed to practice their religion in France and retain their civic rights while the Church lost its right to special privileges. In addition, Napoleon emphasized the idea that the loyalty of the people was due to the state and not to the monarch. Before the French Revolution, individual merit was subordinated to the importance of noble lineage. The Revolution tried to eliminate these beliefs and replace them with the idea that all individuals were equal in the eyes of the government. Napoleon enshrined this concept when he attempted to create a new aristocracy—the Legion of Honor—based on merit. These ideas traveled with his armies into occupied and annexed states and led to the beginning of the breakdown of the old order.

156. (C) In France under the ancien régime, the Estates-General was an assembly of the different classes (estates) of French subjects. It had a separate assembly for each of the three estates, which were called and dismissed by the king. The Estates-General met intermittently from about 1302 until 1614, and then not again until 1789. There were three estates in France: the First Estate (clergy), Second Estate (nobility), and Third Estate (commoners and all others). At the time of the French Revolution, the First Estate comprised about 100,000 Catholic clergy (all numbers are estimates) and owned about 10 percent of the land in France. All property of the First Estate was tax exempt, and they collected taxes in the form of tithes. The Second Estate consisted of about 400,000 nobles and owned about 25 percent of the land. They also paid no taxes, but collected them in the form of seigneurial dues and rents. The nobility had a near-monopoly over high government, army, and church offices. The Third Estate comprised about 24 million people—the bourgeoisie, workers, peasants, and everyone else in France—and owned about two-thirds of the land. Unlike the First and Second Estates, the Third Estate paid all the nation's taxes. The Third Estate's resentment led to the French Revolution of 1789.

157. (D) Simón Bolívar (1783–1830), born into a wealthy creole family in Venezuela, admired both the American and French Revolutions. Bolívar led a failed revolutionary movement in Venezuela (1810–1814) and fled to Jamaica, where he wrote *La Carta de Jamaica* to justify revolution and republican government in Spanish America. He returned to Venezuela and began another revolt in 1816. In 1819, his army crossed the flooded Apure valley, climbed the bitterly cold Andean passes, and defeated the surprised Spanish at Boyacá in one of the great campaigns of military history. The same year, Bolívar became president of Greater Colombia (present-day Colombia, Venezuela, Ecuador, and Panama). Venezuela's freedom was secured following his victory at Carabobo (1821), and Ecuador was liberated when Bolívar and Antonio José de Sucre won the Battle of Pichincha (1822). Bolívar also commanded the rebel forces that freed Peru from Spanish rule. In 1826, he convened representatives of the new South American republics in Panama to try to unify Spanish America. Bolívar declared himself dictator in 1828, and the next night, he barely escaped assassination by jumping from a high window. Separatist movements in Venezuela and Ecuador undermined the union, and many people opposed his power and arbitrary methods. In poor health and disillusioned, Bolívar resigned the presidency in 1830 and died of tuberculosis the same year.

158. (D) The French Revolution created numerous forms of government, but a limited monarchy was not one of them. The Revolutionary era saw a bewildering number of constitutions. The most famous is the Constitution of 1791, which included the Declaration of the Rights of Man and established a short-lived constitutional monarchy. The turmoil of the Revolution led to a new Constitution in 1793, which was ratified but never applied. The Constitution of 1795 resulted from the Thermidorian Reaction and established the five-man Directory. Yet another new constitution in 1799 established the Consulate under Napoleon after his coup of 18 Brumaire; this was revised again in 1802 to make Napoleon Consul for Life. Another constitution in 1804 created the First French Empire with Napoleon as emperor; he crowned himself Emperor of the French on December 2, 1804. After Napoleon's defeat at Waterloo, the Bourbon Restoration returned the monarchy to power until the uprisings of the July Revolution of 1830.

159. (C) In 1944, Eric Williams wrote *Capitalism and Slavery*, in which he argued that the English Industrial Revolution only occurred because of the profits from the slave trade. Williams claimed plantation owners, shipbuilders, and merchants connected with the slave trade and sugar production in the Caribbean made large fortunes. This money helped provided the excess capital that allowed England to rule the world in the 1700s and 1800s. He further argued that the British abolition of their slave trade in 1807 was motivated primarily by economics and not by humanitarianism. Williams's theory excited and angered many people and caused a tremendous increase in the study of the slave trade. In general, scholars found that the slave trade actually formed only a small share of the Atlantic trade of any European country. On the other hand, many historians still support Williams's basic thesis that Caribbean slavery fueled the rise of industrial capitalism in Britain. Eric Williams eventually served as prime minister of Trinidad from 1962 to 1981 and led Trinidad and Tobago to independence.

160. (D) The Articles of Confederation, written in 1777, established the government of America as a "firm league of friendship" in which each state kept its "freedom and independence." The Articles created a loose union of almost independent states. The authors intentionally created a weak national government with no national supreme court or president. The Declaration of Independence had objected that Great Britain's government was too powerful and too far away; American rebels now tried to avoid both problems. By 1786, the Articles had served the nation well. Under the Confederation Congress, America had fought and won the Revolution and negotiated a favorable peace treaty with England. The same Congress had organized national departments of war, foreign affairs, finance, and the post office and created a system to deal with settlers who wanted to move to western lands. America was at peace, and most of its people seemed contented.

161. (A) The Napoleonic Code is the name for the French civil code, drafted by a commission of four judges and established in 1804. This law code forbade privileges based on birth, allowed freedom of religion, assured property rights, and specified that government jobs go to the most qualified. However, the Napoleonic Code curtailed women's rights in many aspects of life and attempted to restrict them to the private sphere of the home. The new laws obligated a husband to support his wife, but the man alone controlled any property they held in common. A wife could not sue in court, sell or mortgage her own property, or contract a debt without her husband's consent. The Civil Code modified the laws from the Revolutionary period that had been favorable to women. Divorce was still possible but now severely restricted for women, and the new law judged a wife's infidelity far more harshly than a husband's.

162. (D) The US Constitution begins with a single, very long sentence known as the Preamble. A preamble is an introduction to a formal document. The Preamble to the Constitution opens with the words, "We, the People of the United States." This announced that the national government would draw its power directly from the people of the country. The Preamble also lists the positive goals of the new document: "to form a more perfect Union, establish Justice, insure domestic Tranquility, provide for the common defense, promote the general Welfare, and secure the Blessings of Liberty to ourselves and our Posterity." Each of these phrases referred to a supposed specific weakness in the "less perfect" government established by the Articles of Confederation. The beautiful phrasing of the Preamble was probably written by Gouverneur Morris.

163. (D) The term *Industrial Revolution* describes a set of changes that brought steam-driven machinery, large factories, and a new working class first to Great Britain, then to the rest of Europe, and eventually to the rest of the world. By 1830, more than one million people in Britain depended on the cotton industry for employment and cotton cloth made up half of England's exports. The British Reform Bill of 1832 increased the number of British voters by about 50 percent. However, voting still depended on owning property, and only one in five Britons could vote. The Reform Act of 1884 doubled the electorate, but universal male suffrage did not come to Great Britain until 1918.

164. (E) Simón Bolívar (1783–1830) led Colombia, Venezuela, Ecuador, and Peru to independence. José de San Martín (c. 1778–1850) is the national hero of Argentina. Bernardo O'Higgins (1778–1842) was a Chilean independence leader who, with José de San Martín, freed Chile from Spanish rule. Antonio José de Sucre (1795–1830) was a Venezuelan independence leader and the general at decisive battles at Pichincha and Ayacucho that ensured Peru's independence. Valeriano Weyler (1838–1930) was a Spanish soldier in charge of repressing the Cuban independence movement in the 1890s.

165. (A) In 1791, inspired by the French Revolution, slaves in the sugar-rich French colony of Saint-Domingue (present-day Haiti) rose in a 10-year revolt against their colonial overlords. Through the 1790s, François-Dominique Toussaint Louverture, a former slave, led the forces that defeated the Spanish, British, and French armies that attacked Haiti. In 1801, Napoleon sent a 20,000-man French army under General Charles Leclerc to Haiti and forced Toussaint's surrender. But the Haitians, aided by guerilla forces in the mountains and by yellow fever that weakened the invaders, drove out the French. In 1804, Jean-Jacques Dessalines declared Haitian independence. The Haitian Revolution remains the only example of a successful long-term slave revolt. The slave-owning President Jefferson was strongly pro-French, and he assured France that he would be happy to supply a fleet and help "reduce Toussaint to starvation."

166. (E) The Treaty of Paris (1783) ended the American Revolution. In the treaty, the British made numerous concessions. They granted America unconditional independence and extremely generous boundaries: all the land between the Appalachian Mountains and the Mississippi River. The United States was granted fishing rights off Newfoundland and Nova Scotia and guaranteed freedom of navigation on the Mississippi River. The British also promised to withdraw garrisons from the west "with all convenient speed." In making these concessions, the British totally ignored the rights or wishes of their Indian allies. The only American concession was a promise to recommend to state governments that they return Loyalist property seized after the American Revolution. The British did not forgive colonial American debts owed to Great Britain.

167. (B) Austrian prince Metternich (1773–1859) has been both praised and criticized for his role at the Congress of Vienna. In 1813, Metternich played a key role in the creation of the Quadruple Alliance (Great Britain, Austria, Prussia, and Russia) against Napoleon. Although Metternich wanted to check French power, he did not want to destroy the country because he feared it would upset the European balance of power. The period from 1815 to 1848 is sometimes called the Age of Metternich because for these 33 years, it seemed as if he was the arbiter of Europe. However, Metternich's system depended upon the suppression of nationalist movements; the revolutions of 1848 forced Metternich to flee to England.

168. (B) Antoine Lavoisier (1743–1794) is considered the founder of modern chemistry. Lavoisier discovered both oxygen (1778) and hydrogen (1783), helped construct the metric system, and assembled the first large list of elements. Lavoisier's classification of substances is the basis of the modern distinction between chemical elements and compounds and of the system of chemical nomenclature. He also discovered that although matter may change its form or shape, its mass always remains the same. Lavoisier held various government posts from 1775 to 1794; in 1794, Jean-Paul Marat accused him of various crimes and he was guillotined. Carl Linnaeus (1707–1778) was a Swedish botanist and zoologist who originated modern scientific classification of plants and animals. Georges Cuvier (1769–1832) helped establish the fields of comparative anatomy and paleontology by comparing living animals with fossils. Mary Anning (1799–1847) was a world-famous British paleontologist who made important finds in Jurassic-age marine fossil beds. Charles Lyell's (1797–1875) *Principles of Geology* popularized the idea that the earth was shaped by slow-moving forces still in operation.

169. (E) The key tool in spinning had always been the spindle, which elongates the strands of fiber and then twists them together to make thread or yarn. In 1765, the British inventor James Hargreaves devised a "spinning jenny" that imitated the function of spinning wheels. The jenny's operator manually turned a wheel that spun a series of 24 to 100 spindles, each simultaneously drawing out the roving and twisting it into thread. In 1769, Richard Arkwright invented the spinning frame, which separated the functions of drawing and twisting. The spinning frame lowered production costs dramatically because it ran hundreds of spindles continuously on inexpensive waterpower. Samuel Crompton invented the spinning mule in 1779; it got its name because it was a hybrid of Hargreaves's spinning jenny and Arkwright's spinning frame. In 1789, Samuel Slater, an apprentice of Arkwright's, immigrated to America. Slater had (illegally) memorized the design of Arkwright's machinery. His opening of Slater's mill in Pawtucket, Rhode Island, marks the beginning of the American Industrial Revolution. These machines required little or no skill to operate, and tending spinning frames, mules, and jennies became women's work, and then the work of children.

170. (D) The American Declaration of Independence (1776) declared, "a decent respect to the opinions of mankind requires that they should declare the causes which impel them to separation." For that reason, the Declaration contains a long list of grievances, specifically aimed at King George III (rather than Parliament). However, the final draft does not discuss the American slave trade. In Thomas Jefferson's rough draft, the slave-owning Virginian did rail against King George III for sustaining the slave trade. However, southern whites were equally upset by Lord Dunmore's 1775 proclamation that offered freedom to slaves who joined the British cause. When Jefferson's draft was presented to the Continental Congress, both northern and southern slaveholding delegates objected to the paragraph's inclusion, and the entire paragraph was removed.

171. (D) In the three decades from 1700 to 1730, about 10,000 slaves per decade were imported into British North America. Then the numbers began to increase: 1731–1740, 41,000; 1741–1750, 59,000; 1751–1760, 42,000; 1761–1770, 70,000. Although less than 5 percent of the total number of slaves sent from Africa were imported into British North America, by 1825, the southern states of the United States had the largest slave population of any country in the Western Hemisphere. In 1680, people of African descent made up less than 5 percent of the American population. Their percentage rose almost every year, peaking at 21 percent in 1770. The transatlantic slave trade continued at fairly high levels after the American Revolution until the legal slave trade ended in 1807.

172. (C) Romanticism was a new artistic movement that developed in the late 1700s and early 1800s. Romantic writers rebelled against the Enlightenment's emphasis on reason. They instead focused on the importance of deeply felt emotions, of individual genius, and of a sentimental rather than scientific relationship to nature. Wolfgang von Goethe's *The Sorrows of Young Werther* (1774) is often considered to have begun the movement; it told the story of a lovesick youth who rejects all appeals to reason and commits suicide. Important romantics include the British poets William Wordsworth, John Keats, Samuel Coleridge, and William Blake; the American writers Edgar Allan Poe and James Fenimore Cooper; and French writers such as Victor Hugo and Alexandre Dumas, père.

173. (D) The British victory in the French and Indian War had raised the British debt from 73 million pounds in 1754 to 137 million pounds in 1763. In 1754, the annual expenditures of the British government totaled 8 million pounds; in 1763, just the yearly interest on debt was 5 million pounds. However, taxes in Britain were already at an all-time high. The British government felt that the war had been fought for the benefit of the American colonists, and they should pay their fair share; American taxes were considerably less than British taxes. The new taxes were never intended to be permanent, but to last only until Britain made some headway in paying off its debt. Grenville informed American assemblies that unless they raised the money for their defense, the Stamp Act would be imposed. The colonists knew they were not paying their fair share of taxes but resented having to pay internal taxes that they did not levy themselves. The Americans never considered "no taxation without representation" a serious position; they did not want representation in Parliament, as they knew their minority presence there would simply justify oppression.

174. (D) Children became the focus of new attention by the European elite in the 1700s. This was partly the result of a decreasing child mortality rate and partly because of new Enlightenment ideas. Jean-Jacques Rousseau's *Émile, or On Education* (1762) offered an educational approach to gently draw the best out of children rather than repressing their natural curiosity and love of learning. The Enlightenment taught the middle and upper classes to value their children and to expect their improvement through education. In the 1730s, no shops specialized in children's toys in Britain; by 1782 such shops could be found throughout the country (the jigsaw puzzle was invented by John Spilsbury in 1762). In America, educated or wealthy Americans, who were often members of Episcopal or Presbyterian churches, usually treated their children leniently. Most yeomen and tenant farmers were much stricter and more authoritarian, especially in families belonging to Baptist and Congregational churches.

175. (C) No boycott against British cloth or tea in the 1760s and 1770s could succeed without the support of women. The Daughters of Liberty were a colonial women's group who displayed their patriotism by boycotting British goods following the passage of the Townshend Acts. They used traditional skills to weave yarn and wool into fabric known as *homespun*. Women organized spinning matches, bees, and demonstrations and were lionized by patriots for making America less dependent on British textiles. Their work did not compensate for the loss of British imports, which had averaged about 10 million yards a year, but it inspired support for nonimportation in hundreds of communities. Many of these women also opposed the Tea Act and signed agreements publicly pledging that they would not buy tea. They experimented to find substitutes, such as the use of boiled basil leaves to make a tea-like drink called Liberty Tea. In the Edenton Tea Party (October 1774), 51 women in Edenton (NC) signed an agreement to boycott tea and other English products and then sent the document to British newspapers.

176. (A) The Berbice Slave Uprising (1763–1764) began on plantations on the Canje River in Berbice; the area was a Dutch colony from 1627 to 1815 and is in present-day Guyana. The slaves rebelled against inhumane treatment and took control of the region. They were led by Cuffy (d. 1763), a west African sold into slavery and now a national hero of Guyana. Although the freedom fighters numbered about 3,000, they were eventually defeated with help from neighboring French and British colonies. The anniversary of the slave rebellion (February 23) has been Republic Day in Guyana since 1970.

177. (E) William Wilberforce (1759–1833) is acknowledged as the leader of the British movement to abolish the slave trade. In 1785, he became an evangelical Christian and came into contact with anti-slave-trade activists Thomas Clarkson, Granville Sharp, Hannah More, and Charles Middleton, who persuaded Wilberforce to take up abolitionism. Wilberforce headed the parliamentary campaign against the British slave trade for 26 years until the passage of the Slave Trade Act of 1807. In later years, he supported the campaign for the complete abolition of slavery. That campaign led to the Slavery Abolition Act of 1833, which abolished slavery in most of the British Empire.

178. (D) The Petition of Right (1628) was a statement of civil liberties sent by Parliament to Charles I. It was initiated by Edward Coke based on earlier statutes and charters and asserted four basic principles: no taxes could be levied without consent of Parliament; no subject could be imprisoned without cause (the right of habeas corpus); no soldiers could be housed in private homes; and martial law could not be used in time of peace. Although the petition was an important safeguard of civil liberties, Charles I soon violated its spirit. The right to counsel was not guaranteed by any documents of the English Revolution.

179. (B) Napoleon crushed the Austrians at Marengo and Hohenlinden in 1800. The British navy proved its superiority in the Battle of Trafalgar (1805), but Napoleon trounced the Austrians and Russians in December 1805 at Austerlitz, usually considered his greatest victory. After maintaining neutrality for a decade, Prussia declared war on France, but Napoleon destroyed the Prussian army at Jena and Austerdadt (1806) and then defeated the Russians again at Friedland (1807). Napoleon was eventually defeated in Russia (1812), again at Leipzig at the Battle of the Nations (1813), and finally at Waterloo (1815). He was banished to the remote island of St. Helena, off the coast of western Africa, where he died in 1821 at the age of 52. The Battle of Sedan (1870) was a catastrophic French defeat in the Franco-Prussian War and decided the war in favor of Prussia.

180. (C) In 18th-century Britain, agricultural output increased 43 percent and population increased 70 percent. This agricultural revolution was not the result of new technology, but was based on aggressive attitudes toward investment and management of land. One major change was the decision by British landowners to consolidate their holdings by pressuring small farmers and villagers to sell their land or give up their common lands. The big landlords then fenced off (enclosed) their property. Once enclosed, it was the private property of the owner, who eliminated traditional community grazing rights such as mowing meadows for hay or grazing livestock on common land. Enclosure normally required an act of Parliament, but wealthy landowners controlled Parliament and used the government to steal the public land. By 1800, six million acres of common land had been enclosed. Most villagers and small landowners could not afford the court fees to resist enclosure and were forced to sell to landlords. The countryside became depopulated (described in Oliver Goldsmith's "The Deserted Village," 1770) as a landless proto-working class moved to cities to provide the labor for the new textile industries.

Chapter 8: 19th-Century United States and Europe

181. (E) The Congress of Vienna was an international conference held from September 1814 to June 1815 that was called to remake Europe after the defeat of Napoleon. The representatives of the major powers (Austria, Great Britain, Russia, Prussia, and France) made many territorial decisions in order to create a balance of power that would preserve the peace. France lost all territory conquered by Napoleon and would now be ruled by Louis XVIII; the Dutch Republic was united with the Austrian Netherlands (present-day Belgium) to form a single kingdom under the House of Orange; Norway and Sweden were joined under a single ruler; Switzerland was declared neutral; Russia was given Finland and the Duchy of Warsaw (Poland); Prussia was given most of Saxony and parts of Westphalia and the Rhine Province; and a German Confederation of 38 states under the Austrian Emperor was created from the previous 360 of the Holy Roman Empire.

182. (C) Adam Smith (1723–1790) believed that individual interests and desires were aligned with those of the greater society. In *The Wealth of Nations* (1776), Smith insisted that individual self-interest, even greed, was compatible with society's best interest. Smith believed this was accomplished by the laws of supply and demand that served as an "invisible hand" to maintain society. He argued that the division of labor in manufacturing increased productivity and generated more wealth for the individual. To maximize the effects of market forces and the division of labor, Smith endorsed a concept called *laissez-faire* to free the economy from government intervention or control.

183. (D) Karl Marx (1818–1883) and Friedrich Engels (1820–1895) published the *Communist Manifesto* in 1848. They attacked utopian socialists as fanciful dreamers and declared that true communists must work for the downfall of the bourgeoisie and the ascendancy of the proletariat. For Marx and Engels, the history of society was "the history of class struggles." The bourgeoisie overthrew the feudal nobility in the French and English Revolutions and now exploited the proletariat by controlling the means of production and rendering workers virtually powerless. Competition among workers creates wage-labor and drives down wages to create even greater profits for the bourgeoisie. Marx and Engels were optimistic, however, that workers would inevitably rise to power through revolution against capitalism. The *Communist Manifesto* states that the ultimate goal of communists was the abolition of the old society based on class conflict and the foundation of a new society without classes and without private property. Unlike most utopian socialists, Marx and Engels embraced industrialization because they believed it would eventually bring on the proletarian revolution.

184. (C) The Battle of Bull Run (July 1861) took place just outside of Washington, D.C., and was a Confederate victory. The Union capture (April–May 1862) of New Orleans, the Confederacy's largest city, made it impossible for the South to use the Mississippi River as a transportation artery. At Antietam (September 1862), the Union checked Robert E. Lee's first invasion of the North. Gettysburg and Vicksburg, both in July 1863, are considered the turning points of the Civil War. Gettysburg ended Lee's second invasion of the North and doomed any hope of foreign intervention for the Confederacy. Vicksburg gave the Union complete control of the Mississippi River.

185. (B) In 1800, Spain returned the territory of Louisiana to France; Napoleon hoped to use this area as a breadbasket for the rich French sugar plantations in the Caribbean. These French ambitions terrified Americans; in the era before railroads, almost all American commerce west of the Appalachians followed various river systems to the Mississippi, where it was floated to New Orleans. However, after France's failure to defeat the Haitian rebellion, Napoleon decided to rid himself of the entire problem. In 1803, President Thomas Jefferson sent agents to Paris to buy New Orleans and the Gulf Coast for $2 million. To their shock, French Foreign Minister Talleyrand offered them the entire Louisiana Territory. After the briefest hesitation, the United States purchased 827,000 acres for $15 million, or about 3.5 cents an acre (about $220 million in 2012 money). The purchase more than doubled the size of the United States. Faced with this bargain, Jefferson reversed his long-standing belief in strict construction and argued that the implied powers of the president allowed this action. The Senate approved the treaty purchase 24 to 6.

186. (A) Serfs were emancipated in Prussia in 1810 and in Austria in 1848, yet more than 40 million serfs remained in Russia in 1850. Their lack of mobility, and the feudal ideology of the nobility, impeded the modernization of Russia. However, sympathetic portrayals of serfs, such as in Ivan Turgenev's *A Hunter's Sketches* (1852), led to a spirit of reform. When Alexander II (1818–1881) came to power in 1855, he emancipated 22 million privately owned serfs in 1861 and 25 million state-owned peasants a few years later. Unfortunately, the newly freed serfs were not given land along with their personal freedom. Instead, they were forced to "redeem" the land they farmed by paying the government through long-term loans, which in turn compensated the original landowners. In the end, most peasants ended up owning less land than they had tilled as serfs.

187. (C) By the 1800s, upper-class women's costumes were elaborate, ornate, and dramatic, especially in contrast to men's plain garments. Women's clothes often featured constricting corsets, long voluminous skirts, bustles, and low-cut necklines for evening wear. In *The Theory of the Leisure Class* (1900), Thorstein Veblen noted that both the rich and the poor attempted to gain and signal status through *conspicuous consumption* and *conspicuous leisure*. The "conspicuous" element was absolutely necessary because the anonymity of urban and industrial culture guaranteed that only the crassest display of wealth, such as the over-the-top mansions at Newport, Rhode Island, would be noticed. In fashion, constraining clothing on women demonstrated a man's social standing by advertising how little his wife did. Two examples of this were the corset and bound feet. Both made it impossible for a woman to even attempt to do anything constructive, thereby clearly displaying male wealth and power.

188. (D) Free trade refers to a government policy that does not discriminate against imports or interfere with exports by applying tariffs (to imports) or subsidies (to exports). Under a free trade policy, prices supposedly reflect supply and demand and determine how resources are allocated. Natural resources, labor, and markets are basic components of a modern industrial economy; however, free trade may or may not be present.

189. (E) Probably no more than 100,000 Americans in total joined antebellum utopian movements. However, they represented a serious critique of the capitalist environment. Utopians believed that the expanding market economy corrupted human virtue, and they searched for an antidote to the Industrial Revolution in a genuinely radical and totally new order. New Harmony, Indiana, was a utopian town established in 1825 by Robert Owen (1771–1858), a self-made millionaire and social reformer. Before it disbanded in 1828, New Harmony recorded several firsts in the United States: first kindergarten, first free public school, first free library, first school with equal education for boys and girls. Brook Farm was a utopian community in West Roxbury, Massachusetts, in the 1840s. Residents tried to balance labor and leisure while working together for the benefit of the greater community. Brook Farm was never financially stable and closed in 1847. Nathaniel Hawthorne was a founding member of Brook Farm; he later fictionalized his experience in *The Blithedale Romance* (1852). The Oneida Community in central New York was a religious community established by John Humphrey Noyes (1811–1886) in 1848. Residents of Oneida held property in common and stressed the subordination of selfish desires to the greater good. The members practiced complex marriage and common care of children. Oneida was a financial success, manufacturing steel traps, sewing silk, and preserving fruits and vegetables. They began the famous tableware business in 1877, but the community was reorganized as joint stock company in 1881.

190. (C) The managerial revolution describes a revolutionary shift between 1840 and 1920 in which the modern business enterprise replaced traditional family-owned-and-operated business. In the 1800s, companies became so large that they outgrew control by a single owner. Now, responsibilities were divided and given to a class of salaried managers who ran these new enterprises within a carefully designed hierarchy. Corporations in railroads, iron, oil, and meat production created separate departments along functional lines and introduced modern cost-accounting procedures. The salaried middle manager became a key layer of command between owners and workers.

191. (A) A small border war over the dusty land between the Rio Grande and the Nueces River made the United States a world power. After winning the Mexican-American War (1846–1848), the United States took the Mexican provinces of California and New Mexico (which contained the future states of Nevada, Utah, and Arizona). These lands increased the size of the United States by more than 20 percent. The victory completed American expansion across North America to the Pacific Ocean. The harbors of San Francisco and San Diego opened the door to American trade with Asia. The rich farmland of California helped feed the nation. At the same time, Mexico lost more than 500,000 square miles, more than one-third of its territory. Los Angeles, Phoenix, Santa Fe, Las Vegas, and Salt Lake City all became American cities. The debate over whether slavery should be allowed in the new territories was a major cause of the American Civil War (1860–1865). The United States suffered 13,000 dead out of about 100,000 who fought in the Mexican-American War. Only about 2,000 Americans died in military action; the rest died from diarrhea, dysentery, measles, and other diseases. About 50,000 Mexicans died defending their homeland.

192. (C) The Peterloo Massacre (also called the Manchester Massacre) occurred at St. Peter's Field in Manchester, England, on August 16, 1819. The end of the Napoleonic Wars in 1815 led to periods of unemployment. The Corn Laws, passed by Parliament, favored wealthy landowners at the expense of most urban dwellers. A crowd of about 70,000 men, women, and children gathered peacefully under the leadership of Henry Hunt to demand reform of parliamentary representation and repeal of the Corn Laws. A cavalry charge into the crowd resulted in about 15 deaths and more than 400 injuries. The government's endorsement of the action created widespread anger throughout Britain and added moral force to the reform movement. However, the Peterloo Massacre's actual impact on reform in Britain is greatly disputed.

193. (C) The Treaty of Ghent (December 1814) returned Anglo-American relations to the conditions of 1812. The treaty did not mention impressment or neutral maritime rights. This seemed to indicate that the War of 1812 was pointless. However, the war had crucial direct and indirect results. It was disastrous for most Native American tribes. Defeats suffered by Indians in the northwest and south forced them to sign treaties that opened land to American expansion. The possibility of military resistance to white expansion ended with Tecumseh's death and the neutralization of the British. The War of 1812 stimulated tremendous economic changes. Prewar trade restrictions and the war itself led to increased production of manufactured goods. New England merchants, unable to prosper in shipping, invested capital in manufacturing and sped the impact of the industrial revolution in the United States. A wave of American nationalism followed the Treaty of Ghent, sometimes known as the Era of Good Feeling. Ironically, one of most decisive effects of the failed American invasions of Canada was a Canadian determination never to be invaded or absorbed by the United States. The militias' performance in the War of 1812 was a disgrace, and the ineffective militias were gradually phased out.

194. (C) In general, the birthrate began to fall dramatically in western Europe and the United States in the 1800s (it had been decreasing in France since the 1700s). In the United States, women bore an average of seven children in 1800, five in 1860, and four in 1900; these numbers include immigrants with large-family traditions. Abstinence and withdrawal were common methods of birth control. However, the decline in birthrate was also aided by the spread of modern birth control devices such as diaphragms and condoms. As a last resort, abortion was widespread, although some states began to restrict it in the United States in the 1830s. Smaller families and fewer births changed conditions for women; birth and infant care no longer occupied a woman's entire lifetime and childhood developed as distinct period of life.

195. (B) Reconstruction was the period in United States history from about 1863 to 1877 in which three problems were considered: what to do about the former slaves in the South, what to do about the former rebels in the South, and who would decide. The Confederate states had to be restored to the Union and provided with loyal governments, and the role of the emancipated slaves in Southern society had to be defined. Reconstruction was incredibly lenient, with the former white rebels suffering no long-term negative sanctions (only one execution and few imprisonments). Organizations such as the Ku Klux Klan used violence to keep African Americans and white Republicans from voting, and Southern whites recovered complete power after 1877. African Americans were liberated from slavery (Thirteenth Amendment) and acquired the right of citizenship (Fourteenth Amendment) and the right to vote for black men (Fifteenth Amendment), but the latter two rights were ignored in the white "redemption" after the war. The results were the one-party *solid South* and increased racial bitterness. Although blacks had tilled the land for decades, if not centuries, they were given no land and no reparations. Many became indebted sharecroppers. Between 1877 and 1950, the American South was organized as a terror state in which blacks asserted their rights at the risk of their lives.

196. (A) In 1856, the Bessemer process was invented simultaneously by Henry Bessemer in England and William Kelly in the United States. Unlike puddling furnaces that produced wrought iron, Bessemer converters produced steel—harder and more durable—in large amounts with little labor. However, the Bessemer process only operated with expensive, low-phosphorus iron. The open-hearth furnace, developed in 1868, handled low-quality iron, so it was now possible to produce steel in large quantities and large dimensions ideally suited for railroad track and locomotives. In 1885, three-quarters of American steel went into steel rails, but then demand diversified. Steel was used in skyscrapers, trolley lines, subways, pipes, battleships, and then automobiles. The scale of business enterprise rose dramatically, the skills of the puddler, heater, and hand roller became obsolete, and gang labor was replaced by ore- and metal-handling equipment. The face-to-face relationships of workers with employers disappeared, replaced by a hierarchy of professional managers. The typical American steel-worker of 1900 worked an 84-hour week tending machines in an impersonal, bureaucratic business organization.

197. (C) Lithography (from the Greek word *lithos*, meaning "stone") was a new artistic technology invented (c. 1798) by German engraver Alois Senefelder that spread across Europe and the United States in the 1800s. An artist would use a greasy crayon to trace an image on a flat stone; the grease attracted the ink, while the blank areas repelled it. The inked stone was then embedded in a printing press that could produce thousands of identical images. Lithographs in relatively inexpensive daily and weekly newspapers helped educate a mass audience about social and political problems created by industrial and urban growth. In the United States, the firm of Currier and Ives (1857–1898) produced more than 7,000 lithographs, appealing to virtually every popular taste and interest. Eventually, the perfection of chromolithography and a proliferation of photographs, stereographs, and engravings undermined the popularity of lithography.

198. (A) The Orange Riots were not related to labor unrest. They took place in New York City in 1870 and 1871 and involved violent conflict between Irish Protestants (called Orange-men) and Irish Catholics, with the participation of the police and National Guard. The 1871 riot was particularly bloody; more than 60 people died (mostly Irish laborers) and 150 people were wounded. The cause of the fighting was primarily social and religious. The other four choices are all examples of class warfare in the Gilded Age.

199. (D) Giuseppe Mazzini (1805–1872), along with Giuseppe Garibaldi (1807–1882) and Camillo Benso di Cavour (1810–1861), were the outstanding figures of the Risorgimento (resurgence), the period leading to unification of Italy. Mazzini worked for a revolution against Austrian rule in northern Italy from a young age. In 1831 he organized a secret political society called Young Italy to promote Italian unification. During the revolutions of 1848, uprisings occurred in Milan, the Papal States, and the Two Sicilies. Mazzini returned to Italy and in 1849 was one of the leaders of the Roman republic. After its fall, he resumed propagandizing from abroad and organized unsuccessful uprisings in Milan (1853) and southern Italy (1857). Mazzini supported Giuseppe Garibaldi's expedition to Sicily, but unlike Garibaldi, he opposed a monarchy and remained a republican. Mazzini's relations with Cavour were strained. Although both worked for Italian unification, Cavour believed the best method was to rely on a foreign power (France) for help, while Mazzini supported revolution based on direct popular action.

200. (B) In 1823, President James Monroe gave a speech to the US Congress that is now known as the Monroe Doctrine. Monroe declared that the Western Hemisphere was closed to new European colonization and that the United States would consider any attempts to extend Europe's political influence into the Western Hemisphere as dangerous to American interests. However, the United States would not interfere with already existing colonies in the Western Hemisphere or in European affairs. The Monroe Doctrine was and remains an American foreign policy position and nothing more. No one is forced to obey it, the republics of South America never agreed to it, and Monroe's speech made little impression on the great powers of Europe at the time.

201. (B) In the 1820s, Robert Peel (1788–1850), the secretary for home affairs, revised the criminal code to reduce the number of crimes punishable by death and introduced a municipal police force in London. In 1824, laws prohibiting labor unions were repealed. In 1829, Catholics were permitted to sit in Parliament and hold most public offices. The Reform Bill of 1832 was the culmination of this trend; it increased the number of British voters by about 50 percent. The bill gave representation to new cities in the industrial north for the first time and took away seats from the *rotten boroughs*—those areas with very small populations (the most famous being the uninhabited Old Sarum). The Reform Bill of 1832 set a precedent for the widening of suffrage, but voting still depended on owning property, and only about one in six Britons could vote. The Reform Act of 1884 doubled the electorate again, but universal male suffrage did not come to Great Britain until 1918.

202. (E) The Hudson River School was America's first homegrown artistic movement, active from about 1825 to 1875. It was led by Thomas Cole, Asher Durand, and Frederic Church, who painted the beauties of American scenery and approached nature with reverence. They were influenced by 19th-century European romanticism. Lacking the long history of Europe, they instead glorified the American landscape as a form of patriotism. They were particularly attracted by the grandeur of Niagara Falls and the scenic beauty of the Hudson River valley, the Catskill Mountains, and the White Mountains. In 1825, only one 1 of every 10 American paintings was a landscape; by 1850, 9 out of 10 were landscapes.

203. (D) The Paris Commune was the government that briefly ruled Paris from March through May 1871. The conditions in which it formed, its controversial decrees, and its violent end make the Commune's rule one of the most controversial incidents of the time. The defeat of France in the Franco-Prussian War (1871) led to the fall of Napoleon III's empire. However, most Parisians opposed the national government, headed by Adolphe Thiers, as too conservative, too royalist, and too ready to accept a humiliating peace with Prussia. Thiers fled to Versailles, and the Parisians elected a self-governing municipal council known as the Commune of 1871. Parisians quickly developed a wide array of political clubs, local ceremonies, and self-managed, cooperative workshops. The Communards were not united and expressed a bewildering set of secular political programs. While the victorious Prussians affected neutrality outside the city, the French troops of the Versailles government began a siege of Paris to regain control. After five weeks, the troops entered the city in May. The Communards fought desperately, throwing up barricades, shooting hostages (including the archbishop of Paris), and burning important buildings. On May 28 the Commune was finally defeated. Severe reprisals followed, resulting in more than 18,000 Parisian dead and almost 7,000 deported. Memories of the bloody Paris repression embittered political relations between radicals and conservatives in France for many years.

204. (E) The so-called walking city was common in Europe and the United States before 1830. A major characteristic was congestion caused by extremely high population density. In 1819, London had 800,000 people but was only three miles across. Walking cities retained a clear distinction between city and country, a legacy from the days of city walls. American cities were rarely walled but still had no sprawl and little blurring of urban/rural lines. Neighborhoods in preindustrial cities contained a mixture of functions. Except for waterfront warehouses and prostitution, no urban neighborhoods were exclusively commercial or residential. Factories were nonexistent, and most production was by artisans in small shops. Public buildings, hotels, churches, warehouses, shops, and homes were all interspersed. This meant a short commute from work. In 1815, even in the largest cities, only 1 in 50 people traveled more than one mile to work. The most fashionable addresses were close to the center of the city. In Europe, people who lived outside the walls and away from palaces and cathedrals lived in inferior surroundings. Suburbs were considered slums, and the word often had a pejorative connotation.

205. (B) In 1854, war broke out between Russia and the Ottoman Empire (present-day Turkey), England, France, and Sardinia. The main cause of the war was the *eastern question*— who would control the European territory of the decaying Ottoman Empire. British and French troops, enemies for centuries, ironically fought together to defend the Ottoman Empire's territory. They landed in Crimea in September 1854 and waged a long siege of the well-fortified Russian naval base of Sevastopol on the Black Sea. Generals on both sides displayed their incompetence (most famously in the "Charge of the Light Brigade"), and governments failed to provide soldiers with even minimal supplies, sanitation, or medical care. More than 700,000 men died, two-thirds from disease and starvation. When the Peace of Paris was signed in March 1856, Russian involvement in southeastern Europe had been checked and Russo-Austrian relations had cooled. The defeat was cataclysmic for Russia, as its autocracy was forced to abolish serfdom, begin overdue internal reforms, and try to revive the empire. The work of Florence Nightingale was perhaps the most positive outcome of the war. Although officially neutral, Americans as a whole were anti-British and pro-Russia.

206. (B) The Catholic Church felt threatened by the growing rationalism in the 1800s, as well as the state-building in Italy and Germany that competed for people's traditional loyalties. Pope Pius IX (reigned 1846–1878) issued *The Syllabus of Errors* (1864), which attacked secularism, modernism, and liberalism. In 1870, the First Vatican Council approved the dogma of papal infallibility that proclaimed that the pope's utterances must be regarded by Catholics as divinely revealed truth on issues of morality and faith. Liberal Catholics had to submit to the new dogma or be excommunicated. In 1854, the pope's announcement of the doctrine of the Immaculate Conception (that Mary was born without original sin) was followed by an outburst of religious fervor, especially among women. In 1858, a peasant girl from Lourdes in southern France, Bernadette Soubirous, began having visions of the Virgin Mary. Crowds of mostly women besieged Lourdes to drink from a miraculous spring that was claimed to cure ailments. Railroad tracks were laid to Lourdes in 1867, and it became a pilgrimage site for millions of Catholics; an estimated 200 million people have visited the shrine since 1860.

207. (D) Musical nationalism emerged in the Romantic era in the mid-1800s as a reaction against the mainstream European classical tradition, which always seemed to be German, French, or Italian. Nationalistic music usually explored folk themes from rural life; the popular view was that folk music represented the "true" music of a nation. This new music aided movements for national liberation and self-determination that grew in the 1800s. Czech composer Antonín Dvorák (1841–1904) employed popular national melodies in his *Moravian Duets* (1876) and *Slavonic Dances* (1878). Norwegian composer Edvard Grieg's (1843–1907) music for Ibsen's play *Peer Gynt* (1875) integrated rural legends into music for urban audiences. In 1876, Richard Wagner (1813–1883) premiered his *Der Ring des Nibelungen* based on a medieval German legend, and it was hailed as a triumph of German nationalism. Isaac Albéniz (1860–1909) was a Spanish Catalan composer known for his piano works based on Spanish folk music.

208. (A) The *cult of domesticity* refers to a primarily upper- and middle-class ideology in western Europe and the United States in the 1800s. The cult of domesticity, mainly but not solely created by men, stated that a woman's true role centered on maintaining home and nurturing family, which would serve as a rock of traditional value in a radically changing economy. Women's virtues—piety, purity, and submissiveness—were said to be best nourished in the home as mother, daughter, sister, and wife. Female influence should be indirect, subtle, symbolic, and private. Mothers ensured the future of the nation by rearing children in a spiritual and virtuous environment. Education, religion, morality, and culture all filled the void left by the loss of productive economic functions of women in the Industrial Revolution (e.g., food preparation, textile manufacture). This domestic ideal limited paying jobs that middle-class women could hold outside the home. Eventually, women turned the concept inside out; if women were pure, nurturing, and beneficial, then reform, healing, and political involvement were natural concerns.

209. (B) In the late 1800s and early 1900s, governments in western Europe and the United States began to allow professional people to decide who would and would not be admitted to the professions. The middle class from the early 1800s had derived its position from family background and stature within the local community. The new middle class placed a higher value on education and individual accomplishment. Growing numbers of doctors, lawyers, managers, professors, and journalists tried to build organizations that could stabilize and/or exalt their position in society. As late as 1880, any patent medicine salesman, frustrated politician, or literate person could claim to be a doctor, lawyer, or teacher. Gradually, new professional organizations established rigorous standards for certification and restricted admission to reduce competition and keep out "undesirables"—minorities and women. In the United States, membership in the American Medical Association rose from 8,400 in 1900 to 70,000 in 1910. By 1920, two-thirds of doctors were members. Many qualified people were kept from working because they lacked the requisite credentials (e.g., the exclusion of female midwives from medicine).

210. (C) American businessmen in the late 1800s exalted individual initiative but often begged the government for assistance. They demanded that liability be limited in the case of bankruptcy. High tariffs were intended to keep out foreign competition and favor American businesses. Generous land grants enabled railroad entrepreneurs to become rich. In 1886, the US Supreme Court granted corporations the rights of natural persons under the Fourteenth Amendment in *Santa Clara County v. Southern Pacific Railroad*. (Corporations retain that right as of 2012.) The corporate merger movement tried to restrict competition, and businessmen demanded exemptions from antitrust legislation. They also wanted the state (via the army and National Guard) to break strikes and impose labor discipline, such as in the railroad strikes of 1877 or the Pullman Strike of 1894.

211. (A) William Wordsworth (1770–1850) wrote the sonnet "The World Is Too Much with Us" in 1807. Wordsworth was a leader of the Romantic movement in England that included John Keats, Samuel Taylor Coleridge, and Percy Bysshe Shelley. Wordsworth's early works were strongly influenced by the republicanism of the French Revolution, although as the years passed, he grew increasingly conservative. Wordsworth's personality and poetry were influenced by his love of nature, especially the scenes of the Lake District in northwest England where he spent most of his adult life. Wordsworth's use of the language of ordinary speech was criticized at the time, but it revolutionized English poetry.

212. (D) The Industrial Revolution led to enormous urban growth. By 1850, half the population of England lived in towns compared to a quarter of French and Germans. In the 1830s alone, London grew by 130,000 people and Manchester by 70,000. Between 1841 and 1846, Paris grew by 120,000 people; from 1827 to 1847, Vienna's population increased by 125,000; between 1815 and 1848, Berlin's increased by 180,000; and between 1837 and 1900, Prague's grew by 96,000. Between 1820 and 1860, New York City's population increased from 152,000 to 1.2 million; Philadelphia's from 64,000 to 565,000; and Chicago's from a small settlement to 112,000. Massive rural emigration and not natural increase accounted for the majority of this surge. Agricultural improvements increased the food supply, but the land could no longer support the people living on it. City life and factories enticed peasants faced with hunger and poverty. They also attracted emigrants: the Irish to English cities, Italians to French cities, and Poles to German cities. The influx caused serious overcrowding and led to disease and sanitation problems. In 1850, London's 250,000 cesspools were only emptied once or twice a year. Human waste ended up in rivers and then contaminated drinking water. From 1830 to 1832, and again from 1847 to 1851, devastating cholera epidemics swept across Asia, Europe, and the United States, killing more than a million people.

213. (E) Tecumseh (1768–1813) was chief of the Shawnee in present-day Ohio famous for his organizational and military abilities. Tecumseh believed that Native American land was the common possession of all Native Americans and that land could not legally be ceded by, or purchased from, an individual tribe. When Americans refused to accept this principle, Tecumseh attempted to unite the Native Americans of the old Northwest, the South, and the eastern Mississippi valley. However, his hopes of a great alliance failed with the defeat of his brother, The Prophet (Tenskwatawa), at Tippecanoe (present-day Indiana) in 1811. In the War of 1812, Tecumseh and most Native Americans fought with the British, but he was killed in the Battle of the Thames (near present-day Chatham, Ontario) in 1813. The other choices were all brilliant Native American leaders, but they did not attempt to create intertribal alliances to fight the American invasion.

214. (B) Florence Nightingale (1820–1910) was an English nurse who is considered the founder of modern nursing. When the Crimean War began, she escaped the confines of middle-class domesticity by organizing a battlefield nursing unit of 38 female nurses to care for the British sick and wounded. Through sheer determination, she secured medical supplies and personnel for her hospital and improved the sanitary conditions of the troops. After the war, she laid the foundation of professional nursing by establishing (1860) a nursing school at St. Thomas' Hospital in London, the first secular nursing school in the world. International Nurses Day is celebrated around the world on her birthday.

215. (A) The decision of the first seven Southern states to secede from the Union was precipitated by the election of Abraham Lincoln to the presidency in November 1860. The US Constitution says nothing about secession, so several Southern governors imitated the original constitutional conventions by calling for the election of delegates (even though five of the seven states joined the United States after 1787). South Carolina was the first to secede (December 20), followed by six more—Mississippi, Florida, Alabama, Georgia, Louisiana, and Texas—by February 1, 1861. Only Texas had a popular vote (there was no popular ratification of the original US Constitution either). Although President Lincoln expressly said he would not touch slavery in the South, secessionists hoped to protect the status quo before any threat could materialize. The Confederate Constitution expressly guaranteed protection for slavery in the territories. Four other Southern states (Virginia, Arkansas, Tennessee, and North Carolina) seceded in May and June (1861) after the shelling of Fort Sumter. Stephen Douglas was a staunch Unionist.

216. (D) Otto von Bismarck (1815–1898) was known as the Iron Chancellor of Germany. In 1862, William I, king of Prussia, appointed him prime minister; in direct violation of the constitution, Bismarck dissolved parliament and collected taxes for the army without legislative approval. After Germany defeated Denmark in 1864, Bismarck engineered a quarrel with Austria over Schleswig-Holstein. This squabble led to the Austro-Prussian War (1866), which ended after seven weeks with the complete defeat of Austria. The victory allowed Bismarck to drive Austria from the German Confederation and to create a North German Confederation under Prussian leadership. Bismarck then deviously published the Ems Dispatch, a telegram that created a nationalist paroxysm and caused the Franco-Prussian War (1870–1871). As Bismarck anticipated, the southern German states rallied to the Prussian cause and France was crushed. In 1871 William I was proclaimed German emperor and Bismarck became chancellor with virtually complete control of foreign and domestic affairs. Over the next two decades, Bismarck used a system of alignments and alliances to turn Germany into the virtual arbiter of Europe. Bismarck's record in domestic policy was mixed, but between 1883 and 1887, laws were passed providing for sickness, accident, and old-age insurance; limiting woman and child labor; and establishing maximum working hours. The Bismarckian era ended when William II became kaiser in 1888; Bismarck was dismissed in 1890.

217. (D) *Vertical integration* refers to the merger of two businesses that are at different stages of production, for example, a food manufacturer and a chain of supermarkets. Vertically integrated companies are united through a common owner; usually each member produces a different product or service. In that way, vertical integration is the opposite of horizontal integration, which is the merger of businesses that are at the same stage of production, such as two supermarkets or two food manufacturers. Steel manufacturer Andrew Carnegie (1835–1919) introduced the concept and use of vertical integration in the later 1800s. The Carnegie Steel Company controlled not only the mills where the steel was made, but also the mines where the iron ore and coal were extracted, the ships and railroads that transported the iron ore and coal to the factory, and the coke ovens where the coal was cooked. By the late 1880s, Carnegie Steel was the largest manufacturer of pig iron, steel rails, and coke in the world.

218. (B) In 1848, a women's rights convention met in Seneca Falls, New York. Elizabeth Cady Stanton wrote its famous Declaration of Sentiments, which reads in part, "We hold these truths to be self-evident: that all men and women are created equal." This feminist document arose out of the gender segregation of the early abolition movement in the United States and Great Britain. Early feminists attacked the legal and social inequality of women, drawing parallels between the position of women and slaves (inability to vote or control property, exclusion from education and key occupations). The Declaration of Sentiments was signed by 68 women and 32 men (including Frederick Douglass) and invited widespread ridicule. However, in 1848, New York passed a pioneering law that protected the property of married women in event of the death or incapacitation of their husbands.

219. (D) In 1790, the entire United States produced only 3,000 bales of cotton. Cotton grew well in many areas of the South, but the seeds were so difficult to remove from the fiber that it took an entire day to hand-clean a single pound of cotton. In the 1790s, a number of inventors developed a machine to separate the seeds from the fiber of cotton. The cotton gin (short for *engine*) was simply a hand-cranked cylinder with metal teeth. However, now it was possible to clean 50 pounds of cotton a day. By 1811, South Carolina and Georgia were producing 60 million pounds of cotton a year. Farmers then rushed into Alabama and Mississippi. Between 1820 and 1860, the number of slaves in Alabama increased from 41,000 to 435,000. In 1859, the prewar peak of production, planters sent more than 4 million bales of cotton to New England and European textile mills. This was about 60 percent of the world's cotton. By the Civil War, cotton exports accounted for 60 percent of the value of all American exports.

220. (C) The quotation is from President Andrew Jackson's State of the Union address of 1830. Jackson supported the forced removal of the Cherokee Indians from Georgia, where they had lived for centuries. After the American Revolution, most Cherokee had adopted the "civilizing" philosophy, raising cotton, accumulating property, and even acquiring slaves. They established a written law code in 1808, and in 1817, passed articles of government giving only the National Council the authority to sell lands. Sequoyah devised an 85-letter alphabet in 1821. White Georgians wanted Cherokee land and felt confident that Andrew Jackson, a ruthless slave-owning Indian fighter, would support the expulsion of the southern tribes. Jackson pushed the Indian Removal Act (1830), which expelled 100,000 Indians to territories beyond the Mississippi River. The debates in Congress were extremely bitter, and the act only passed the House of Representatives by a 102 to 97 vote. The Cherokee appealed to the US Supreme Court; in *Worcester v. Georgia* (1832), Chief Justice John Marshall stated that Georgia's laws violated treaties and the US Constitution. Both Georgia and President Jackson ignored the decision. Thousands of Georgians streamed onto Cherokee lands, and the US army forced the Cherokee to follow the Trail of Tears to Oklahoma in 1838. An estimated 4,000 out of 15,000 Native Americans died on the 1,200-mile march. (The other answer choices all opposed the Indian Removal Act.)

221. (D) In the 1800s, scientific research promoted public health and disease control. John Snow (1813–1858) contributed to the formation of the germ theory when he traced the source of the 1854 cholera outbreak in London to a specific water pump at the geographical center of the outbreak. Ignaz Semmelweis (1818–1865) was a Hungarian physician whose work demonstrated that hand-washing could drastically reduce the number of women dying after childbirth. Although Semmelweis was ridiculed by the medical establishment of the time, he eventually became known as the "savior of the mothers." Louis Pasteur (1822–1895) advanced the *germ theory*—the idea that certain organisms such as bacteria and parasites cause diseases. Pasteur demonstrated that heating milk and wine to a certain temperature (pasteurization) killed those organisms and made food safe. In the 1860s, English surgeon Joseph Lister (1827–1912) connected the germ theory of bacteria to infection and developed antiseptics for treating wounds. Using carbolic acid for sterilization, as Lister suggested, hastened the decline of puerperal fever, a condition caused by the dirty hands of physicians and midwives that killed innumerable women after childbirth. Robert Koch was the first scientist to devise a series of tests to assess the germ theory of disease. Koch discovered the bacteria that created anthrax, tuberculosis, and cholera, and he essentially created the field of bacteriology.

222. (B) After Reconstruction, southern whites passed Jim Crow laws (blacks were forcibly prevented from voting) segregating public facilities from drinking fountains to hotel rooms. In some cases, the purpose was to keep African Americans from advancing: for example, schools and hospitals for blacks provided inferior education and care. In other cases, the purpose was purely psychological: the creation of separate water fountains cost extra money but served to intimidate blacks and remind them of their inferior status. Jim Crow laws were declared constitutional by the Supreme Court in 1896 in the case of *Plessy v. Ferguson*. By an eight to one vote (John Harlan dissenting), the Court ruled that "separate but equal" facilities were constitutional. This ruling was not overturned for 58 years until *Brown v. Board of Education* in 1954. De facto segregation in the northern states was also the rule, but actual Jim Crow laws were rare.

223. (E) Literary realism is an approach that tries to faithfully describe life without idealization or subjective prejudice. Realists wanted to avoid unusual occurrences and wrote on new subject matter such as factories, slums, workers, bosses, corrupt politicians, petty criminals, and social outcasts. The popularity of realism was affected by interest in the scientific method, the rejection of romanticism, and Charles Darwin's theory of natural selection. Honoré de Balzac (1799–1850) wrote a series of detailed novels, collectively entitled *The Human Comedy* (*La Comédie humaine*), which presented a panorama of French life after the fall of Napoleon. Émile Zola (1804–1902) developed a school of realism known as naturalism; his masterpiece, *Germinal,* is a novel about life in a mining town. Stephen Crane (1871–1900) is known for *The Red Badge of Courage* (a young boy's experience in the Civil War) and *Maggie* (a girl's decline into prostitution), a theme taken up in greater detail by Theodore Dreiser (1871–1945) in *Sister Carrie* (1900).

224. (A) After Napoleon's defeat in 1815, the Congress of Vienna established a nominally independent Polish kingdom united with the czar of Russia. The western provinces of Poland were given to Prussia, Galicia was given to Austria, and Krakow was made a separate republic. A Polish nationalist revival led to a general insurrection in 1830 (known as the November Revolution) in Russian Poland. The Poles were defeated (1831) at Ostrołęka, and Nicholas essentially annexed Poland. Thousands of Poles emigrated, especially to Paris, which became the center of Polish nationalist activities. Their intellectual hero was the poet Adam Mickiewicz (1798–1855), whose mystical writings portrayed the Polish exiles as martyrs of a crucified nation. However, in 1846, a Polish peasant revolt in Galicia turned on Polish nobles and led to the annexation of Krakow by Austria. After crushing another revolt in 1864, Alexander II began a program of Russification to reduce the threat of rebellion by national minorities within the Russian Empire. A similar policy of Germanization occurred in Prussian Poland. Only in Austrian Galicia did the Poles enjoy a considerable degree of autonomy.

225. (C) In 1848, a series of revolutionary explosions rocked western and central Europe. In Germany, Hungary, Italy, France, and parts of the Austrian Empire, popular movements attacked conservative royalty and demanded democracy, national self-determination, and economic reforms. Lack of cooperation among the revolutionary movements, and the loyalty of the armies to old authorities, eventually led to the defeat of the insurgents. Middle-class reformers feared working-class demands and often sided with conservatives. Although every one of the revolutions of 1848 was put down, the uprisings spread the idea of *consent of the governed*, essentially ended feudalism in central Europe, began the German and Italian unification movements, and established Hungary as an equal partner with Austria under Hapsburg rule.

226. (C) The great Russian novelist Leo Tolstoy (1828–1910), the author of *War and Peace* (1869), did not desire to overturn the social order; instead, he believed that Russia needed spiritual regeneration. *Anna Karenina* (1877) tells the story of an impassioned, adulterous love affair, but it also includes a subplot involving the spiritual quest of Levin, a former progressive landowner, who eventually rejects modernization and idealizes the Russian peasantry's tradition of stoic endurance. After the 1870s, Tolstoy became known for his extreme moralistic and ascetic views. His literal interpretation of the ethical teachings of Jesus caused him to become a fanatical Christian anarchist and pacifist, preaching simplicity of life. His ideas on nonviolent resistance, expressed in works such as *The Law of Love and the Law of Violence* (1908), inspired Mohandas Gandhi and Martin Luther King Jr.

227. (C) Baron Georges Haussmann (1809–1891) was a French city planner famous for his bold alterations in the layout of Paris under Napoleon III between 1853 and 1870 (the Second Empire period). Haussmann's renovation of Paris created the city's modern appearance, with long, straight, wide boulevards bordered by cafés and shops. To create adequate traffic circulation, Haussmann widened the irregular medieval streets and alleyways. He cut new boulevards through dense residential areas, in the process evicting thousands of poor people and destroying their homes. Ultimately, 85 miles of new streets were created, many lined with showy dwellings for the wealthy. Haussmann deliberately placed Paris's great railway stations in a circle outside the old city and provided them with broad approaches. He created vast open spaces and vistas for the enhancement of Place de l'Opéra, the Étoile, and the Place de la Nation, which became the focus points for radiating avenues. Haussmann also laid out the vast Bois de Boulogne, as well as many smaller parks. Dramatic changes in the urban environment made Paris and many other European cities the backdrop for displays of state power and national solidarity.

228. (E) The idea of a railroad was not new in 1800; miners had used iron tracks since the 1600s to haul coal with wagons pulled by horses. Richard Trevithick (1771–1833) invented the locomotive (1804), but George Stephenson (1781–1848) built the first public railroad line to use steam locomotives. Despite being illiterate until age 18, Stephenson designed his first locomotive in 1814 to haul coal in Killingworth. In 1825, Stephenson built the *Locomotion* for the Stockton and Darlington Railway in northeastern England, the first public steam railroad in the world. His locomotive, the *Rocket*, defeated the competition in a contest in 1829 and was used on the Liverpool-Manchester Railway. Stephenson established his company as the chief builder of steam locomotives in Great Britain, the United States, and most of Europe. Stephenson's rail gauge of 4 feet 8.5 inches, known as *Stephenson gauge*, is the standard gauge throughout the world.

229. (B) The "Sick Man of Europe," a phrase attributed to Tsar Nicholas I, was a nickname first used in the mid-1800s to describe the Ottoman Empire. The Ottoman decline was particularly pronounced from about 1827 to 1908, when the empire was reeling from Russian imperialism, economic problems, and national uprisings. The Ottoman Empire took its first foreign loans during the Crimean War (1853–1856) and soon found itself in heavy debt to the European powers. Russia was victorious in the Russo-Turkish War (1877–1878), and Romania, Serbia, and Montenegro formally proclaimed independence from the Ottoman Empire. A Bulgarian state was reestablished after almost 500 years of Ottoman domination. The Congress of Berlin (1878) allowed Austria-Hungary to occupy Bosnia and Herzegovina, and Great Britain to take Cyprus. From 1878 to 1908, the "Sick Man of Europe's" possessions were under constant pressure.

230. (A) The rise of consumer capitalism in the 1800s transformed the scale of consumption similar to the way that industrial capitalism transformed the scale of production. Department stores, founded after 1850, were the center of the new consumer culture; they possessed excitement, sensory stimulation, a profusion of goods, and large crowds. Department stores changed the experience of shopping; the incredibly tantalizing displays, luxury of decor, and seasonal attractions inspired bewilderment and wonder among shoppers. Many people's first experience of elevators, electric lights, and plate glass was at the department store. Attractive salesgirls were hired to inspire customers to buy. Shoppers no longer bargained over prices; instead, they reacted to sales, a new marketing technique that could incite a buying frenzy. Department stores appealed to women, who came out of their domestic sphere into a new public role as shoppers. They took newly constructed mass transportation to the central business district, where they walked without male supervision.

Chapter 9: Southeastern Asia

231. (C) James Cook (1728–1779) was a noteworthy English explorer whose three major voyages introduced the British into the Pacific Ocean area. Cook joined the British navy in 1755 and worked his way up to command (1768) on an expedition to chart the transit of Venus. He returned to England in 1771 after circumnavigating the globe and exploring the coasts of New Zealand. On this long voyage, Cook did not lose a single man to scurvy because of his frequent replenishment of fresh food. Cook next commanded (1772–1775) an expedition to the southern Pacific; he explored the Antarctic Ocean and the New Hebrides and visited New Caledonia. Cook sailed again in 1776; he visited and named the Sandwich Islands (Hawaii) and unsuccessfully searched the coast of northwestern North America for a Northwest Passage. On the return voyage he was killed by natives in an incident on Hawaii. On his three journeys, Cook visited about 10 major Pacific island groups, made the first European contact with many indigenous peoples, and mapped lands from New Zealand to Hawaii in greater detail and on a scale not previously achieved. (Cook sailed within 75 miles of the Antarctic coast in 1773; the first landing on mainland Antarctica may have been by American sealer John Davis in 1821.)

232. (E) After defeating the Mongols, the Ming dynasty embarked on a period of trade and exploration. The Yongle emperor dispatched his advisor, Zheng He (1371–1433), on seven overseas expeditions between 1405 and 1433. In general, Zheng He's fleet followed long-established and well-mapped trade routes, although these were not always familiar to the Chinese. One of Zheng He's fleets supposedly contained 62 ships and 28,000 soldiers. His fleets visited Arabia, Brunei, the eastern coast of Africa, India, the Malay Archipelago, and Thailand, giving and receiving goods along the way. At one time, historians believed Chinese maritime commerce ended after Zheng He because of the Hai jin (literally "sea ban") order imposed during the Ming and Qing dynasties. However, it is now thought that the Chinese continued to dominate southeastern Asian commerce until the 19th century. Almost all historians disagree with the hypothesis that Zheng He reached America in 1421.

233. (A) In Australian Aboriginal mythology, the Dreaming is the sacred era in which ancestral spirit beings formed the Creation. According to Aboriginal belief, all life—human, animal, bird, and fish—is part of a vast network of relationships that can be traced back to the great spirit ancestors of the Dreaming. In the Dreaming, the ancestors shaped the flat landscape into its present features and each tribe possessed a traditional area of the land that was theirs alone. The concept of the Dreaming remains important in the spiritual lives of Australian Aboriginal people.

234. (B) Goa, located in southwestern India, is currently India's smallest state by area; Panaji is the capital and Vasco da Gama the largest city. The Portuguese first conquered Goa in 1510 under Afonso de Albuquerque. They held the area as an overseas territory of Portugal in India for the next 450 years. Goa has two World Heritage Sites: the Bom Jesus Basilica and the churches and convents of old Goa. In the 1500s, Goa was one of the largest cities in Asia, with about 300 churches and 40,000 people. The appearance of the Dutch in the early 1600s led to its decline. When India became independent in 1947, the Portuguese retained Goa as a colony, but the Indian army took over Goa in just two days in 1961. Kochi is famous for its ancient Jewish community; Coromandel was Dutch India; Tranquebar was Danish India; Puducherry was French India.

235. (A) Ferdinand Magellan (c. 1480–1521) was a Portuguese navigator whose expedition for Spain (1519–1522) became the first to circumnavigate the earth. Magellan sailed from Spain in September 1519 with five vessels and about 265 men. The ships wintered in South America, and on October 21, 1520, Magellan discovered and entered the strait that bears his name. He reached the Pacific in November, and his three-ship fleet then headed northwest across the Pacific. No land was sighted for nearly two months, and the sailors suffered intensely. On March 6, 1521, Magellan reached the Marianas, and 10 days later the Philippines, where he was killed (April 27). Two remaining vessels reached the Moluccas, where they loaded spices. The *Trinidad* was eventually wrecked, but the *Victoria*, commanded by Juan Sebastián del Cano, sailed across the Indian Ocean and rounded the Cape of Good Hope. After more adventures, and with only 18 men, the *Victoria* reached Spain on September 6, 1522, thus completing the first voyage around the world. The voyage proved definitively that the earth was round and revealed the Americas as an entity completely separate from Asia.

236. (D) Multatuli, born Eduard Douwes Dekker (1820–1827), was one of the Netherlands's greatest writers. His most famous work, the novel *Max Havelaar* (1860), exposed the brutality of Dutch colonial rule in Indonesia. Dekker went to Java in 1838 and held several different positions over the next 18 years. He resigned in 1856 and returned to the Netherlands; he published *Max Havelaar* under the pseudonym of Multatuli (derived from the Latin, meaning, "I have suffered much"). *Max Havelaar* satirized the greed, religious hypocrisy, and moral bankruptcy of the Dutch bourgeoisie and their rule in Indonesia. His criticism had a tremendous effect in Holland and eventually led to reforms in Java. The book was a huge success and read all over Europe. (The other answer choices are native Indonesian writers of the early 20th century.)

237. (C) Between 1787 (Charles Dickens was born in 1812) and 1868, the British government transported more than 160,000 convicts on 806 ships to various Australian penal colonies. These colonies were intended to alleviate pressure on overburdened British correctional facilities and help settle Australia. The First Fleet arrived at Botany Bay in January 1788 and relocated to Port Jackson (present-day Sydney), where they established the first permanent European colony (New South Wales) on Australia on January 26. The vast majority of the convicts sent to Australia were English and Welsh (70 percent), Irish (24 percent), or Scottish (5 percent). Most were thieves who had been convicted in the large cities of England; about 20 percent of the early convicts were women who worked in "female [textile] factories." Governor Arthur Philip (ruled 1788–1792) created a labor system in which people, whatever their crime, were employed according to their skills as brick makers, clerks, carpenters, nurses, servants, cattlemen, shepherds, and farmers. By the mid-1830s, only about 6 percent of convicts were locked up. However, they often worked long hours under horrible conditions. The number of convicts was far less than the number of immigrants who arrived in Australia in the 1851–1871 gold rush. In 1852 alone, 370,000 immigrants arrived in Australia. By 1871 the total population had nearly quadrupled to 1.7 million people.

238. (E) The Moluccas (also known as the Maluku Islands) are an archipelago that is part of present-day Indonesia. The islands were known as the Spice Islands by the Chinese and the Europeans. The Moluccas were famous as the original home of nutmeg, mace, and cloves. The Portuguese visited the islands around 1512 and established a trading center at Ternate. In 1641, Portuguese Molucca was captured by the Dutch, who destroyed trees on all other islands to keep the spice supply in check. The fighting to control these small islands became intense in the 1600s and 1700s; the Dutch considered the tiny island of Run (less than two square miles) more valuable than their colony of New Amsterdam (New York). The mystique of the Spice Islands finally vanished when the British captured Banda Neira in 1810 and transferred nutmeg seeds and trees to Ceylon, Grenada, Singapore, and other British colonies.

239. (A) Kamehameha I (1758–1819), also known as Kamehameha the Great, conquered the Hawaiian Islands and established the Kingdom of Hawaii in 1810. Under his rule, a unified legal code was instituted and the islands became prosperous. By developing alliances with the major Pacific colonial powers, Kamehameha helped preserve Hawaii's independence. He used the products he collected in taxes to promote trade with Europe and the United States, but he insisted on the preservation of Hawaii's ancient customs and religious beliefs. Kamehameha did not allow non-Hawaiians to own land, and this wise idea remained in force until 1848. The kingdom of Hawaii remained independent until it was overthrown by the United States in the 1890s.

240. (C) Willem Janszoon (c. 1570–1630) was a Dutch navigator and colonial governor, and probably the first European to have seen the coast of Australia. Dirk Hartog (1580–1621) was a Dutch explorer and the first European to leave behind an artifact of his visit to Australia. Abel Tasman (1603–1659) was a Dutch explorer, best known for his voyages of 1642 and 1644. Tasman was the first to sail around Australia and reach the islands of Van Diemen's Land (present-day Tasmania) and New Zealand and sight the Fiji Islands. William Dampier, an English explorer and privateer, landed on the northwest coast of Australia in 1688 and again in 1699 on a return trip. William Barents (c. 1550–1597) was a Dutch navigator and explorer, but he sailed in the far north.

241. (B) The Toungoo dynasty ruled Burma (Myanmar) from the mid-1500s until 1752. King Minkyinyo founded the dynasty at Toungoo, south of Ava (present-day Inya). At its peak under King Bayinnaung, the Toungoo empire included Siam, Manipur, the Chinese Shan States (including Rakhine and Taninthayi), and Lan Xang. It was the largest empire in the history of southeastern Asia. However, it collapsed only 18 years after Bayinnaung's death in 1599 under attacks by Rakhine forces aided by Portuguese mercenaries. King Anaukpetlun (reigned 1605–1628) defeated the Portuguese in 1611 and reestablished a smaller kingdom based in Ava. In the early 1600s, the kingdom's population was about two million, and it enjoyed a brief period of prosperity before declining in the early 1700s. The Toungoo dynasty collapsed in 1752.

242. (B) Spain gained control of the Philippines in 1571; it was the only important part of the Spanish Empire outside of the Americas. The route between Acapulco (on the Pacific coast of Mexico) and Manila (capital of the Philippines) had a monopoly on Spanish trade with Asia. Silks and porcelain from China, spices from the Moluccas, and lacquerware from Japan were purchased with silver from New Spain. The Asian items were then exported to New Spain on galleons, transported by land across Mexico to Veracruz, and loaded on the Spanish treasure fleet for Spain. This route was the alternative to the voyage west across the Indian Ocean and around the Cape of Good Hope. By going through Mexico, the Spanish avoided stopping at ports controlled by competing powers. The Manila-Acapulco galleon trade began in 1565 with the discovery of the ocean passage by Andrés de Urdaneta and continued until 1815, when the Mexican War of Independence disrupted the route. It took at least four months to sail across the Pacific Ocean from Manila to Acapulco. The flood of silver into China via the Philippines made Ming China one of the greatest importing and exporting nations of the 17th century. However, the Ming government could not control the resulting inflation, and economic difficulties led to the takeover by the Qing dynasty in 1644.

243. (A) Sikhism is a monotheistic religion founded by the mystic Nanak (c. 1469–c. 1539) and the following nine Sikh Gurus (from 1469–1708) in the Punjab region of India. The last teaching is the holy scripture of Sikhism known as the Adi Granth. As of 2012, Sikhism was the fifth-largest organized religion in the world; Amritsar (in India) is the holy city. World-wide, there are about 25 million Sikhs, of which about three-quarters live in the Punjab (they constitute about 60 percent of the state's population). In 1699, Gobind Singh (1666–1708), the tenth and final guru, instituted certain basic practices of Sikhism such as wearing a turban, carrying a dagger, and never cutting the hair or beard. After an initiatory rite, the initiate takes the surname Singh (lion). Gobind Singh also created the military fraternity called the Khalsa. By the late 1700s, Sikhs had conquered most of the Punjab and established various feudal states. Their greatest leader was Ranjit Singh (1780–1839), who established a Sikh kingdom in the Punjab. The Sikhs make up about 2 percent of India's population.

244. (D) A gamelan is a musical ensemble from Indonesia, usually from the islands of Bali and Java. It is basically a percussion orchestra featuring a variety of instruments such as xylophones, drums, gongs, bamboo flutes, and bowed and plucked strings. In some cases, there are vocalists. A gamelan refers to a set of instruments that are built and tuned to stay together. In Indonesia, gamelan often accompanies dance, *wayang* puppet performances, or rituals and ceremonies.

245. (A) The Battle of Plassey in 1757 was a decisive British East India Company (BEIC) victory over the Nawab (local prince) of Bengal and his French allies. Many historians date British rule in India from this crucial battle. The battle was preceded by the attack and plunder of Calcutta by Siraj-ud-Daulah (the last independent Nawab of Bengal) and the "Black Hole of Calcutta" tragedy. The British sent reinforcements under Robert Clive from Madras to Bengal and recaptured Calcutta. Clive then seized the French fort of Chandernagore. Siraj-ud-Daulah had a numerically superior force and made his stand at Plassey. The British, knowing they were outnumbered, conspired with some of Siraj-ud-Daulah's leaders before the battles, who then assembled their 45,000 troops near the battlefield but made no move to join the battle. As a result, Siraj-ud-Daulah's army was defeated by roughly 3,000 British soldiers. At a cost of 23 killed, Robert Clive now controlled Calcutta and Bengal and acquired numerous concessions for taxes and trade. The British used this revenue to increase their military might and push the other European colonial powers out of southern Asia.

246. (C) Polynesia is a region of Oceania made up of more than 1,000 islands scattered over the central and southern Pacific Ocean. Some of the main islands include Samoa, Tonga, the Cook Islands, Tuvalu, and French Polynesia. The indigenous people who inhabit the islands of Polynesia have many similarities in language, culture, and beliefs. The Polynesians achieved an advanced society without the use of metals, which were extremely limited on their islands. They generally developed stratified societies with definite class distinctions between commoners and the elite. The polytheistic Polynesians revered gods of agriculture and war; in many early Polynesian societies, a terraced pyramid seems to have been a place of worship. The population of Polynesia grew significantly after 1000 CE. Trade networks grew where islands were closely grouped together, giving Polynesian peoples opportunity for cultural and economic interactions.

247. (B) Ayutthaya was a kingdom in present-day Thailand that existed from 1350 to 1767. King Ramathibodi I (Uthong) founded Ayutthaya as the capital of his kingdom in 1350; the city, positioned on a bow in the Chao Phraya River (about 55 miles north of present-day Bangkok), was well positioned for defense and trade. By 1550, the kingdom's vassals included city-states in the Malay Peninsula, Sukhothai, and parts of Cambodia. Eventually, the kingdom expanded its borders to roughly those of modern Thailand, except for in the north. Ayutthaya was generally friendly toward foreign traders, including the Chinese, Vietnamese, Indians, Japanese, and Persians, and later, the Europeans. The court of King Narai (1656–1688) had links with King Louis XIV of France, whose ambassadors compared the city in size and wealth to Paris. After Narai's death, however, his successor initiated a 150-year period of relative isolation. Ayutthaya's main religion was Theravada Buddhism, but Mahayana Buddhism and Catholicism (from French missionaries who arrived through China in the 1600s) were also practiced. In 1767, Burma totally destroyed Ayutthaya.

248. (C) Moai are large human figures (more than 800) carved from rock between 1250 CE and 1500 on the Polynesian island of Easter Island. About half are still at Rano Raraku, the main moai quarry. However, hundreds were transported from there and set on stone platforms (*ahu*) around the island's perimeter. Almost all moai have overly large heads making up about three-fifths the size of their bodies. Historians conjecture that the moai are the faces of deified ancestors; they may also have been the embodiment of powerful living or former chiefs. The tallest moai, called Paro, was 33 feet high and weighed 82 tons; the heaviest erected was a shorter but squatter moai at Ahu Tongariki weighing 86 tons. It is not known exactly how the moai were moved across the island.

249. (E) The Joseon (Chosun) dynasty ruled Korea from about 1392 to 1910, the last royal/imperial dynasty in Korean history. The dynasty was founded after the overthrow of the Goryeo kingdom. Much of modern Korean etiquette, culture, societal attitudes, and even language stems from this period. The Joseon dynasty was responsible for the movement of the capital to Seoul (1394). In the 1400s, printing with movable metal type (invented two centuries earlier) became widely used and the Korean alphabet was developed. The 1592 invasion by the Japanese shogun Toyotomi Hideyoshi was repelled only after six years of great devastation. Manchu invasions in the early 1600s made Korea (1637) a tributary state of the Qing dynasty. The Joseon rulers reacted by severely limiting foreign contacts with Europeans, for which the country became known as the Hermit Kingdom. After 1650, Korea experienced a period of peace and economic prosperity, but it was eventually forcibly annexed by Japan in 1910.

250. (D) The historic city of Malacca (2010 population: 483,000) is located on both sides of the Malacca River near its mouth into the Strait of Malacca in the Malay Peninsula (Malaysia). Until the 17th century, Malacca was a leading commercial center of southeastern Asia. It was founded about 1400 and quickly gained wealth as a center of trade with China, Indonesia, India, and western Asia. Its Muslim sultans extended their power over the nearby coast of Sumatra and the Malay Peninsula as far north as Kedah and Pattani; Malaysia is currently the world's largest Muslim nation by population. In 1511, Malacca was captured by the Portuguese under Afonso de Albuquerque; the Dutch then captured Malacca in 1641 after a long siege. The Dutch swung the center of commerce to Sumatra, and Malacca's trade also declined because of the silting of its port.

Chapter 10: Imperialism

251. (E) Imperialism refers to the control of a territory or country by a more powerful nation in order to dominate the area politically, socially, and/or economically. Europeans, Americans, and the Japanese basically used four different patterns to dominate other areas. Colonies were areas in which the controlling power had a direct influence over the government and literally owned the territory. Protectorates were regions that were allowed to keep their own governments but were controlled by an outside power. Spheres of influence, common in China, were areas that granted special investment or trading privileges to another country. Economic imperialism refers to control of a region by private businesses rather than by an outside government. A garrison state is a 20th-century concept referring to a state organized to serve primarily its own need for military security and military power.

252. (E) After the Industrial Revolution, rubber was in great demand in Europe, Japan, and the United States. At the Berlin Conference (1885), Leopold II of Belgium (1835–1909) was given personal control over the rubber and ivory trade of the Congo region of Africa. In 1891, Leopold issued a decree requiring the local chiefs to supply men to collect rubber, essentially without payment. Male rubber tappers and porters were mercilessly exploited and driven to death. Leopold's agents held the wives and children of these men hostage until they returned with their rubber quota. Those who refused or failed to supply enough rubber had their villages burned down, their children murdered, or most notoriously, their hands cut off. By 1908, worldwide outrage forced the Belgian government to take control of the Congo and some of the worst practices ended. Historians estimate that approximately 10 million people died during Leopold II's 23-year reign of terror.

253. (D) In the 1850s, the British East India Company (BEIC) made several unpopular moves in India. The political expansion of the BEIC at the expense of native princes and of the Mughal court aroused both Hindu and Muslim Indians. The harsh land policies carried out by Governor-General Dalhousie and then Lord Canning threatened many Indians' traditional landholdings. The BEIC's attempts to introduce free market competition in India undermined the traditional power structure in the villages, placing the peasants at the mercy of merchants and moneylenders. In 1853, the aged Bahadur Shah II (last of the Mughal emperors) was told that the dynasty would end with his death. Indian soldiers, already dissatisfied with their pay, feared that the British wanted to force them to adopt Christianity. They became even more outraged when, in 1857, the British furnished the soldiers with cartridges (for guns) coated with grease made from the fat of cows (sacred to Hindus) and of pigs (forbidden to Muslims). In 1857, angry sepoys rose against their British officers and the rebellion swept across northern and central India.

254. (B) The best-known explorer and missionary in Africa was the Scottish clergyman David Livingstone (1813–1873). For 30 years, Livingstone crisscrossed Africa, generally traveling light and getting along with native peoples. Livingstone was the first European to see the waterfall that he renamed Victoria Falls, and one of the first Europeans to make an east-west transcontinental journey across Africa. He vehemently opposed the slave trade, which remained a profitable business for some African rulers. In 1866, Livingstone set out to search for the source of the Nile. After he did not communicate with anyone for a number of years, American newspaperman Henry Stanley went to Africa to find him as part of a *New York Herald* newspaper stunt in 1869. Stanley found Livingstone on the shores of Lake Tanganyika in October 1871 and greeted him with the famous words "Dr. Livingstone, I presume?" Livingstone's explorations, missionary travels, and "disappearance" made him one of the greatest British heroes of the 1800s.

255. (C) In general, African and Asian bravery was no match for Maxim guns, repeating rifles, and rapid-fire artillery. However, there were a few exceptions. At the Battle of Adowa in 1896, Menelik II's forces annihilated the Italian army, which suffered 7,000 killed. As a result, Italy recognized the independence of Ethiopia. The Battle of Isandlwana took place in present-day South Africa in 1879 when a contingent of 1,800 British and Native troops met approximately 20,000 Zulu warriors in the first engagement of the Anglo-Zulu War. The Zulus had traditional iron spears, cowhide shields, and a few old muskets and rifles; the British were armed with state-of-the-art breech-loading rifles and two artillery pieces. Despite the disparity, the Zulus led by Cetshwayo overwhelmed the poorly led and badly deployed British, killing more than 1,300 troops. The Zulu army suffered about 1,000 killed in the battle. Unlike the Italians in Ethiopia, the British mounted renewed expeditions and eventually defeated the Zulus.

256. (A) New Guinea, located in the southwestern Pacific Ocean, is the world's second largest island (after Greenland). The first European contact with New Guinea was by Portuguese and Spanish sailors in the 1500s. In 1828, the Netherlands claimed the western half of the island. In the 1870s and 1880s, the French sent four failed expeditions to establish a colony on present-day New Ireland. In 1883, the British colony of Queensland annexed southeastern New Guinea. However, the British government revoked Queensland's claims and formally assumed direct responsibility in 1884. That same year, Germany claimed northeastern New Guinea as the protectorate of German New Guinea. Essentially, the Netherlands controlled the western half of New Guinea, Germany the northeastern part, and Great Britain the southeastern part. The political history of the island continued to be complex after 1900.

257. (D) In 1884–1885, the imperialist nations met in Berlin to prevent the competition for colonies in Africa from starting a European war. At the Berlin Conference, hosted by Otto von Bismarck, the European countries divided Africa between them. The European powers recognized Belgian King Leopold II's private claims to the Congo Free State but called for free trade on the Congo and Niger Rivers. Among the numerous territorial agreements, Portugal was awarded Mozambique in the east and Angola in the west. The signatories also agreed that no European power could claim any part of Africa unless it had set up government offices there. This *Principle of Effectivity* intensified the so-called Scramble for Africa because even within areas designated as their sphere of influence, the European powers still had to take possession under the Principle of Effectivity. No representatives of any African peoples attended the conference.

258. (E) In the late 1800s, several ideas helped Americans adjust to the idea of the United States as an imperial power. Racial theories advocated by historians, professors, clergy, and missionaries informed people that the United States conquered other people not for the sake of conquest but because it was the "white man's burden" to uplift the less civilized. This idea was used to subjugate Native Americans from 1860 to 1890, and it was now applied to Hawaiians, Samoans, Cubans, Panamanians, and Filipinos. Josiah Strong, a Congregational minister, was a fervent expansionist who championed overseas missionary work. Strong's bestseller, *Our Country: Its Possible Future and Its Present Crisis*, was published in 1885 and sold 175,000 copies. This quotation is from a long chapter entitled "The Future of the Anglo-Saxon Race." Strong's work helped justify the American annexation of Samoa, the American coup that overthrew the government of Hawaii, and the acquisition of an empire after the Spanish-American War. Of course from the African and Asian perspective, the Anglo-Saxon genius for colonizing was more accurately described as brutal rule by overwhelming force and bloody terror. The other answer choices are all anti-imperialists who argued against the annexation of the Philippines.

259. (B) In the late 19th century, the Qing dynasty became the victim of European, Russian, and Japanese imperialism. Because no single European country controlled China in the way that Great Britain controlled India, China was divided into "spheres of influence." Germany dominated Shandong province, Jiaozhou (Kiaochow) Bay, and the Hwang-Ho valley. Russia's sphere of influence was the Liaodong Peninsula, including access to Darien and Port Arthur. Russia also negotiated the right to build a railroad across Manchuria, thereby dominating a large portion of northwestern China. The United Kingdom controlled Weihaiwei and the Yangtze valley, while France controlled Guangzhou Bay and several other southern provinces. The United States, lacking a sphere of influence in China, grew alarmed at being excluded from Chinese markets. In 1900, several powers agreed to the United States' Open Door policy, which advocated freedom of commercial access and non-annexation of Chinese territory.

260. (C) The discovery of diamonds at Kimberly in 1871 led to a massive influx of foreign prospectors across the borders of the Orange Free State. Then, gold was discovered in the South African Republic in 1886. This made the Transvaal the richest nation in southern Africa; however, the country lacked the manpower and the industrial base to develop the resources. Therefore, the Transvaal government reluctantly allowed the immigration of mostly British Uitlanders (foreigners). Soon, the number of Uitlanders in the Transvaal exceeded the number of Boers. The Jameson Raid of 1895–1896, instigated by Cecil Rhodes and led by Leander Starr Jameson, was intended to encourage an Uitlander revolt in Johannesburg and undermine the Boers in Paul Kruger's Transvaal Republic. However, the Uitlanders did not support the raid, and Transvaal forces captured Jameson's men before they reached Johannesburg. Although the Jameson Raid was ineffective, it was the inciting factor in the Boer War.

261. (E) While several of the answer choices are valid, the main impulse behind American expansion was the need to find markets for surplus production. Between 1865 and 1898, American wheat production rose by 256 percent, corn by 222 percent, coal by 800 percent, and steel rails by 523 percent. In newer industries, crude oil production increased from 3 million barrels in 1865 to 55 million barrels in 1898; in the same period, steel ingot production rose from 20,000 long tons to almost 9 million tons. Total American exports grew from $71 million in 1830 to $281 million in 1865 to $1.2 billion in 1898. The United States moved from fourth in the world in manufacturing in 1870 to first in 1900. However, after the Panic of 1893, many American businessmen and politicians concluded that American production far exceeded what the country could consume. They saw huge profits beckoning in heavily populated areas of Latin America and Asia. They wanted their share of these markets to stay competitive with European countries. By 1900, the United States exported 15 percent of its iron and steel products, 25 percent of its sewing machines, and 70 percent of its cotton. In 1900, only 4 percent of American exports went to China or Japan, but businessmen dreamed of a day when every Asian resident bought an American shirt or sewing machine.

262. (D) In the 1700s and 1800s, scientists argued that different human groups such as blacks, whites, Jews, and Slavs were biologically different and that some groups were better than other groups. Herbert Spencer in Britain and William Graham Sumner in the United States erroneously extended Charles Darwin's emphasis on competition and natural selection to the idea of "survival of the fittest" (the phrase is Spencer's, not Darwin's) of nations and individuals. Americans (like the British, the Germans, and the Japanese) declared themselves the fittest, and in a nation-eat-nation world, this gave them a bogus scientific rationale to dominate other peoples and places. "The White Man's Burden," Rudyard Kipling's famous 17-stanza poem that seemed to justify imperialism, first appeared in the United States in an 1899 issue of *McClure's Magazine*. Ernst Haeckel's *biogenetic law* (now discredited), expressed in the phrase "ontogeny recapitulates phylogeny," was also popular at the time. The theory suggested that the development of the individual repeated the development of race. Thus, primitive people were actually in a state of arrested development and, like children, needed supervision and protection. ("Root hog, or die" was a rural American saying; the expression means, "provide for yourself or do without and die.")

263. (D) Cecil Rhodes (1853–1902) was an English-born businessman and politician in South Africa. He was the founder of the diamond company De Beers, which in 2010 marketed more than a third of the world's rough diamonds and at one time marketed 90 percent. Rhodes was one of the richest men in the world and a fervent believer in British colonial imperialism. He helped Britain extend its African empire by one million square miles and was the founder of the state of Rhodesia (present-day Zimbabwe), which was named after him. One of Rhodes's pet ideas was a continuous "red line" of British dominions from north to south, with a Cape-to-Cairo railroad to unify the possessions. However, as of 2012, a Cape-to-Cairo railroad remains uncompleted.

264. (D) In the Teller Amendment (1898), the United States had promised not to annex Cuba, a land long desired by expansionists. Therefore, it seemed obvious that a similar policy would be applied to the Philippines, a remote land few Americans had even heard of before 1898. However, American imperialists (such as Indiana Senator Albert Beveridge) used a series of well-crafted arguments appealing to American destiny, Anglo-Saxon superiority, and patriotism to argue for Philippine annexation. Annexationists praised the Philippines as a crucial link to the lucrative China trade. Imperialists also held the crucial card; the United States already possessed the Philippines. No one could imagine returning it to Spain, handing it to another power, or making it independent. Yet critics of Philippine annexation insisted that by imposing its power on others, the United States violated its beliefs in self-determination and liberty. They believed expansion would lead to greater executive power, an expensive standing army, entangling foreign alliances, and increased taxes. Southerners worried about any policy that might add nonwhites and introduce "inferior blood" into the national community. Ultimately, Philippine annexation was approved by two votes (57–27; two-thirds was needed) and an amendment that promised independence as soon as Filipinos formed a stable government was defeated by one vote.

265. (E) Colonialism was devastating for most Africans, who lost control over their traditional lands to European overlords. The transition from individual farm plots and subsistence agriculture to cash-crop plantations forced Africans to work in European-owned businesses. This reduced food crops for individual families and led to food shortages. The new political units formed by the European imperialist powers interfered with traditional African village life and imposed political divisions that disregarded African linguistic, ethnic, and cultural groups. The artificial boundaries drawn by Europeans remain an ongoing problem. On the other hand, hospitals were constructed and sanitation was improved, while schools boosted literacy rates. Infrastructure was created or improved, but railroads, public works, telephones, and telegraphs were all initially designed primarily for the use of the imperialist powers.

266. (C) In the early 1870s, most Mexicans opposed foreign investment in their railroads or lands, remembering American greed in the Mexican War. Many Americans would not invest there anyway; after the French had been expelled from Mexico in 1866, the nation had been plagued by political instability that made investment risky. In 1876, Porfirio Diaz (1830–1915) took power in Mexico in a coup and began a 35-year rule that lasted until 1911. Diaz ruthlessly restored order in Mexico by crushing political opponents and bandits alike. He encouraged foreign investment through tax exemptions and land grants. Diaz sold three-quarters of Mexico's mineral wealth to foreign interests; in 1910, Americans owned 186 of 208 mining companies in Sonora. Mexico became a land of peace even though half of the rural population was bound to debt slavery. The United States supported Diaz because order in Mexico had made it safe for American investors and corporations. By 1913, American investments in Mexico totaled about $1 billion.

267. (A) Singapore was a trading center in the Srivijaya empire before it declined in the 1300s. Thomas Stafford Raffles engineered the cession of the sparsely populated island to the British East India Company in 1819, and he founded the modern city of Singapore that same year. In 1824, Singapore was only a small fishing and trading village, but the British presence attracted Chinese and Malay merchants. The port grew rapidly, soon overshadowing Penang and Malacca in importance. The development of Malaya under British rule in the early 1900s made Singapore one of the leading ports in the world for the export of tin and rubber. A large British naval base was built in the 1920s and 1930s, but in a brilliant campaign through Malaya, the Japanese conquered Singapore in 1942. The city is now an independent nation.

268. (B) José Martí, the hero of the Cuban independence movement, supposedly asked, "Once the United States is in Cuba, who will get her out?" After the Spanish-American War, the United States had no intention of allowing Cuba to lead an independent existence. In November 1900, a Cuban constitutional convention met in Havana and drafted the framework for a new government. The United States used the threat of indefinite army occupation to pressure the Cubans into accepting the Platt Amendment (named after Orville Platt, expansionist senator from Connecticut). In its original form, the Platt Amendment was a rider attached to the Army Appropriations Bill in March 1901. The Platt Amendment made Cuba an American protectorate. Cuba agreed to make no treaties with foreign powers but allowed the United States to intervene in internal Cuban affairs. Cuba also agreed to sell or lease lands for American naval bases; in 1903, the United States leased a site in Cuba on Guantánamo Bay for a naval base that it still possesses in 2012. Under American pressure, the Platt Amendment was included in the constitution of Cuba in June 1901 and also in the treaty between the United States and Cuba in 1903. The American army left Cuba in 1902 but returned to occupy the country from 1906 to 1909 and again in 1917 to 1922. Most provisions of the Platt Amendment were repealed in 1934 as a part of President Franklin Roosevelt's Good Neighbor Policy.

269. (A) The opening (1869) of the Suez Canal increased the strategic importance of Ethiopia, and several European powers sought influence in the area. Ethiopian Emperor Menelik II (1844–1913) was a wily negotiator who attempted to modernize Ethiopia and consolidate his own rule in a unified nation. When the Italians invaded Ethiopia in 1895, Menelik's forces crushed them at Adowa (1896). In the Treaty of Addis Ababa (1896), Italy recognized the independence of Ethiopia, and it was never colonized by a European nation. However, Italy invaded Ethiopia again with more success in 1935.

270. (E) In the 1700s and early 1800s, British traders wanted Chinese silks, porcelain, and tea. This led to a huge trade imbalance because Chinese merchants would accept only silver bullion from the Europeans. As a result, the British needed to find a valuable commodity that Chinese merchants would accept in bulk, and they discovered it in opium. In 1839, the Qing dynasty attempted to enforce its prohibitions on the importation of opium; Lin Zexu confiscated a large quantity of opium at Guangzhou (Canton) and destroyed it. The British responded by sending gunboats to attack several Chinese coastal cities. China was defeated in the First Opium War and forced to sign the Treaty of Nanking (1842), which ceded Hong Kong to Britain and opened certain ports, including Shanghai and Guangzhou, to British trade and residence. Within a few years other European powers signed similar treaties with China.

271. (D) The so-called New Imperialism in the 1800s and early 1900s depended on a constant need to expand trade. Overseas territories guaranteed favorable markets for the home country's products because competitors could be excluded. The "Second" Industrial Revolution required a number of exotic resources such as rubber, copper, oil, manganese, and other resources that were not found in the industrial states themselves. If the Japanese wanted oil and rubber to industrialize, they had to either trade for them or take them. Many nations tied their prestige to building an empire, and those originally without colonies (such as Germany and the United States) struggled to catch up. Advances in medicine, such as the use of quinine against malaria, enabled outsiders to penetrate Africa and other places with tropical forests without being wiped out by deadly diseases and parasites. The astonishing power of new weapons such as the Maxim machine gun, the repeating rifle, and rapid-fire artillery allowed small numbers of men armed with these weapons to defeat large numbers of men without them. The slave trade is associated with the "Old" Imperialism.

272. (C) Extraterritoriality is the state of being exempt from the jurisdiction of local law. It was one of several provisions of China's unequal treaties with Japan, the United States, and European powers that caused long-standing bitterness and humiliation among the Chinese. In China, extraterritoriality meant that if a European, American, or Japanese person had a dispute with a Chinese person, the former would have the right to be tried in a court under the laws of his or her own country. Extraterritoriality was imposed upon China in the Treaty of Nanking (1842) resulting from the First Opium War. By 1900, the extraterritoriality system had been extended to about 90 treaty ports and covered 300,000 foreign residents. Extraterritoriality in China ended only after World War II.

273. (C) When China invaded Korea in 1894, Japan responded by sending troops to Korea to fight the Chinese. In the Sino-Japanese War, Japan drove the Chinese from Korea and began the takeover of coal- and iron-rich Manchuria. The peace treaty (1895) gave Taiwan to Japan. Japan's influence in Manchuria was confirmed in its stunning victory in the Russo-Japanese War (1905). In the Treaty of Portsmouth, Japan received Russia's lease on the Liaodong Peninsula, including Port Arthur, and control of the southern portion of the Chinese Eastern Railway. Japan completely annexed Korea in 1910. Patriotic Koreans intensely disliked the Japanese presence, and the March First Movement was series of demonstrations for Korean national independence that began on March 1, 1919, in Seoul and spread through the country. About two million Koreans participated in 1,500 demonstrations. It took a year for Japan to suppress the movement; by that time, about 7,000 people had been killed by the Japanese police and soldiers.

274. (D) *Unequal treaties* refers to a series of more than 20 treaties imposed on Qing dynasty China by the United States, Japan, and the European powers during the 1800s and early 1900s. (The term less frequently refers to treaties imposed on Tokugawa Japan and Joseon dynasty Korea.) These treaties were not negotiated by nations treating each other as equals but were imposed on China after a war or the threat of war. Unequal treaties forced the Qing to pay large amounts of reparations, open up ports for trade, permit foreign "spheres of influence," and allow extraterritoriality. In some cases, China was forced to cede or lease territories such as Hong Kong to Great Britain and Macau to Portugal. China and Great Britain signed the first unequal treaty after the First Opium War (the Treaty of Nanking in 1842). Other notorious unequal treaties include the Tianjin Treaty in 1858, the Beijing Treaty in 1860 (after the Second Opium War), and the Treaty of Tientsin in 1885 (after the Sino-French War).

275. (E) In 1881, a conservative Sudanese Muslim sect known as the Wahhabis rallied around Muhammad Ahmad (1844–1885), who in 1881 declared himself the Mahdi—the prophesied redeemer of Islam. The Mahdi resolved to resist the Anglo-Egyptian push to control the Sudan; in 1883, his warriors overwhelmed a 4,000-man Egyptian force near al-Ubayyid and seized their rifles and ammunition. The charismatic Mahdi then defeated an 8,000-man Egyptian relief force in the Battle of El Obeid. The Anglo-Egyptian government sent soldiers under Charles Gordon, who had achieved fame as leader of the Qing dynasty's "Ever Victorious Army" during the Taipeng Rebellion. However, the Mahdi's army wiped out Gordon's force at Khartoum in 1885. The Mahdi then formed an Islamic government that imposed modified Shari'ah (Islamic law). Six months after the capture of Khartoum, Muhammad Ahmad died of typhus. In 1898, a large force under General Kitchener (of World War I fame) and armed with modern weapons defeated the Mahdi's successor (Khalifa) at the bloody battle of Omdurman; about 10,000 Sudanese were killed while Kitchener's force lost only 47 men.

276. (B) Ram Mohan Roy (1772–1833) was an Indian reformer who is usually considered the founder of Indian nationalism. Roy knew Sanskrit, Persian, and Arabic classics as well as English, Greek, and Latin works. Roy believed that India could learn from European technology, education, and culture without losing its identity. He was a founder of Hindu College in Calcutta, which provided an English-style education for Indians. Roy challenged traditional Hindu culture such as rigid caste distinctions, child marriage, suttee, and purdah—the isolation of women in separate quarters. (The other choices are all Indian nationalist leaders of the 1900s.)

277. (B) During the American Civil War, Emperor Napoleon III of France used a large French army to install Maximilian I of Austria and his young wife Carlotta, daughter of King Leopold I of Belgium, on the throne of Mexico. Most Mexicans opposed this government and, led by Benito Juárez (1806–1872), they fought a guerrilla war against it. Maximilian's regime never acquired much local support but rested solely on French bayonets. With the American army on the border, Mexican resistance mounting, French public opinion against the venture, and a war with Prussia looming, Louis Napoleon removed the soldiers in 1867. Maximilian rejected abdication and decided to stay on. He assumed command of his forces at Querétaro, but after a siege from March to May 1867, he was captured and fell before a firing squad.

278. (A) In German South West Africa (now Namibia), the Germans stole the land and cattle of the native Herero and Nama and forced them to pay high taxes. In 1904, the Herero, frustrated with the treaty of protection they had signed with the Germans, began a great revolt. Led by Samuel Maharero, they destroyed some farms and killed about a hundred people. In response, German General Lothar von Trotha devised a plan to annihilate the Herero nation. The Germans surrounded the Herero at the Battle of Waterberg, leaving only one route for them to escape into the Omaheke desert. The Germans then sealed off the last water holes and erected fencing to prevent any Herero who fled the violence from returning. An estimated 20,000 to 100,000 Herero and Nama died of starvation and thirst. In 1985, the United Nations classified the incident as genocide. In 2004, at the 100th anniversary of the massacre, a German minister commemorated the dead on site and apologized for the crimes on behalf of all Germans.

279. (C) Senegambia as a political unit was created by competing French and English colonial interests. The competition began in the 1500s when both nations established trading centers in the region, the French on the Senegal River and the English on the Gambia River. In 1758, the British captured major French trading bases along the Senegal River area and formed the crown colony of Senegambia. The unified region collapsed in 1779 when the French recaptured Saint Louis and burned the major British settlement in the Gambia region. The Treaty of Versailles (1783) created the current balance between France and England in the region. Saint Louis, Gorée, and the Senegal River region were restored to France, and the Gambia was left to the British. As a result, Gambia (which gained independence in 1965) is wedged into the middle of Senegal (independent in 1960).

280. (D) In 1902, the Venezuelan government under Cipriano Castro refused to pay its debts. As a result, Great Britain, Italy, and Germany blockaded the country and the Germans bombarded Fort San Carlos in 1903. Under American pressure, the Europeans agreed to arbitrate the dispute, accepting for the first time that the United States intended to dominate South America. In his presidential message in 1904, Theodore Roosevelt declared that the United States had the right to exercise an "international police power" over Latin America and intervene in its domestic affairs. This position is known as the Roosevelt Corollary to the Monroe Doctrine. Throughout the 1900s, the United States constantly intervened in the Caribbean to supposedly "maintain order." Whereas Monroe's "doctrine" had warned European nations not to intervene in the Western Hemisphere, Roosevelt's corollary justified American intervention in Latin America.

281. (E) From 1826 to 1893, the United States recognized the independence of the kingdom of Hawaii, a group of eight major islands about halfway between California and Asia. Between 1876 and 1885, annual sugar production in Hawaii rose from 26 million pounds to 174 million pounds. In 1887, the United States supported the new "Bayonet Constitution," imposed by intimidation, which gave political power to wealthy white residents. By 1888, Americans owned 75 percent of Hawaii's wealth but made up less than 10 percent of the population. The McKinley Tariff of 1890 caused a crisis in Hawaii by eliminating the protection for Hawaiian sugar; wealthy Hawaiian plantation owners viewed annexation to the United States as the best solution. In 1891, the new Queen Liliuokalani adopted the cry of "Hawaii for the Hawaiians" and attempted (January 14, 1893) to institute a new constitution by royal decree. Plantation owners appealed to US Ambassador John Stevens to help overthrow the Hawaiian government. On January 16, Stevens ordered 150 US Marines to land in Honolulu, where they surrounded the royal palace in order to intimidate the queen. The next day, Stevens recognized a new government headed by pineapple magnate Sanford Dole. Two weeks later, Stevens unilaterally proclaimed Hawaii an American protectorate. In 1993, the US Congress apologized to Native Hawaiians "for the overthrow of the Kingdom of Hawaii."

282. (B) In the 1800s, Christian missionaries from European countries moved into Vietnam and won some converts. Threatened by growing Western influence, Vietnamese officials tried to suppress Christianity by killing missionaries. Using this as an excuse, France invaded the area in 1858 and took control of southern Vietnam. France then took northern Vietnam following its victory over China in the Sino-French War (1884–1885). French Indochina was formed in 1887 from present-day Vietnam and Cambodia; Laos was added after the Franco-Siamese War (1893). The confederation lasted until 1954.

283. (B) The Samoan archipelago, with its fine harbor of Pago Pago on the island of Tutuila, commands important ocean lanes in the Pacific about 3,000 miles south of Hawaii. As interest in Asian trade and coaling stations grew, Samoa became more valuable. In 1878, the United States signed an unequal treaty with Samoa gaining the use of Pago Pago. In 1879, Germany and Great Britain also secured treaty rights in Samoa from native princes. The Samoan crisis began in 1888 when the Germans deposed the Samoan king and a civil war broke out between pro- and anti-German factions. In 1889, one British, three German, and three American warships gathered in crowded Apia Harbor in western Samoa. However, in March 1889 a hurricane struck Samoa and all six American and German warships were wrecked. The Tripartite Convention of 1889 established a three-power protectorate over Samoa, with the restored native dynasty ruling in name only. After the Spanish-American War, the British were bought out and Germany and the United States divided the islands between them. Germany received the two largest islands, but the United States got Tutuila and the harbor at Pago Pago, which it still possesses in 2012.

284. (D) In the Hay-Pauncefote Treaty (1901), the British conceded to the United States the right to build a transoceanic canal alone. President Theodore Roosevelt chose a Panamanian route for the canal site, but Panama was a province of Colombia at the time. In 1903, when Colombia refused American terms for a canal (a 99-year lease on a six-mile-wide canal zone in exchange for $10 million plus annual rent of $250,000), President Roosevelt denounced them as "inefficient bandits" and "contemptible little creatures." In November 1903, the Panamanians staged a revolution against Colombia with American warships preventing any Colombian troops from smashing the revolt. The United States instantly recognized the new republic on November 6, and the Hay–Bunau-Varilla Treaty (November 17) granted the United States exclusive and perpetual control of the canal zone, now 10 miles wide, for the same terms offered Colombia. The new Panamanian government protested the Hay–Bunau-Varilla Treaty. It was known as "the treaty that no Panamanian signed" because Philippe Bunau-Varilla, who claimed to represent Panama, was not a Panamanian citizen, had not been in Panama for 17 years, and never returned there. In 1979, the United States returned the Panama Canal Zone to Panama.

285. (A) The Boxer Rebellion (1899–1900) arose from Chinese resentment at the Manchu inability to protect China from foreign intrusion. This feeling was intensified by China's humiliating defeat by Japan in the Sino-Japanese War (1895). The Boxers belonged to a secret society called *I Ho Ch'uan* (Chinese for "righteous harmonious fists," hence the English name "Boxers"). They combined anti-Western ideology with a complicated series of exercises that followers believed made them invulnerable to bullets. There is dispute as to whether the Boxers were primarily heroic anti-imperialists or futile opponents of inevitable change. However, they eventually numbered more than 100,000 and encouraged violent attacks on foreigners and Chinese Christians, especially in the northern Chinese provinces of Zhili, Shanxi, and Shandong. Empress Dowager Cixi initially supported the movement in secret, but then declared war on all foreign powers. Southern China remained peaceful, but as many as 30,000 foreigners and Chinese Christians were killed in the north. In the most dramatic episode, the foreign legations in Beijing were besieged for 45 days before a 20,000-man multinational relief force drove the Boxers and the Chinese government from the capital. Coalition forces then killed thousands of villagers in reprisals. Foreign troops were stationed in Beijing, and the Europeans imposed indemnities so severe that the Qing could not pay them. As a result, the Chinese Revolution of 1911 established the Republic of China.

286. (B) The United States was shocked when Filipinos did not seem to desire benefits of so-called "American civilization" if it meant colonial rule. In 1896, before the Spanish-American War, native Filipinos had begun a revolt to win their independence from Spain. The leader of that movement, Emilio Aguinaldo, now led the resistance to American rule and proclaimed an independent Philippine Republic in January 1899. The majority of Filipinos probably supported him. The revolt eventually became a savage guerilla war that was finally squashed by 60,000 American soldiers. The United States suffered 4,200 deaths, 10 times the number in the Spanish-American War. Filipino casualty numbers remain controversial; estimates range from 40,000 to 200,000 killed. Ironically, in order to defeat the Filipinos, the United States used the same "reconcentration" policy it had so vehemently condemned in Cuba. Of the 30 American generals who fought in Philippines, 26 had gained experience fighting Native Americans in the west, and the war took on trappings of a racial crusade. In March 1901, American soldiers captured Aguinaldo, and the fighting soon ended.

287. (B) In New Zealand, the native Maori were descended from seafaring people who reached New Zealand from Polynesia around 1200. Over several centuries in isolation, the Maori developed a unique tribal culture with their own language, mythology, crafts, performing arts, and after about 1450, a prominent warrior culture. However, European settlers were attracted by New Zealand's mild climate and good soil. These settlers introduced sheep and cattle and were soon exporting wool, mutton, and beef. In 1840, when Great Britain annexed New Zealand, there were about 100,000 Maori and about 2,000 Europeans. As colonists poured in, they took over Maori land, leading to fierce conflicts, but by the 1870s, the resistance crumbled. In 1896, there were about 45,000 Maori and more than 700,000 Europeans. Between 1840 and 1890, the Maori lost 95 percent of their land. (In 2010, there were about 660,000 Maori in New Zealand, about 15 percent of the national population.) In 1907, New Zealand became independent with its own parliament, prime minister, and elected legislature, although the country preserved close ties with the British Empire.

288. (C) Cuba and Puerto Rico were the last of Spain's once-extensive Latin American empire. A Cuban revolt had already been defeated in the Ten Years' War (1868–1878). Sugar was Cuba's lifeblood, but the United States (not Spain) imported more than 90 percent of the crop. Just as in Hawaii in 1890, a change in United States tariffs brought on a revolution. The Wilson-Gorman Tariff of 1894 increased the tax on Cuban sugar 40 percent and trade collapsed. With Cuba's economy in ruins, poverty and unemployment led to discontent with Spanish rule and a revolt broke out in 1895. Cuban rebels launched a guerilla war and adopted the deliberate policy of devastating the island so completely that the Spanish would leave. The Spanish committed more than 200,000 soldiers but could not quell the revolt. In 1896, Spanish General Valeriano Weyler organized a brutal "reconcentration" policy that moved native Cubans into camps and destroyed the rebellion's popular base. Cubans died by thousands in these camps, victims of unsanitary conditions, overcrowding, and disease. News of "Butcher" Weyler's policies created a tidal wave of American support for Cuban independence. Twice in 1896, the US Congress passed resolutions welcoming the future independence of Cuba.

289. (E) The Sepoy Mutiny, also known as the Indian Rebellion of 1857, began as a mutiny of sepoys of the army of the British East India Company's (BEIC). It quickly erupted into civilian rebellions in northern and central India. The rebellion posed a threat to BEIC power until it was suppressed by the British army in 1858. The rebellion was marked by savage atrocities on both sides. At the rebellion's end, the British government abolished the BEIC and assumed direct control of India. Expropriation of land was discontinued, religious toleration decreed, and Indians admitted to the civil service. Some Indians view the uprising as India's First War of Independence.

290. (D) The Boer War (1899–1902) was fought between Great Britain versus the South African Republic (Transvaal) and the Orange Free State. The Boers (people of Dutch ancestry) resented British control of southern Africa. Anti-British sentiment, led by Paul Kruger, increased after the discovery (1886) of gold brought thousands of prospectors (mainly British) into the Transvaal. The Boer government denied the Uitlanders (foreigners) citizenship and taxed them heavily. The Jameson Raid (1895–1896), a botched coup attempt by British colonial leaders, helped incite the Boer War, which began in 1899. The Boer forces scored impressive early victories, but the British sent massive reinforcements in 1900 and captured Johannesburg, Pretoria, and Bloemfontein. Yet the Boers continued to fight a devastating guerrilla war under Jan Smuts, Christiaan de Wet, and Louis Botha. The British responded by herding more than 150,000 black Africans and Boers, mostly women and children, into reconcentration camps. More than 25,000 Boers died of starvation, disease, and exposure in these camps; about 85 percent of the dead were children. The British then built chains of blockhouses and sent troops through the guerrilla country. In 1902, the British forces (about 350,000) finally defeated the Boer troops (about 60,000). The Treaty of Vereeniging (1902) ended hostilities with the annexation of both republics to the British Empire. Battlefield casualties were light (about 7,000 each side), but adding deaths from disease and the camps brings the total dead to 75,000 British, Boer, and black African lives. The war left much bitterness, which affected the political life of South Africa for decades.

Chapter 11: Ming and Qing China

291. (C) The Qing granted commercial rights to the Portuguese, Dutch, and British. However, they were vigilant about and successful at controlling trade relations through the mid-1700s. The Qing fiercely protected Chinese culture. In 1724, Christianity was banned. In 1757, the Chinese instituted the Canton system, which limited the ports in which European traders could do business with China. It also forbade any direct trade between European merchants and Chinese civilians. Instead, European employees of major trading companies had to trade with an association of Chinese merchants known as the *Cohong*. The European (and soon the American) presence was restricted to Canton (present-day Guangzhou) during the trading season.

292. (A) After ridding China of the Mongols, the Ming dynasty embarked on a period of intensified interest in the trade and exploration of the Eastern Hemisphere. Chinese Emperor Yongle wanted to explore other lands and display the splendors of the Ming dynasty. He dispatched his advisor, Zheng He, on most (but not all) of his overseas expeditions. The other four choices are later emperors of the Ming dynasty.

293. (D) In the early 1300s, the Yuan dynasty began to decline. Excessive taxation caused a succession of peasant uprisings and the ruling class became unstable; there were eight emperors from 1308 to 1333. During this period, corruption and bribery became severe problems, and the Mongol army gradually lost effectiveness. Many ethnic Han Chinese chafed under the Four Class system. The Mongols classified the population of China into a hierarchy of four groups: Mongols, non-Han (mostly Islamic population), northern Chinese, and at the very bottom were the southern Chinese. In 1368, the leader of a Hongjin (red headband) peasant uprising, Zhu Yuanzhang, conquered the Yuan capital of Dadu (present-day Beijing). The Yuan dynasty collapsed, and the Chinese established the Ming dynasty (1368–1644).

294. (C) Wang Yangming (1472–1529) was a Chinese scholar and official whose interpretation of Neo-Confucianism influenced philosophy in eastern Asia for centuries. He is best known for his theory that knowledge and action are codependent. Wang Yangming developed the idea of innate knowing, arguing that every person knows from birth the difference between good and evil. Such knowledge is intuitive and not rational. Wang upheld the typical optimistic Neo-Confucian premise of the goodness of human nature. His preferred method of seeking knowledge was through *Jing zuo* ("quiet sitting"), a practice that strongly resembles Zen (Chan) meditation. His philosophy spread across China and Japan, and he is regarded one of the four greatest masters of Confucianism along with Confucius, Mencius, and Zhu Xi.

295. (E) The Tang dynasty (c. 618–907 CE) comes first chronologically and the Qing dynasty (1644–1911) comes last. In the middle are the Song (c. 960–1270), the Yuan (1271–1368), and the Ming dynasties (1368–1644).

296. (E) The Ming dynasty began to decline just as Europeans began to sail toward China. In the 1600s, natural disasters, epidemics, famines, and crop failures crippled the Chinese economy, resulting in widespread peasant revolts. Huge quantities of silver entered China in the 1500s as a result of international trade, but this influx shrank significantly in later Ming years, which damaged the economy. At the same time, Manchu forces gained control over most of Inner Mongolia in 1632. Although the Ming fought the Manchu, they also used Manchu warriors to fight peasant rebellions within their own borders. In 1640, starving Chinese peasants, unable to pay their taxes and no longer in fear of the Chinese army, began to form into huge bands of rebels. In 1644, the Ming emperor invited Qing warriors from nearby Manchuria to help him quell a peasant uprising. Instead, the Qing captured Beijing and ousted the emperor. The Qing (or Manchu) dynasty ruled China from 1644 to 1912, the last dynasty in China's history.

297. (C) Kangxi (1654–1722) was an early emperor of the Qing dynasty; his rule of 61 years makes him the longest-reigning Chinese emperor in history. Kangxi extended Manchu control and promoted learning in the arts and sciences. He conquered the feudal states of southern China, took Taiwan (1683), blocked Russian expansion on the Amur River in the Treaty of Nerchinsk (1689), and pushed into Outer Mongolia (1697). He earned a positive reputation for his repeated tax reductions, attention to water conservation, and imperial tours of inspection. He actively encouraged and rewarded people to reclaim the wasteland. In the early years of his reign, he employed Jesuit missionaries to map the empire and to teach mathematics and astronomy. Kangxi also ordered the compilation of a dictionary of Chinese characters, cleverly winning support from the Han Chinese scholar-bureaucrats. Kangxi's reign brought about long-term stability and relative wealth after years of war and chaos. By the end of his reign, the Qing controlled China, Taiwan, Manchuria, Inner and Outer Mongolia, and Tibet.

298. (A) Chinese trade with Europeans in the 17th and 18th centuries was substantial even though the Qing placed restrictions on foreign merchants. The Europeans bought large quantities of tea, silk, and porcelain. In exchange, the Chinese merchants received huge sums of silver, which created a rising class of merchants in Chinese coastal cities. Carved jades were popular exports from China to Europe during the 19th century. Slavery did exist during the Qing dynasty, but slaves were generally not sold to European merchants.

299. (D) The patriarchal family continued to reign supreme under the Qing dynasty. Upon marriage, a woman became part of her husband's family, and women could not divorce their husbands. Since daughters were often considered a social and financial liability, female infanticide was not uncommon despite efforts by Confucian moralists, Buddhist teachings, Christian missionaries, government officials, and imperial edicts to stop the practice. Although most girls were not educated, the daughters of the elite classes were often taught to read and write. Foot binding remained a part of Chinese society into the 20th century and even spread to some middle-class families. The Manchu leaders of the Qing dynasty never adopted foot binding and tried to stop its popularity.

300. (B) Christianity had made inroads in China at the end of Ming dynasty in the late 1500s. Jesuit fathers who were well versed in science, such as Adam Schall von Bell and Ferdinand Verbiest, won the confidence of Chinese emperors. The Jesuits tried to convert the imperial court and the elite to Christianity without touching Chinese customs and beliefs such as ancestor veneration and state sacrifices to heaven. Many aspects of Catholicism resembled Buddhist practices, such as the use of incantations, bells, ceremonial prayers, processions, pictures, and relics. Emperor Kangxi was at first friendly to the Jesuits working in China; in 1692, he issued an edict of toleration of Christianity, and by 1700, the Jesuits had made many converts to Christianity. However, in the early 1700s, a Chinese Rites controversy arose in the Catholic Church over whether Chinese folk religion rituals and offerings to ancestors constituted idolatry. In 1715, Pope Clement XI, supported by the Dominicans, ruled against tolerating these practices among Chinese Roman Catholic converts. Kangxi was particularly angered, and he banned Christian missions in China. This controversy hampered Christian efforts to gain converts in China until it was revised in 1939 by Pope Pius XII.

301. (B) Qing dynasty China reached its largest extent during the 18th century, when it ruled all of China proper as well as Manchuria (northeastern China), Inner Mongolia, Outer Mongolia (from the late 1600s), Xinjiang, Tibet, and Taiwan. In addition, many surrounding countries, such as Korea (Joseon dynasty), Vietnam, and Nepal, were tributary states for much of this period.

302. (E) The Qing dynasty was run by pastoral nomads from Manchuria known as Manchu. The Manchu represented only about 30 percent of the population in China. Because they were not Han Chinese, the Manchu were resented, especially in the south. However, they had assimilated a great deal of Chinese culture before conquering China, and they realized that to dominate the empire, they would have to compromise. As a result, the Manchu retained many institutions of the Ming and earlier Chinese dynasties. They continued Confucian court practices and temple rituals over which the emperors had traditionally presided. The Manchu also continued the Confucian civil service system. Although Chinese were barred from the highest offices, Chinese officials were more common than Manchu office holders outside the capital, except in military positions. Neo-Confucian philosophy, emphasizing the obedience of subject to ruler, was enforced as the state creed. The Manchu emperors supported Chinese literary and historical projects of enormous scope, which helped preserve much of China's ancient literature. However, the Manchu worked hard to prevent their absorption into the majority Han Chinese population. Han Chinese were prohibited from migrating into the Manchu homeland, intermarriage between the two groups was forbidden, and the Chinese were not allowed to learn the Manchurian language.

303. (C) The Forbidden City, in the middle of Beijing, was the Chinese imperial palace from the Ming dynasty to the end of the Qing dynasty. For almost 500 years, it served as the home of emperors and their households, as well as the ceremonial and political center of the Chinese government. The Forbidden City was constructed from 1406 to 1420. The complex eventually consisted of more than 800 buildings and covered about 170 acres. The Forbidden City was declared a World Heritage Site in 1987. Topkapi Palace in Istanbul was the official residence of the Ottoman sultans for approximately 400 years (1465–1856); it also served as a setting for state occasions and royal entertainments.

304. (D) The Taipeng Rebellion against the Qing government (1851–1864) may have been the deadliest conflict in world history until World War II; the death toll from fighting, plague, and famine is estimated at 20 to 30 million people. Some of the rebels' grievances related to European imperialism and the increased foreign presence in China, while others reflected anger at Confucian society and discontent with the rule of the northern Manchu in southern China. These complaints merged with Taipeng ideology, a strange mix of Protestant Christianity and Chinese religious ideas. Hong Xiuquan, the leader of the rebellion, claimed he was the younger brother of Jesus Christ and preached a new vision of society: equality among all believers, abolition of private property, no opium use, no gambling, and no foot binding. At first, the rebellion was successful; the Yangtze valley fell quickly and Nanjing (renamed Tianjing) was taken in 1853. However, the rebels were defeated when they tried to capture Beijing, and the next few years were ones of bloody stalemate. Ultimately, the Qing put together powerful regional armies (such as under Zeng Guofan), bought modern armaments, and hired European advisors (such as British General George Gordon) to lead the troops. In 1864, Qing forces captured Nanjing and went on a rampage, perhaps killing as many as 100,000 people, ending the rebellion.

305. (D) The culture of Ming dynasty China was generally conservative despite the country's foreign contacts. This was a natural reaction to the previous Yuan dynasty, dominated by Mongols from the north. The major cultural innovations in the Ming dynasty took place in pottery and ceramic manufacture. Kiln makers investigated new techniques in design and shapes and showed a renewed interest in color and painted design. There was also an openness to foreign forms such as in blue-and-white ware and cloisonné enamelware. During the Ming dynasty, Chinese monochrome porcelain became famous throughout the world, with imitations created in Vietnam, Japan, and Europe. In the 1400s, technical refinements in the preparation of the cobalt used for underglaze blue decoration led to spectacular ceramic ware. In the late Ming period, China exported porcelain around the world on an unprecedented scale.

306. (A) The Hundred Days' Reform was a failed reform movement in 1898 in the late Qing dynasty. It was undertaken by the young Guangxu emperor (1871–1908) and his reform-minded supporters, but it ended in a coup by powerful conservative opponents led by Empress Dowager Cixi (1835–1908). The sweeping reforms were a response to China's defeat by Japan in the First Sino-Japanese War (1895). Under the influence of reformers Kang Youwei and Liang Qichao, Guangxu believed that China could modernize by imitating constitutional monarchies such as Japan and Germany. The reforms included modernizing the traditional exam system and creating a new education system that emphasized math and science instead of Confucian texts. Following Japan's lead, the reformers sought to build up military strength and industrialize China through manufacturing, commerce, and capitalism. The ambitiousness of the reform effort hindered its success. Empress Dowager Cixi and General Ronglu removed Guangxu from power; he lived under house arrest until he died in 1908. The failure of the movement actually helped the revolutionary forces within China; changes within the establishment were seen to be hopeless, and the overthrow of the Qing government appeared to be the only viable way to save China.

307. (B) The "Four Great Classical Novels" of Chinese literature are regarded by scholars as the most influential of premodern Chinese fiction. In chronological order, they are *Water Margin* (14th century), *Romance of the Three Kingdoms* (14th century), *Journey to the West* (16th century), and *Dream of the Red Chamber* (18th century). They were written during the Ming and Qing dynasties and are well known to most Chinese readers. They are among the world's longest (some consist of more than 120 chapters) and oldest novels and have influenced the creation of many stories, theatrical works, movies, games, and other entertainments throughout eastern Asia. *Soul Mountain* is one of the most famous works of Gao Xingjian, the first Chinese writer to win the Nobel Prize in Literature (in 2000).

308. (B) Macao is an area in southeastern China on the estuary of the Pearl River, about 40 miles west of Hong Kong and 65 miles south of Guangzhou (Canton). Macao was the oldest permanent European settlement in eastern Asia; it did not develop until 1535, when Portuguese traders obtained the rights to anchor ships in Macao's harbors. In 1557, the Portuguese established a permanent settlement in Macao, and it prospered as a port for nearly 300 years. With the gradual silting up of its harbor and the rise of Hong Kong in the 1800s, Macao lost its preeminent position as a port and became identified with smuggling and gambling. In 1999, Portugal returned Macao to China.

309. (C) The White Lotus Rebellion (1796–1804) broke out in 1796 among impoverished settlers in the mountainous region that separates Sichuan province from Hubei and Shaanxi provinces. It began as a tax protest led by the White Lotus Society, a secret Buddhist religious society that forecast the coming of the millennium, advocated the restoration of the Ming dynasty, and promised personal salvation to its followers. The rebels were initially successful, but the rebellion was crushed by the Qing government under Emperor Jiaqing (reigned 1796–1820) in 1804. However, the uprising weakened Qing control, ended the myth of the military invincibility of the Manchu, and perhaps contributed to the greater frequency of rebellions in the 19th century. By some estimates, the White Lotus Rebellion caused the deaths of about 15 million people.

310. (E) The Yongle Emperor (1360–1424) ruled the Ming dynasty from 1402 to 1414. As emperor, he moved the capital from Nanjing to Beijing and constructed the Forbidden City. Yongle had the Grand Canal repaired (it had deteriorated during the Yuan dynasty) to supply the new capital of Beijing with a steady flow of southern goods and foodstuffs. He commissioned most of the exploratory sea voyages of Zheng He. During his reign, the monumental Yongle Encyclopedia (22,000 volumes) was completed. Yongle respected and worked hard to preserve Chinese culture by designing monuments such as the Porcelain Tower of Nanjing. However, he is also known for his despotism and cruelty.

Chapter 12: Tokugawa Japan and the Meiji Restoration

311. (C) A major goal of the daimyo, who reunified Japan in 1600, was the establishment of order after the chaotic warfare of the 1500s. The Tokugawa period (1600–1867) was distinguished from the medieval period by its relative peace, commercial development, and urbanization. Agriculture improved as new seeds, tools, and the use of fertilizer created higher outputs. The resulting food surpluses led to increased population. To control the daimyo, the Tokugawa shoguns required them to maintain expensive residences in Edo (Tokyo) and live there on a rotating schedule. The daimyo also had to contribute to the upkeep of shrines, temples, and roads; this caused a financial burden for the daimyo and moderated their power. Shogun Tokugawa Ieyasu enforced the suppression and persecution of Christianity from 1614. In 1633, Shogun Iemitsu forbade traveling abroad; in 1639, he reduced contacts with foreigners to very limited trade relations with China, and the Netherlands in the port of Nagasaki. In addition, all foreign books were banned (until 1720). Despite Japan's isolation, domestic trade improved, and new art forms like kabuki and woodblock prints became popular. Tokugawa Japan had a strict hierarchical order: at the top stood the samurai, followed by the peasants, artisans, and merchants. The members of the four classes were not allowed to change their social status.

312. (E) Before the Meiji era, men controlled Japanese society and relegated women to relatively powerless roles except for their position as mothers and wives. The Meiji Restoration made only slight changes in this order. However, as Japan urbanized and industrialized, women won opportunities for paid employment outside the home. By 1900, the booming textile industry employed more than half a million workers, about two-thirds female. Politically, Japanese women were granted a few more rights in marriage and divorce in the Meiji Civil Code (1898) but were still kept under unfair restrictions. For example, women could now divorce their husbands on grounds of cruelty, desertion, or serious misconduct, but not for infidelity. A woman could also legally own her own land, but once she married, she needed her husband's consent for all contracts. Japanese women were prohibited by law from joining political parties and attending political meetings; they did not receive the vote until 1946. The most important change of the Meiji Restoration probably involved education. In 1873, the Fundamental Code of Education required everyone to attend school regardless of gender.

313. (B) Matsuo Basho (1644–1694) was the greatest of the Japanese haiku poets. He was born near Kyoto and moved to Edo (Tokyo) in 1667. Basho became the master of the genre by combining the ideal of *karumi* (lightness of touch), an intense love of nature, and the influence of Zen Buddhism. He spent much of his life traveling, relying on the hospitality of temples and fellow poets. When he was not traveling, Basho was a semirecluse, living on the outskirts of Edo in a hut. The concise and impressionistic nature of his poetry has influenced many modern poets, especially Ezra Pound and the Imagists (1920s), and the Beat generation (1950s and 1960s).

314. (A) In the 1500s, Japanese feudalism began to wane. Some of this was caused by European influence, which began in Japan in 1543. Soon afterward, Portuguese merchants arrived with trade items including firearms. The Portuguese landed on Tanegashima Island, and until modern times, firearms were colloquially known in Japan as "Tanega-shima." Oda Nobunaga and Toyotomi Hideyoshi, who virtually unified Japan in the late 1500s, made extensive use of guns in their armies. As a result, daimyo were forced to fortify their castles to withstand artillery. The protective walls of the castles attracted artisans and merchants to settle the land surrounding the castles; eventually, some of these settlements became centers of bureaucracy. In 1549, the Christian Jesuit missionary Francis Xavier established Japan's first mission at Kagoshima. By 1600, a few hundred thousand Japanese had converted to Christianity; the Jesuits took control of the port city of Nagasaki and trade flourished.

315. (D) Katsushika Hokusai (1760–1849) was Japan's most renowned woodblock print artist. He is famous for his woodblock print series, *36 Views of Mount Fuji* (created between 1826 and 1833), which includes the internationally recognized print, *The Great Wave off Kanagawa*. In all, Hokusai left more than 30,000 works, including silk paintings, woodblock prints, picture books, travel illustrations, erotic illustrations, and sketches. The Great Wave print continues to be popular throughout the world. The other answer choices are all famous Japanese woodblock printmakers of the period, but not as famous as Hokusai.

316. (D) In 1867, discontented daimyo and samurai led a revolt that unseated the shogun and "restored" the 15-year-old emperor Mutsuhito (1852–1912) to power. When he was crowned emperor, Mutsuhito took the name Meiji, which means "enlightened rule." He moved from the old imperial capital in Kyoto to the shogun's palace in Edo, which was renamed Tokyo ("eastern capital"). The emperor reigned 44 years from 1868 to 1912, a period known as the Meiji Restoration. At the time of his birth, Japan was an isolated, preindustrial, feudal country dominated by the Tokugawa shogunate. By the time of Emperor Meiji's death in 1912, Japan had undergone a political, social, and industrial revolution at home and emerged as one of the great powers in the world.

317. (C) Oda Nobunaga (1534–1582) was the first of the three unifiers of Japan. He was known for his ruthless use of power and his vision to bring all of Japan "under a single sword." Nobunaga's life was one of continuous military conquest; he eventually conquered a third of Japanese daimyo before his death. In order to unify the country, Nobunaga attacked Buddhist monasteries that opposed his rule. He destroyed the Buddhist monastery of Mount Hiei, whose warrior monks were famous in Japan, and slaughtered about 3,000 fleeing monks, women, and children. Nobunaga supported Christian missionaries to counterbalance other powerful Buddhist monasteries. He embraced Western innovations, especially firearms. At the Battle of Nagashino, Nobunaga used new tactics that completely changed Japanese warfare. He also instituted a specialized warrior class and appointed his retainers to positions based on rice production and not land size. In 1582, Nobunaga was assassinated by a disgruntled general from his inner circle. He was replaced by one of his aides, Toyotomi Hideyoshi.

318. (E) Japan developed in relative isolation for more than 200 years under the Tokugawa shogunate. Internal commerce expanded, agricultural production grew, and bustling urban areas developed. By 1800, however, there were signs of discontent in Tokugawa society. Many daimyo needed money in a commercial economy, but they were cash poor; a daimyo's wealth was in land. Lesser samurai lacked the wealth to live as well as urban merchants. Merchants in turn resented their lack of status. Peasants suffered under heavy taxes. The social hierarchy began to break down as the merchant class grew powerful while some samurai became financially dependent on them. The Tokugawa shogunate's emphasis on traditional values irritated important segments of society. Foreign pressure deepened the unrest; many Japanese felt the shogun should have taken a stronger stand against United States and European intrusions in the 1850s and 1860s. The Tokugawa shogunate was overthrown in 1867.

319. (C) In the early 1600s, the Tokugawa shogunate suspected that foreign traders and missionaries were actually the forerunners of a European military assault. In 1614, Catholicism was officially banned and all missionaries ordered to leave. A campaign of persecution followed, with thousands of converts killed, tortured, or forced to renounce their religion. This eventually led to a revolt from 1637 to 1638 known as the Shimabara Rebellion. In this revolt, about 30,000 Christians, *ronin*, and peasants faced a samurai army of about 100,000 sent from Edo. There is no evidence that Europeans directly incited the rebellion, but Shimabara was a Christian area and the rebels used many Portuguese motifs and Christian icons. The Shimabara Rebellion was a rare instance of serious unrest during the Tokugawa shogunate. The rebellion was crushed at a high cost to the shogun's army and Amakusa Shirō, the rebel leader, was beheaded. Christians were associated with disloyalty and were formally persecuted until the 1850s. The Shimabara Rebellion convinced many Tokugawa policy makers that foreign influences were more trouble than they were worth. This led to Japan's national seclusion foreign relations policy (*sakoku*). Under *sakoku* ("locked country"), no Japanese could leave the country on penalty of death. The government monopolized foreign policy and expelled traders, missionaries, and foreigners except for the Dutch and Chinese merchants restricted to the man-made island of Deshima in Nagasaki Bay.

320. (D) The Russo-Japanese War (1904–1905) grew out of the rival imperialistic ambitions of Russia and Japan to control Manchuria and Korea. The Russians wanted a warm-water port on the Pacific Ocean; Vladivostok was not ice-free, but Port Arthur (present-day Lushunkou, China), on the extreme southern tip of the Liaodong Peninsula in southern Manchuria, could be used all year. When negotiations proved useless, the Japanese attacked Port Arthur in 1904 without a declaration of war. A series of quick Japanese victories astounded the world. The Japanese bottled up the Russian fleet at Port Arthur, occupied the Korean peninsula, captured Port Arthur after a bloody siege, and defeated the Russians at Mukden (present-day Shenyang, China). The capstone was the complete destruction of the Russian Pacific fleet at Tsushima by Admiral Togo's fleet in May 1905. US President Theodore Roosevelt's mediation resulted in the Treaty of Portsmouth (New Hampshire). Russia recognized Korea as part of the Japanese sphere of influence and agreed to evacuate Manchuria; Japan would annex all of Korea in 1910. Russia also signed over its 25-year leasehold rights to Port Arthur (renamed Ryojun by the Japanese) and ceded the southern half of Sakhalin Island to Japan. All these areas of conflict between Russia and Japan would be renegotiated after World War II. The loss of the war also destabilized Imperial Russia, leading to the Russian Revolution of 1905.

321. (D) When the Meiji emperor was restored as head of Japan in 1868, the nation was primarily preindustrial and militarily weak. When the Meiji period ended with the death of the emperor in 1912, Japan had a highly centralized, bureaucratic government, including a constitution (1889) establishing an elected Diet (legislature). The constitution also eliminated legal distinctions between classes, leading to a loss of all privileges for the samurai. The emperor retained autocratic power, and voting rights were sharply limited. Meiji leaders made the economy a major priority. They encouraged businesses to adopt Western methods, set up a modern banking system, built railroads, and organized a telegraph and postal system. To develop industry, the government often built factories and sold them to wealthy business families. With such support, business and banking dynasties, known as zaibatsu, soon ruled over industrial empires. The Meiji reformers set up schools and a university and introduced compulsory education. Perhaps most important, Japan developed a cult around the emperor and the powerful army and navy, with all men subject to military service. Japan regained complete control of its foreign trade and legal system, and by winning wars against China (1895) and Russia (1904–1905), established full independence and equality in international affairs.

322. (B) Geisha are traditional female Japanese entertainers whose skills include performing various Japanese arts such as classical music, classical Japanese dance, and clever conversation. Geisha (or *geiko* in Kyoto dialect) might attend guests during meals, banquets, and other occasions, making them feel at ease with conversation, drinking, and dance performances. The line between geishas and courtesans (prostitutes) has varied over Japanese history. (Prostitution was legal in Japan until the 1900s.) The first geishas emerged in the 1700s, when the profession still included many men; by 1800, the position of a geisha was considered a female occupation. Some women would have sex with their male customers, whereas others would entertain strictly with their art forms. Geisha flourished as artists and entertainers, but the profession declined after World War II.

323. (C) Kabuki is a classical Japanese dance-drama, known for the elaborate costumes and makeup worn by some of its performers. Kabuki was influenced by the older Noh plays (which originated in the 1300s), but it was less refined and included comedy and melodrama. Kabuki uses more characters than the older form of Noh and features much more stage action including lively and exaggerated movements. Ironically, kabuki was founded by a woman. In 1603, Izumo no Okuni began performing a new style of dance drama in the dry riverbeds of Kyoto. However, women were banned from playing kabuki roles in 1629. Instead, men known as *onnagata* play female roles. Kabuki, both in classic and modern forms, continues to be popular in Japan, while Noh is restricted to a few theatrical groups. Bunraku is a form of traditional Japanese puppet theater that also became popular in the Tokugawa period. Chikamatsu Monzaemon (1653–1725), one of the first professional kabuki playwrights, produced several famous bunraku plays.

324. (E) The Battle of Sekigahara (1600), sometimes known as the Battle for the Sundered Realm, cleared the path to the shogunate for Tokugawa Ieyasu. When Toyotomi Hideyoshi died suddenly in 1598, a succession struggle ensued. Tokugawa was Toyotomi's main general and most likely successor. His opponents rallied around the Toyotomi clan, official heirs to the shogunate. Tokugawa's victory at Sekigahara established him as the shogun and virtual dictator of Japan. His dynasty ruled Japan in relative peace until the Meiji Restoration in 1867.

325. (E) In the early 1600s, the Tokugawa shoguns decreed that no foreigners could enter Japan and no Japanese could travel outside a 15-mile limit. For more than 200 years, Japan closed its ports to foreign trade. The main exception was the artificial fan-shaped harbor at Nagasaki (constructed 1634) known as Deshima, where the Dutch operated a limited trading concession under humiliating conditions. This Japanese policy was known as *sakoku*—self-imposed isolation. Between 1641 and 1847, about 606 Dutch ships arrived at Deshima. In 1720 the ban on Dutch books was lifted, causing Japanese scholars to flood into Nagasaki to study European science and art; Nagasaki became a center of *rangaku* ("Dutch learning").

326. (A) The Meiji Restoration (1867–1912) modernized Japan sufficiently to resist European and American imperialism. This did not depend on the effectiveness of the samurai, but on the industrialization of Japan that created a modern military capable of defeating the Chinese (1895) and the Russians (1904–1905). One of the reasons for the collapse of the

Tokugawa shogunate had been the government's inability to resist American threats and the resulting unequal treaties. It was Japan's lack of natural resources, especially coal, iron, rubber, and oil, that set the country on an imperialist course into Korea, Manchuria, China, and ultimately Southeast Asia.

327. (B) In 1895, a modernizing Japan easily defeated China in the First Sino-Japanese War. Japan used its victory to gain treaty ports in China and control over the island of Taiwan. Ten years later, Japan's armies defeated Russian troops in Korea and Manchuria, and Japan's navy destroyed almost the entire Russian fleet. In the 1905 Treaty of Portsmouth (New Hampshire), Japan gained control of Korea as well as part of Manchuria. In 1910, Japan annexed Korea outright. The Gentlemen's Agreement (1907) technically was not related to Japanese imperialism but was an attempt to reduce tensions between the United States and Japan. This informal agreement stipulated that the United States would not impose restriction on Japanese immigration, and Japan would not allow further emigration to the United States.

328. (C) *Zaibatsu* literally means "financial clique" in Japanese. It refers to the industrial and financial business conglomerates of the Japanese Empire. The zaibatsu were so wealthy and powerful that they dominated the Japanese economy from the Meiji Restoration until World War II. The zaibatsu were usually large family-controlled vertical monopolies consisting of a holding company on top, with a banking subsidiary providing finance and several industrial companies dominating specific markets. The Big Four zaibatsu—Mitsubishi, Mitsui, Sumitomo, and Yasuda—all date from before 1900.

329. (B) Japanese modernization accelerated because of support from the government. However, Japan's lack of natural resources such as coal and iron prompted an interest in Manchuria, an area of east Asia that lay at the meeting point of Chinese, Japanese, and Russian spheres of influence. Because of its natural resources, Manchuria was an area of significant strategic importance. The Russian Empire took control over the northern part of Manchuria from a weakened Chinese Empire in 1860 in the Beijing Treaty. Disputes over Manchuria and Korea led directly to the Russo-Japanese War of 1904–1905. The Japanese invaded Manchuria in 1931 and set up the puppet state of Manchukuo. As of 2012, the area was roughly divided equally between China and Russia.

330. (A) In 1852, US President Millard Fillmore ordered Commodore Matthew Perry to take on the delicate task of negotiating trade treaties with isolationist Japan. Perry was instructed to request protection for shipwrecked American seamen, the right to buy coal, and the opening of ports to trade. Perry could use "argument and persuasion," but he was "not to resort to force unless in self defense." Fillmore instructed Perry to impress the Japanese "with a just sense of the power and greatness of our country." In July 1853, Perry anchored his four powerful steamships in Tokyo Bay. The Japanese ordered him to go to Nagasaki, but Perry firmly refused. He presented his requests to Japanese officials along with gifts such as 100 gallons of Kentucky whiskey, two telegraph transmitters, and a working miniature model locomotive. The Japanese knew the British had broken China's trade barriers through military force in the First Opium War (1839–1842), and they understood that the entrance of foreigners into Japan probably could not be stopped. In 1854, the Japanese signed the Treaty of Kanagawa, agreeing to open the ports of Shimoda and Hakodate to the United States. The Japanese concessions, although meager, revolutionized Japanese policy and led to deeper American involvement in Asia.

Chapter 13: Colonial Africa

331. (B) The so-called Benin bronzes are not bronze at all, but a collection of more than 3,000 brass plaques from the royal palace of the Kingdom of Benin (present-day southwestern Nigeria). These plaques were seized by a British force in 1897 and given to various museums and private collectors. Scholars believe "bronzes" had been cast in Benin since the 13th century CE. The plaques depict a variety of scenes, including animals, fish, humans, and life at the court. Many contain depictions of the *oba*, the supreme ruler of Benin, who headed both religious and secular affairs. The *obas* supported guilds of artists to produce objects that honored royal ancestors and glorified history and court life.

332. (A) In general, as Europe and North America grew stronger through slave labor, Africa grew weaker. For every slave taken captive, another probably died in the constant slave raiding in Africa or on the march to the coast. Slave traders demanded the healthiest and the strongest; men usually outnumbered women about two to one. This gender imbalance encouraged some African men to take several wives and helped to change the nature of marriage and kinship in Africa. The slave trade also rewrote the continent's political map; many western African states existed solely as places to supply captives to European slavers. Some African kingdoms, such as Dahomey, became rich based on the slave trade. Neighboring African kingdoms, fearing invasion, then purchased as many guns as possible. By 1730, Europeans shipped about 180,000 guns a year into the Gold and Slave Coasts. The slave trade and guns threw the continent into chaos. In the 1600s, the western African economy stopped growing as many people entered the more lucrative business of trading slaves for European money, textiles, and metalware.

333. (B) In the 1600s and 1700s, southern Africa was filled with numerous quarreling ethnic groups. The most prominent of these groups were the Zulu, who rose to power in the early 1800s under Chief Shaka (reigned 1818–1828). Shaka organized an army of as many as 40,000 Zulu warriors and reduced many of the Zulu's former enemies to vassals. Shaka is credited with uniting many of the northern Nguni people and the Ndwandwe into the Zulu Kingdom, the nation that dominated a large portion of southern Africa. Shaka was murdered by his half brother, Dingane, in 1828. Shaka's diplomatic skills and military energy made him a great Zulu chief. Some historians have praised his military genius, while others have condemned the brutality of his reign.

334. (D) The centralized kingdom of Kongo in west central Africa prospered as a result of its commercial relationship with Portuguese merchants beginning in the 1480s. King Afonso I (c. 1456–c. 1543) ruled the Kongo from 1509 to his death. Virtually everything that historians know about the area at that time is derived from his long series of letters, written in Portuguese, to the Portuguese kings Manuel I and João III. The letters give many details about the country, and several complain about the behavior of Portuguese officials in the slave trade. Afonso welcomed European technology but refused to adopt Portugal's legal code or sell land to foreigners. Afonso converted to Catholicism and tried to convert the people by establishing the church and church schools in Kongo and financing them from tax revenues.

335. (A) Many eastern African rulers and merchants converted to Islam after contact with Muslims involved in the Indian Ocean trade. These elite readily saw the commercial value of conversion to Islam. However, the common people of eastern African villages were originally reluctant to convert. One source of controversy between sub-Saharan eastern Africans and the Islamic faith was the treatment of women. Many African societies tended to offer significantly greater gender equality than did traditional Islamic societies. In the 1700s, when eastern African commoners did begin to convert to Islam, they maintained some of their tribal beliefs and blended them with the precepts of Islam. For example, sub-Saharan women who converted to Islam often did not wear the veil usually required in traditional Islamic societies.

336. (E) Anansi the spider is one of the most important characters of western African and Caribbean folklore. The Anansi stories were exclusively oral, and Anansi was linked with skill and wisdom in speech. Scholars believe the Anansi tales originated with the Ashanti people in Ghana because the word *Anansi* is from the Akan language and simply means "spider." The stories later spread to other Akan groups and then to the West Indies, Surinam, and the Netherlands Antilles with the African diaspora. Anansi is a spider but often acts and appears as a man. In the stories, Anansi might bring rain, stop fires, create the sun, stars, and moon, or teach people techniques of agriculture. Other stories deal with Anansi's attempts to trick people or convince women of his sexual prowess. In many cases, Anansi's tricks ultimately backfire on him.

337. (C) Cape Colony on the southern tip of Africa had been established by the Dutch in 1652. It was seized by Great Britain in 1795, and the ethnic Dutch found themselves in conflict with the British over land usage and racial policies. Between 1835 and 1843, about 12,000 people of Dutch ancestry moved north and east out of the Cape Colony to escape British control—this was known as the Great Trek. The *Voortrekkers* (as they were known) migrated beyond the Orange River and eventually founded the republics of Natal, Transvaal, and the Orange Free State. In their move northward, they clashed with Africans (mainly the Zulu) who inhabited the land. After initial setbacks, the *Voortrekkers* defeated these powerful African kingdoms through the skilled use of horses, guns, and defensive laagers (encampments). Most trekkers remained in the high veld (an area of open grassland) of the interior. They formed isolated communities and a unique identity, calling themselves "Afrikaners." They also developed a hybrid language—Afrikaans—based on Dutch with strong French, Malay, German, and African influences. The Afrikaans-speaking descendants of these people would later be called *boere* ("farmers"). *Trek* is an Afrikaans term, originally meaning a journey by ox wagon.

338. (E) Western Africa had a history of powerful empires such as Ghana, Mali, and Songhai. In the area known as Guinea, farther to the south, there were smaller kingdoms such as Benin. In 1500, most western Africans farmed or worked at pottery, weaving, and metalworking. These cultures had well-developed governments and laws. Many trade routes connected the African kingdoms to each other and to northern Africa. When the Portuguese first appeared in western Africa in the 1400s, the natives thought of them as just another trading partner. The Portuguese offered guns and iron products for ivory and gold. Africans controlled this inland trade because Europeans often got diseases such as yellow fever, malaria, and dysentery. The Europeans provided the demand for slaves but Africans captured the slaves, marched them to the coast, and sold them to Europeans. Before 1800, Europeans only operated in Africa by permission of African rulers.

339. (A) Dahomey was a kingdom in western Africa that flourished in the 18th and 19th centuries in the area of present-day southern Benin. The kingdom prospered in the late 1700s by selling slaves to the Europeans. Dahomey's government was an absolute monarchy almost unique in Africa. The king, surrounded by a magnificent entourage and a centralized bureaucracy, was the unchallenged head of a highly stratified society of royalty, commoners, and slaves. Dahomey was organized for war, not only to expand its boundaries but also to capture slaves. The kingdom reached its zenith under Gezu, who ruled from 1818 to 1858 and waged a military campaign every year during the dry season. The prisoners of war whom he captured were sold into slavery. This provided money for the treasury, increased the annual budget, and kept taxes low. Gezu embellished the court and encouraged the arts. His armies freed Dahomey from the humiliation of paying tribute to the Yoruba's Oyo Empire. After 1840, the kingdom's fortunes changed as Great Britain ended the overseas slave trade. Dahomey exported palm oil instead, but it was far less lucrative than slaves, and an economic decline followed. Dahomey was part of French West Africa from 1894 to 1960.

340. (B) In the 1700s and 1800s, an Islamic revival spread across western Africa. It began among the Fulani people in northern Nigeria and was led by the scholar and preacher Usman dan Fodio (1754–1817). Usman denounced the corruption and greed of the local Islamic rulers and elites and called for social and religious reforms based on Shari'ah (Islamic law). Usman encouraged literacy and scholarship, including for women. He also helped inspire the Fulani herders and Hausa townspeople to resist European infiltration. Usman and his successors set up (1809) a powerful Islamic state in northern Nigeria known as the Sokoto Caliphate. Their success inspired other Muslim reform movements in western Africa between 1780 and 1880.

341. (C) The Suez Canal was planned by the French engineer Ferdinand de Lesseps, who also supervised its construction from 1859 to 1869. As many as 30,000 people worked on the canal at any given period. Altogether, more than a million people from various countries were employed, and thousands of workers died on the project. When completed, the Suez Canal connected the Mediterranean Sea to the Indian Ocean, eliminating the need to go around the Cape of Good Hope in southern Africa.

342. (E) Colonialism had several negative impacts on African women. As the Europeans converted the best land into export-oriented plantations, women lost access to and control of land and became more economically dependent on men. The colonial economy also forced men to seek employment in European economic ventures and took them away from agricultural work in the traditional African economy. If women did not want to face a severe decline in cultivated land, they had to hire labor to substitute for absent male household members. In the new colonial economy, divided between cash crop plantations and subsistence farming, men controlled the cash crops (cocoa, coffee, cotton, palm oil, etc.) and usually the cash that went with paid employment. Women were relegated to now low-status subsistence farming. In addition, because of male migration, many rural areas had twice as many women as men. This damaged the African family; households no longer had fathers, brothers, uncles, and nephews, and male participation in traditional ceremonies, rites, and rituals was distorted. The responsibility of older males to guide and steer young males was abandoned as many men moved to urban areas.

343. (A) As early as 1575, the Portuguese established a small trading post south of Kongo in present-day Angola in order to expand the slave trade into the interior. When the Portuguese attempted to extend their authority, Queen Nzinga Mbande (c. 1583–1663) of the Ndongo and Matamba Kingdoms in southwestern Africa fiercely resisted. For 40 years, the warrior queen led her troops into battle, studied European military tactics, and made strategic alliances with Portugal's Dutch rivals. Nzinga converted to Christianity for reasons more political than religious and adopted the name Dona Anna de Souza. When the Portuguese defeated the Dutch in 1640 and recaptured Luanda, Nzinga retreated to the hills of Matamba, where she established a resistance movement against the Portuguese regime. Even when she was more than 60 years old, Nzinga led her warriors herself. Despite her efforts, she could not ultimately unify her rivals or overcome the superior weaponry of the Portuguese. Her death accelerated the Portuguese occupation of southwestern Africa and led to a massive expansion of the slave trade.

344. (D) The cargo sent to Africa made up more than half of the cost of a slave-trading expedition. Merchandise imported into Africa included cotton textiles, metals, cowry shells, containers, guns and gunpowder, alcoholic drinks, and luxury goods. The two main goods traded by European slavers on the African coast actually came from India—cotton cloth and thousands of pounds of cowry shells packed in barrels. The cowry shells were used as money in many places in western Africa. They originally came from the Maldive Islands near India. Both the cotton and the cowries were usually shipped from India to Europe and then back to Africa.

345. (B) Zanzibar (in present-day Tanzania) consists of two large islands and several smaller ones in the Indian Ocean off the coast of eastern Africa. In the 1800s, it became world famous for its spices, slaves, and ivory. The Portuguese gained control of the eastern African coast in the 1500s, but they had little impact on Zanzibar. In 1698, Arabs from Oman ousted the Portuguese, but they also neglected Zanzibar until the reign of Seyyid Said (1797–1856), who permanently moved his court from Muscat to Zanzibar in 1841. Said brought many Arabs with him, and they gained control of Zanzibar's fertile land, forcing most of the native Bantu-speaking Hadimu to migrate to the eastern part of the island. The Omani sultans also introduced the clove (originally from the Moluccas) in the early 1800s, and Zanzibar became the world's leading clove producer. The Arab elite in Zanzibar dominated much of the eastern African coast (known as the Zanj), including Mombasa, Dar es Salaam, and trade routes extending inland as far as Kindu on the Congo River. The historic heart of Zanzibar city, known as Stone Town, is a World Heritage Site. It was the center of the spice and slave trade and contains a unique mixture of Moorish, Arab, Persian, and Indian architecture.

346. (C) Between 1801 and 1805, US President Thomas Jefferson sent naval vessels to the Mediterranean to defend American ships against the Barbary States of North Africa (Algiers, Morocco, Tripoli, and Tunis). Piracy was a normal source of income for these nations, and most European nations found it easier to pay annual protection money than to fight them. Presidents Washington and Adams had followed this policy, paying more than $2 million in tribute. In 1800, however, the United States and Tripoli quarreled over the proper amount of tribute. Tripoli declared war, and in 1801, Jefferson sent a naval squadron across the Atlantic. No declaration of war was ever issued by the US Congress. Despite several exciting naval adventures, the Americans were unable to capture Tripoli. In 1804, an American force landed in Egypt and, after a hard march across the desert, took the Tripolitan port of Derna. US Lieutenant John Rodgers then negotiated a treaty in 1805. The United States agreed to pay a ransom of $60,000 for American prisoners, and Tripoli renounced all rights to halt or levy tribute on American ships. However, Barbary pirates continued to raid American shipping throughout the Napoleonic war years.

347. (E) The business of slave raiding was left mostly to native Africans. In general, Europeans stayed on the coast of Africa for fear of disease and because they were greatly outnumbered. Some western African kingdoms benefited from the slave trade; Dahomey's army used

European weapons to raid the interior of Africa looking for slaves. The Asante kings also created a huge empire based on slave raiding. Sometimes wars involved large armies that would burn towns and take hundreds of prisoners. African traders often delivered slaves hundreds of miles to the coast. The slaves were tied together, sometimes in groups of 50 or more, with forked logs or bark rope. Groups of chained slaves were called *coffles* and were a common sight in Africa in the 1700s. Many captives died of hunger, thirst, exhaustion, or suicide on these trips.

348. (D) On the African coast, slave traders kept the captives in dark dungeons or open slave pens known as barracoons. A Dutch observer said, "markets of men are kept here in the same manner as those of beasts with us." Slave traders, sometimes called *factors*, lived at each trading post. The factors represented either their country or the company that sent them there. The trading posts were often filled with trade goods and guarded by soldiers. Slave ships, known as slavers, could not simply sail into a port, load up with slaves, and sail away. They had to visit the local ruler, ask permission to trade in his kingdom, and offer gifts. It was not unusual for a ship to visit four different places to purchase 500 slaves. Most slaves spent six months to a year from capture before they boarded European ships. They might spend three of these months waiting on the coast. At the barracoon, ship captains or ship doctors examined the captives. The captives selected to be shipped across the ocean were branded with a hot iron on the back, buttocks, or breast with the mark of the buyer. In some cases, slaves who were rejected were killed.

349. (D) Samuel Ajayi Crowther (c. 1809–1891) was the first African Anglican bishop in Nigeria. Ajayi was 12 years old when he was captured by Muslim raiders in 1821 and sold to Portuguese slave traders. Before leaving port, the British boarded his ship and Ajayi was taken to Sierra Leone and released. He learned English, Latin, and Greek, converted to Christianity, and took the name Samuel Crowther in 1825. In 1841, Crowther journeyed to England, where he was trained as a minister and ordained by the bishop of London. He returned to Africa in 1843 and opened a mission in present-day Nigeria. He began translating the Bible into the Yoruba language and compiling a Yoruba dictionary. In 1843, he published a Yoruba grammar, and later a Yoruba version of the Anglican Book of Common Prayer. Crowther also produced a primer for the Igbo language in 1857, another for the Nupe language in 1860, and a full grammar and vocabulary of Nupe in 1864. In 1864, Crowther was ordained as the first African bishop of the Anglican Church and received a Doctor of Divinity from Oxford University.

350. (A) Dona Beatriz Kimpa Vita (c. 1682–1706) was a popular female prophet in the kingdom of Kongo who effectively merged Christian symbols and traditional Kongolese culture. She was born in the late 1600s, when the kingdom was falling apart; Kimpa Vita was the most important of a number of messianic prophets who proclaimed visions at this time. She believed she was possessed by the spirit of St. Anthony and began preaching in the Kongolese city of San Salvador, which she identified as the biblical Bethlehem. Her call for African unity drew strong support among the Kongolese peasants. Kimpa Vita told her followers that Jesus, Mary, and other Christian saints were really Kongolese, and criticized Catholic priests for refusing to acknowledge this truth. She also taught that God was only concerned with believers' intentions, not with sacraments or good works. Kimpa Vita eventually conspired with one of the contenders for the Kongolese throne. She was captured and burnt at the stake for heresy in 1706 with the support of the Catholic missionaries. Her movement outlasted her brief life, and her ideas appeared in various messianic cults for centuries.

Chapter 14: The Era of the World Wars

351. (B) World War I was one of the deadliest wars in history. Total military and civilian casualties were more than 35 million—about 15 million deaths and 20 million wounded. The Allies lost about 6 million soldiers, while the Central Powers lost about 4 million. The cost was so high, and the returns so meager, that most countries, especially democracies, were reluctant to go to war again only 20 years later. It was their misfortune to be dealing with fascist-led nations such as Italy and Germany who romanticized war and were unafraid to take aggressive actions. At the Munich Conference (September 1938), Great Britain and France allowed Nazi Germany to annex Czechoslovakia's Sudetenland even though Czechoslovakia did not agree and did not attend the conference. The Sudetenland was strategically crucial to Czechoslovakia, as most of its border defenses were located there. The Munich Conference is sometimes known as the Munich Betrayal because France and England had a military alliance with Czechoslovakia that they refused to honor. For the British and the French in 1938, the Sudetenland was not worth dying for, and the Munich Conference reveals the failure of appeasement with adversaries who are willing to fight.

352. (A) The Zimmermann Telegram (or Zimmermann Note) was a 1917 diplomatic proposal from Germany to Mexico to make war against the United States. The proposal was a coded telegram sent by the Foreign Secretary of the German Empire, Arthur Zimmermann, on January 16, 1917, to the German ambassador in Washington, D.C., in the middle of World War I. Zimmermann's telegram anticipated the resumption of unrestricted submarine warfare by Germany, an act that Germany feared would draw the neutral United States into World War I. The telegram instructed the ambassador that if the United States appeared likely to enter the war, he should approach the Mexican government with a proposal for a military alliance. He was to offer Mexico material aid to help it recapture the territory taken from Mexico by the United States after the Mexican-American War, specifically Texas, New Mexico, and Arizona. The proposal was intercepted and decoded by British cryptographers; when the Zimmermann Telegram was revealed in American newspapers on March 1, the revelations infuriated Americans and played a major role in the United States declaration of war on Germany on April 6, 1917.

353. (E) The Provisional Government was the short-lived government of Russia that lasted about eight months, from the abdication of Tsar Nicholas II (March 15, 1917) until the Bolsheviks took power after the October Revolution. The Provisional Government, composed mostly of moderates, was led by Aleksandr Kerensky, a leader of the movement to unseat the tsar. However, instead of ending Russia's involvement in World War I, the Provisional Government launched a fresh offensive against the German and Austro-Hungarian armies in July 1917. This weakened the government's appeal because the rival Bolsheviks promised, "Peace, land, and bread" if they came to power. The dismal failure of the Kerensky Offensive eroded support for the government. Spontaneously elected soviets (councils of workers and soldiers) competed with the Provisional Government for support and often challenged its policies. The Provisional Government was also attacked from the right in an attempted coup by Russian General Lavr Kornilov in August 1917. The Petrograd Soviet helped defeat the coup but gradually gained control of the army, factories, and railways. In late October 1917, the Bolsheviks routed the ministers of the discredited Provisional Government in the October Revolution and placed power in the hands of the soviets.

354. (D) Ivan Pavlov (1849–1936) was a Russian physiologist whose research on classical conditioning laid the foundation for behaviorism (the view that psychology should be an objective science that studies behavior with little or no reference to mental processes). Classical conditioning is a type of learning in which a person or animal learns to link two or more stimuli and anticipate results. Pavlov's interest in the digestive process resulted in a series of experiments exploring the correlation between the nervous system and the autonomic functions of the body. Pavlov experimented with dogs, studying the relationship between salivation and digestion. By applying sound, visual, and tactile stimulation to the dogs, he was able to make the animals salivate whether they were in the presence of food or not. He called this phenomenon the conditioned reflex.

355. (C) In 1929, before the Depression, the Nazi Party had 130,000 members. This was not nearly enough to take power in Germany, but the movement grew exponentially when the Depression destroyed the German economy and left millions unemployed. In the 1930 election, Adolph Hitler blamed the crisis on Jewish financiers and Communists; the Nazis won 18 percent of the vote and became the second-largest party in the Reichstag. In March 1932, Hitler ran for president against incumbent President Paul von Hindenburg and polled 30 percent in the first round and 36 percent in the second against Hindenburg's 49 and 53 percent. Hitler appealed to many Germans because of his promises to revive the economy (by unspecified means), to overturn the Treaty of Versailles, and to save Germany from Communism. In the 1932 election, the Nazis gained their highest total—37 percent—and became the largest party in the Reichstag. In another election in November, support for the Nazis fell to 33 percent; the Nazis interpreted this as a warning that they must seize power before their moment passed. Had the democratic parties united, this could have been prevented, but their shortsightedness made a united front impossible. President Hindenburg appointed Hitler chancellor in January 1933. Hitler then used the Reichstag fire in February as an excuse to suppress his political opponents, eliminate all civil rights, and rule by decree.

356. (C) The Treaty of Versailles was the primary peace treaty at the end of World War I. It was signed after six months of negotiations on June 28, 1919, exactly five years after the assassination of Archduke Francis Ferdinand. The most important and controversial provision required Germany to accept responsibility for causing the war (known as the War Guilt clauses), and therefore to make enormous territorial concessions and pay heavy reparations to England and France. All of the treaty's territorial changes were extremely controversial. France was given Alsace-Lorraine (lost to Germany in 1871) and the demilitarization of Rhineland (remilitarized 1936) as a buffer zone against Germany. The Shandong area in China was conceded to Japan. The Austro-Hungarian Empire was carved into national states for Poles, Czechs, and Hungarians. Other small countries such as Estonia, Latvia, and Lithuania were created as part of a *cordon sanitaire* to quarantine the Bolshevik Revolution in Russia. All former German and Turkish colonies went to victors. Italy acquired new territory but was outraged at missing out on the port of Fiume, which became part of the new nation of Yugoslavia. The Polish Corridor to the Baltic Sea split Germany in half and ran through ethnically German territory; Danzig (Gdańsk), at the corridor's terminus, became a free city under League of Nations control. The German army was reduced to 100,000 and the air force eliminated.

357. (B) The concept of a turning point is a subjective judgment, but most historians consider the Battle of Stalingrad (present-day Volgograd) to be the turning point of World War II. The city was a major transportation center on the Volga River. In September 1942, a German army of more than 500,000 men (including Italians, Hungarians, and Romanians) commanded by Friedrich Paulus began an attack on Stalingrad. Joseph Stalin ordered that the city be held at all costs. After two months of house-to-house fighting, the Germans had taken most of the city. However, the remaining Soviet soldiers continued to hold out, receiving supplies from across the Volga. Adolph Hitler refused, against his general staff's advice, to allow Paulus to withdraw. In November 1942, a massive Soviet counteroffensive of more than a million men under Georgy Zhukov advanced in a pincers movement and encircled the Germans; Paulus surrendered what was left of his army in February 1943. The battle was brutal—total casualties were somewhere between one and two million. The Soviets remained on the offensive for the remainder of the war.

358. (A) On June 28, 1914, Austrian Archduke Francis Ferdinand (1863–1914) and his wife, Sophie, were on a state visit to Sarajevo in Bosnia to shore up support for the Austro-Hungarian Empire. The archduke was shot dead by a Serbian nationalist, Gavrilo Princip (1894–1918), who wanted to unite Bosnia-Herzegovina with Serbia. The Austro-Hungarian government, backed by the Germans, sent a severe ultimatum to the Serbs. Although the Serbs accepted all conditions except one (the presence of Austrian officials in the investigation), Austria-Hungary declared war on Serbia on July 28. While European diplomats dallied, Austria-Hungary, Russia, and Germany all mobilized their armed forces. On August 1, Germany declared war on Russia, and two days later, on France. The Germans invaded Belgium as a route to attack France. This violation of Belgian neutrality prompted Britain to declare war on Germany, and Europe went up in flames.

359. (C) President Woodrow Wilson's Fourteen Points were part of a speech he made to Congress on January 8, 1918. This was one of the lowest points of the war for the Allies, just as the Bolsheviks released details of the secret Allied treaties dividing colonies among them. Wilson's speech was an attempt to counter the resulting cynicism about the war with his vision of a just world in which the rule of law would replace the rule of national passions. Wilson's first five points supported public diplomacy, freedom of the seas, lower tariffs, reductions in armaments, and the decolonization of empires. The next eight dealt with specific details for evacuations of German troops. They included an appeal for self-determination for the Poles, although no formula for determining self-determination or even defining it was included. The final point was the creation of a "general association of nations . . . for the purpose of affording mutual guarantees of political independence and territorial integrity to great and small states alike." Reparations were never one of the Fourteen Points but were important to the French, since almost all the fighting on the Western Front had taken place in France at a tremendous cost.

360. (D) Winston Churchill (1874–1965) held a number of political posts in Britain between 1900 and 1915 including first lord of the admiralty. However, in World War I, he was discredited by the failure of the Dardanelles expedition, which he had championed, and lost (1915) his admiralty post. Churchill was out of office from 1929 to 1939, but he wrote a great deal opposing Indian nationalism. He also warned against Nazi Germany but was often ignored because of his past misjudgments. After the early disasters of World War II, Churchill replaced Neville Chamberlain as prime minister on May 10, 1940. Churchill's energy and stubborn public refusal to make peace until Adolf Hitler was crushed were crucial in rallying British resistance during the grim years from 1940 to 1942. The quotation is from a speech delivered to Parliament on June 4, 1940. In this speech, Churchill had to describe the military disaster in France and warn of a possible German invasion of England without casting any doubt on the ultimate victory. This was the second of three major speeches given during the German invasion of France; the others are designated the "Blood, toil, tears, and sweat" speech of May 13 and the "This was their finest hour" speech of June 18. All three are masterpieces of rhetoric and ensure Churchill's reputation as one of the greatest orators of all history.

361. (C) *Guernica* was painted by Pablo Picasso in response to the bombing of Guernica, a city in Basque country, on April 26, 1937, during the Spanish Civil War. Guernica was bombed by German and Italian warplanes at the request of the Spanish Nationalist forces. The Spanish Republican government commissioned Picasso to create a mural for the Spanish display at the 1937 World's Fair in Paris. *Guernica* shows the tragedies of war and the suffering it inflicts upon innocent civilians. On completion, *Guernica* was displayed around the world and helped to bring the Spanish Civil War to the world's attention. The painting was exhibited at the Museum of Modern Art (MOMA) in New York because Picasso refused to allow it to return to Spain as long as Francisco Franco remained in power. Picasso died in 1973 and Franco died in 1975. After Franco's death, Spain became a democratic constitutional monarchy, and MOMA reluctantly returned the painting to Spain in 1981.

362. (E) The Twenty-One Demands were presented by Japan to the government of China in January 1915. Japan used its declaration of war against Germany (August 1914) as justification for invading Kiaochow, the German sphere of influence in Shandong province in China. The Japanese then secretly presented China with an ultimatum of 21 demands divided into five sections. The first group confirmed Japan's acquisitions in Shandong and expanded Japan's sphere of influence over the railways, coasts, and major cities of the province. The second group expanded Japan's control in southern Manchuria and eastern Inner Mongolia, including rights of extraterritoriality and priority for Japanese investment. The third group gave Japan control of the Hanyeping mining complex, already deeply in debt to Japan. The fourth group barred China from giving any further coastal concessions to any foreign power except Japan. The final group contained a miscellaneous set of demands that would compromise Chinese sovereignty. The Chinese government leaked the full contents of the Twenty-One Demands to the European powers, who were angered by the threat to their own political and economic spheres of interest. At the Versailles Conference, Japan was awarded the German possessions in Shandong over strong Chinese protest. China refused to sign the Versailles Treaty, and Great Britain, Japan's ally at that time, expressed concern over Japan's overbearing, bullying approach to diplomacy.

363. (B) The United Nations Security Council is one of the most important parts of the United Nations. It was created after World War II to maintain international peace and security by establishing peacekeeping operations, international sanctions, and the authorization of military action. Its powers are exercised through U.N. Security Council Resolutions; as of November 2011, there had been 2,018 Security Council Resolutions since 1946. There are 15 members of the Security Council—5 permanent members (China, France, Russia, the United Kingdom, and the United States) and 10 elected nonpermanent members with two-year terms. The permanent members, who were given veto power in the original charter of 1945, are the five main victorious nations of World War II. Germany, Japan, Brazil, and India, despite their political and economic rise in the last 65 years, are not permanent members of the Security Council.

364. (C) At the outbreak of World War I, the Ottoman Empire sided with the Central Powers. In 1915, faced with a stalemate on the Western Front, the Allies tried to gain control of the Dardanelles and Bosporus Straits, open Russia's Black Sea ports, and knock the Ottoman Empire out of the war. However, the Turks' reputation as the "Sick Man of Europe" made the Allies overconfident. By the time the Dardanelles Campaign ended, the Allies had suffered at least 150,000 casualties (50,000 dead), and Turkish casualties have been estimated at 250,000 (85,000 dead). In Turkey, the Dardanelles Campaign laid the groundwork for the creation of the Republic of Turkey in 1923 under Mustafa Kemal Atatürk, a commander at Gallipoli during the campaign.

365. (D) On the single day of October 29, 1929, the New York Stock Exchange lost about 12 percent of its value. This was the beginning of a series of declines that would help bring on the Great Depression. In July 1932, the Dow Jones reached a low of 41.22, a loss of roughly 89 percent from its high of 381.17 in early September 1929 (and 50 percent below 1924 levels). The causes of the crash are controversial, but buying on margin was at least partially contributory. During the 1920s, middle-income citizens began investing in the stock market by buying with money borrowed from their broker, with the stock serving as collateral. Buying *on margin* helped fuel some of the stock market prosperity of the 1920s. At the time, the procedure was not regulated, and many brokers would sell with only 25 percent down and even 10 percent down. Because many people did not have the equity to cover their margin positions when the stock market began to decline, their shares were sold, causing further market declines and further margin calls.

366. (E) World War II was the deadliest military conflict in history. Between 50 and 70 million people were killed, about 2.5 percent of the world's population. The Soviet Union had the most casualties in the war, bearing the brunt of Nazi Germany's offensive as well as its racial policy. More than 20 million Soviet soldiers and civilians died in the war, almost 14 percent of the population. By contrast, the United States had almost no civilian casualties and kept battlefield casualties light by delaying the invasion of France until June 1944. About 418,000 Americans died in World War II, about one-third of one percent of the population.

367. (E) Gerald Nye (1892–1971) was a progressive Republican senator from North Dakota. Nye was an outspoken isolationist who supported the Neutrality Acts in the 1930s. The Nye Committee hearings (1934–1936) outraged many Americans with tales of despicable actions by American corporations during and after World War I. The hearings uncovered the fact that American bankers pressed President Woodrow Wilson to enter World War I to protect the value of their loans to the Allies. After the war, American corporations lobbied against arms control and regularly bribed foreign politicians to improve arms sales between 1920 and 1935. Many American corporations were guilty of tax evasion and profiting from sales to Nazi Germany and Fascist Italy; 26 of the top 100 American companies in 1936 had contractual agreements with Nazis. After Mussolini invaded Ethiopia, American trade with Italy actually increased. When representatives from Dow Chemical were asked if they had sent Italy the materials to make the poison gas that Italians dropped by airplane on helpless Ethiopians, the American businessmen replied, "We do not inquire into the uses of the products. We are interested in selling them."

368. (B) The quotation comes from a proclamation written in 1921 by the Soviet sailors at the Kronstadt naval base on the Gulf of Finland. The Kronstadt uprising was one of many unsuccessful left-wing rebellions against the Bolsheviks after the Russian Civil War. The sailors at Kronstadt were active in the overthrow of Tsar Nicholas II in the February Revolution, but by 1921, they had become disillusioned with the Bolshevik government, the lack of democracy, and the policies of War Communism. On February 28, 1921, the crew of the battleship *Petropavlovsk* passed a resolution calling for a return of full political freedoms. Vladimir Lenin denounced the Kronstadt uprising as a plot by the counterrevolutionary White Army and their European supporters. In March, Leon Trotsky ordered the Red Army to attack the Kronstadt sailors. Casualty figures are disputed but probably range in the thousands.

369. (C) After the Meiji Restoration, the Japanese seemed to view all of Asia as the rightful property of the Imperial Japanese government. However, they could not dominate Asia as long as there were foreign military forces in the Philippines (United States), Hong Kong and Malaya (United Kingdom), Indochina (France), and the oil-rich Dutch East Indies. Japan viewed World War II in Europe as a godsend. With England, France, and the Netherlands reeling, Japan hoped to strike quickly in Asia and hold out long enough to broker a peace accord from a position of strength. After the Western powers placed economic sanctions on Japan, the Imperial government decided on war rather than abandon their plans for Asian conquest. In December 1941, the Japanese attacked Pearl Harbor, Malaya, Burma, Guam, Hong Kong, Wake, and the Philippines. They quickly sank the HMS *Repulse* and HMS *Prince of Wales*, demonstrating the uselessness of battleships without air power. They moved into the southern Pacific, and even Australia was bombed. Singapore, the major British military base in southeastern Asia, fell to the Japanese in February 1942 after a brilliant land campaign through Malaya. The Japanese conquered the oil-rich Dutch East Indies in March, Burma in April, and the Philippines in May 1942. These easy victories left the Japanese overconfident and overextended, and they soon realized they had miscalculated; there was no compromise possible with the United States after the Pearl Harbor attack.

370. (A) In February 1942, President Franklin Roosevelt signed Executive Order 9066 ordering all 110,000 Japanese Americans living in California, Oregon, and Washington to be rounded up and imprisoned in relocation centers. This imprisonment was based on no evidence, but solely on ethnicity. In June 1943, the US Supreme Court upheld the internment order by a 9–0 vote in the case of *Hirabayashi v. United States*. In November 1944, with World War II almost over, the Supreme Court again approved the removal of the Japanese by a 6–3 vote in *Korematsu v. United States*. The opinion, written by Hugo Black, held that the need to protect against espionage outweighed Fred Korematsu's individual rights and the rights of Japanese Americans. Robert Jackson noted in his dissent that Fred Korematsu had been convicted "merely of being present in the state whereof he is a citizen, near the place where he was born, and where all his life he has lived." Frank Murphy's dissent noted the lack of any evidence tying Japanese Americans to sabotage and specifically compared the case to people of German and Italian ancestry, who were treated on a case-to-case basis. The *Korematsu* decision has never been overturned, but in 1988, the US Congress awarded $20,000 and a public apology to each of the surviving Japanese American internees. Fred Korematsu died in 2005.

371. (D) Louvain (present-day Leuven) is the capital of Flemish Brabant in Belgium, about 20 miles east of Brussels. In World War I, the Germans had to move extremely quickly in order to outflank the French before they could fully mobilize. In Belgium, civilians resisted German troops and slowed their advance. In order to crush this resistance, Germans shot hostages, killed priests who encouraged resistance, and lightly punished crimes committed by German soldiers. This was a known as the *Schrecklichkeit* (German for "terror" or "frightfulness") policy. In Louvain, the Germans shot the burgomaster, university rector, and all the city's police officers. The university library was deliberately destroyed by the German army in August 1914; thousands of irreplaceable volumes and Gothic and Renaissance manuscripts were lost. The harsh measures, hastily decided upon in the rush to outflank Allied forces, turned out to be a propaganda disaster for the Germans. The British skillfully used reports like these (and also made some up) to create indignation over the "rape of Belgium." This played a major role in the United States decision to side with England rather than Germany.

372. (D) World War II was virtually unique in American history because of the almost unanimous support of Americans for the war effort. Previous (and subsequent) American wars, such as the War of 1812, World War I, the Civil War, and the Vietnam War were particularly divisive and resulted in large antiwar followings. Before the United States entry into World War II, the large isolationist movement barely modified its stance even after Paris fell to the Nazis and London was bombed. The Japanese assumption that Americans would not die to save the Philippines was probably correct, but they drastically miscalculated when they bombed Pearl Harbor without a declaration of war. The action enraged Americans and guaranteed they would support the war and see it out to the end.

373. (B) These are the opening lines from "The Hollow Men" by T. S. Eliot (1888–1965), written in 1925. The themes of "The Hollow Men" are concerned with post–World War I Europe under the Treaty of Versailles and the difficulty of hope and religious conversion. "The Waste Land" (1922) confirmed Eliot's reputation as the greatest of modernist poets; it expressed the disillusionment and collapse of idealism that followed World War I. He received the Nobel Prize in Literature in 1948.

374. (C) Japan's leaders wanted to control Asia and viewed China, Russia, and the Western powers as obstacles to the empire's prosperity and the fulfillment of Japanese destiny. In September 1931, the Japanese army secretly set off a bomb near some railroad tracks in Mukden (Shenyang) in Chinese Manchuria and then used the explosion as an excuse to invade the territory. The Japanese set up a puppet government in Manchuria and invaded more of China. The League of Nations condemned the invasion, but it imposed no economic sanctions that would have hurt Japan. In 1933, China and Japan agreed to a truce, with Japan occupying territory on the Asian mainland. In 1937, however, the Japanese invaded China again, claiming they were establishing a "new order" in eastern Asia that would liberate the area from European imperialism. Thousands of Chinese were massacred in the so-called Rape of Nanking. Again, the United States and Western powers condemned the action but did nothing more. The United States did not impose sanctions against Japan until 1940, after the beginning of World War II in Europe.

375. (A) The Long March was a massive military retreat by the Red Army of the Communist Party of China to evade the pursuit of the Kuomintang (Nationalist Party) army. There was not one Long March, but a series of marches as various Communist armies in the south escaped to the north and west. The most famous is the march by the First Front Army from

Jiangxi province, which began in October 1934. About 90,000 Communists, both men and women, broke through a siege and escaped in a circling retreat to Shaanxi. The march reportedly covered about 7,000 miles over 370 days, despite constant harassment by Nationalist troops and the armies of provincial warlords. By January 1935, the forces were commanded by Mao Zedong and Zhou Enlai. The route passed through extremely difficult terrain in western China; less than half of the force that left Jiangxi completed the march when it ended in October 1935. The episode solidified Mao Zedong's reputation and leadership of the Communist Party and became an almost legendary event in the triumph of Communism in China.

376. (E) In the 1930s, the United States tried to appear less blatant in dominating Latin America, less eager to send in the American military, and less wary of consulting Latin Americans. President Franklin Roosevelt named it the Good Neighbor Policy in 1933, although the process actually began when President Herbert Hoover repudiated the (Theodore) Roosevelt Corollary of 1904 and took a 10-week goodwill tour to Latin America. Henry Stimson, Franklin Roosevelt's Secretary of State, realized that American imperialism in Latin America made the United States vulnerable to charges of hypocrisy when preaching to Japan about invading other countries. At the Seventh International Conference of American States, in Montevideo (1933), the United States endorsed the concept of nonintervention, an idea that it had blocked in 1920s. However, American economic penetration continued unabated even by the Depression; direct US investments of $1.3 billion in 1929 had increased to $3.5 billion by 1939. American exports to Latin America tripled in the same period. The United States trained the national guards (essentially the secret police) of several bloody dictators, including Rafael Trujillo in Dominican Republic (ruled 1930–1961) and the Somoza family in Nicaragua (ruled 1936–1979).

377. (A) The horrific famine that engulfed Ukraine, the northern Caucasus, and the lower Volga River area in 1932 to 1933 resulted from Joseph Stalin's policy of forced collectivization. The heaviest losses occurred in Ukraine, which had been the most productive agricultural area of the Soviet Union. Stalin regarded the self-sufficient farms of the Ukraine peasants as a threat to collectivization. The wealthier farmers were called *kulaks* and became the primary target of the effort in 1929 to eliminate independent farm holdings and create collective farms. In 1932, Stalin raised the Ukraine's grain quotas by 44 percent; this meant there would not be enough grain to feed the peasants since Soviet law required that no grain from a collective farm could be given to the members of the farm until the government's quota was met. All the grain taken from Ukrainian farmers was exported to European countries, and the money generated from those sales fueled Stalin's Five Year Plan to transform the Soviet Union. The death toll from the 1932–1933 famine is estimated at about six million. As a result, the Ukrainians welcomed the Nazis as liberators when they invaded the area in 1941.

378. (C) Pierre Curie (1859–1906) and his wife, Marie Curie (1867–1934), were scientists who were famous for their research on radioactivity and radium. Marie Sklodowska's father was a professor of physics in Warsaw. In 1891 she went to Paris to study at the Sorbonne, and she married Pierre Curie in 1895. Following A. H. Becquerel's discovery of radioactivity in uranium (1896), Marie Curie began to investigate pitchblende, a complex radioactive, uranium-rich mineral. In 1898, she and Pierre discovered and determined the atomic weights and properties of radium and polonium (named after her native Poland). The Curies refused to patent their processes or to profit in any way from the commercial use of radium. For their work on radioactivity, the Curies shared with Becquerel the 1903 Nobel Prize in Physics;

Marie Curie was the first woman to win a Nobel Prize. In 1906, she became the first female professor at the University of Paris. In 1910 she isolated (with André Debierne) metallic radium and won the 1911 Nobel Prize in Chemistry; she was the first person to be awarded a second Nobel Prize and one of only two people (as of 2012) who have won a Nobel Prize in two different fields (the other is Linus Pauling). She died in 1934 of aplastic anemia brought on by her years of exposure to radiation.

379. (A) The quotation is from Benito Mussolini in the *Enciclopedia Italiana* (1932). The actual definition of fascism is ambiguous because it lacked a systematic ideology (unlike Marxism) other than a negative reaction against socialism and democracy. However, in general, fascists claimed struggle, imperialism, and militarism were positive attributes. They propounded the most extreme interpretation of *social Darwinism*; that survival of the fittest applied to nations as well as peoples or races. Peaceful, complacent countries (e.g., democracies) were doomed to fall before dynamic nations. Fascists glorified the nation; they believed the individual should be totally subordinated to the state, which should control every aspect of national life. Fascist ideology promised salvation from mob rule through an authoritarian leader who embodied the highest ideals of the nation. Fascists were unafraid to use dictatorial methods such as intimidation and even murder by militias and secret police. Germany under Adolph Hitler, Italy under Benito Mussolini, and Spain under Francisco Franco were classic examples of fascist states.

380. (D) The Lend-Lease Act was passed by the US Congress in March 1941 at a time when it was not certain that Great Britain would survive in World War II. The act transferred American food, machinery, and services to nations whose existence was considered vital to the defense of the United States. President Franklin Roosevelt was given the power to sell, transfer, lend, or lease these materials and set the terms for aid. Repayment was to be "in kind or property, or any other direct or indirect benefit which the President deems satisfactory." Opponents of lend-lease argued that the act wiped out the last traces of American neutrality and would inevitably draw the United States into the war. Many famous Americans opposed the act, including Charles Lindbergh. Nonetheless, the Lend-Lease Act passed 317 to 71 in the House and 60 to 31 in the Senate. The initial appropriation was $7 billion; by 1945, about $50 billion ($31 billion for England, $11 billion for the Soviet Union) of goods and services had been distributed to American allies.

381. (D) *Atonality* implies music that lacks a tonal center, or key. Atonality usually describes compositions written from about 1908 to the present day that lack a hierarchy of pitches focusing on a single, central tone; instead, the notes of the chromatic scale function independently of one another. Atonality distorted familiar harmonic music and mirrored the fragmented representation of reality in cubism in painting. Richard Strauss (1864–1949) upset convention by using several keys simultaneously. In *Theory of Harmony* (1911), Austrian composer Arnold Schoenberg (1874–1951) proposed eliminating tonality altogether. A decade later, he invented a new 12-tone scale. Other composers associated with the movement are Alban Berg (1885–1935), Anton Webern (1883–1945), and Olivier Messiaen (1908–1992). The new music distanced modernists from their audiences, increasing the separation between "high" and "low" culture in the 1900s.

382. (A) The Holocaust refers to the genocide of approximately six million European Jews and millions of others during World War II. The murders were part of a systematic program of state-sponsored killing by Nazi Germany (led by Adolph Hitler) throughout Nazi-occupied territory. About two-thirds of the nine million Jews who lived in Europe before 1939 were murdered. About half of those Jews lived in Poland, where the local population often joined with Nazis in exterminating their neighbors. More than one million Jewish children were killed in the Holocaust. The Germans also killed many other civilian groups such as the Rom (known in English as Gypsies), homosexuals, Polish and Soviet citizens, Jehovah's Witnesses, people with disabilities, and political and religious opponents. In total, the Germans murdered between 10 and 11 million civilians.

383. (B) The Treaty of Versailles was the main peace treaty at the end of World War I. It was signed on June 28, 1919, exactly five years after the assassination of Archduke Francis Ferdinand. Probably the most important and controversial provision required Germany to accept responsibility for causing the war (known as the War Guilt clauses) and to pay heavy reparations to England, France, and Belgium. These nations hoped to keep Germany weak for the indefinite future, so they set the reparations total at about 132 billion marks, roughly equivalent to more than $400 billion in 2012. France under Georges Clemenceau particularly demanded heavy reparations, since virtually the entire war on the Western Front had been fought in France and had destroyed the country. However, many economists at the time, notably John Maynard Keynes (quoted in the question), thought these reparations were excessive and counterproductive. The yearly amount paid was reduced in 1924 (Dawes Plan) and in 1929 (Young Plan). Adolf Hitler's rise in popularity was partially based on his attacks on reparations; many Germans refused to accept that they had done anything wrong. Payment ceased completely when the Nazis took power in 1933.

384. (D) German strategy in World War I was based on the Schlieffen Plan, named after Alfred von Schlieffen (1833–1913), chief of the general staff. Schlieffen feared a drawn-out war of attrition against the numerically stronger French and Russians. His plan outlined a way to fight opponents on two fronts by concentrating on one enemy at a time. The Schlieffen Plan called for Germany to deliver a rapid blow to the west that would defeat France in six weeks. The plan assumed that the Russians, notoriously disorganized, would be slow to mobilize and could be initially checked by a holding action. By the time the Russians mobilized, France would have been defeated, and Germany's western armies could be redeployed against Russia. The hammer blow against France was to be an overwhelming sweep of the powerful German right wing through Belgium and northern France. Germany knew Belgian neutrality was guaranteed by Great Britain but was willing to risk war with the British in the gamble that they could quickly defeat France. Ironically, World War I developed quite differently. The Belgians held up the German advance, which was eventually checked outside Paris at the Battle of the Marne. The Germans ended up involved in a lengthy two-front war, yet crushed the disorganized Russians and forced them out of the war. This outcome would be reversed in World War II, when the Germans defeated the French quickly but could not knock the Russians out. In both cases, Germany was the ultimate loser.

385. (E) Every generation writes its own history and interprets the facts based on that knowledge. American historians of the 1920s and 1930s were influenced by the bloodshed of World War I (1914–1918), which many Americans thought served no purpose. Therefore, they interpreted the US Civil War on that basis. Historians claimed slavery was not so bad, the Civil War was avoidable, Andrew Johnson was a principled hero whose removal from office would have been a tragedy, and Reconstruction was evil. The bestselling *Gone with the Wind* (1936) painted the Ku Klux Klan as romantic and heroic. In contrast, most Americans thought the defeat of the Nazis in World War II (1939–1945) was a just cause worth fighting and dying for. Historians after 1945 completely reevaluated the Civil War, claiming it served a valuable purpose in ending slavery. The Civil Rights movement of the 1960s applied the finishing touches: Andrew Johnson was reevaluated as a semialcoholic racist and so-called scalawags and carpetbaggers turned out to be much more heroic than the KKK members who harassed and killed them.

386. **(C)** The British war poets were primarily English soldiers who wrote about their experiences in World War I. For these men, the scale of the war's horror and carnage transformed their lives and attitudes, and they wrote poetry about the war and their hopes and fears in an unsentimental and even cynical style. The shocking, realistic war poetry focused on the horrors of trenches and gas warfare and contrasted with the public perception of the war at home and with the confidently patriotic verse written earlier by poets such as Rupert Brooke. A number of war poets died on active service, most famously Isaac Rosenberg (1890–1918), Charles Sorley (1895–1915), and Wilfred Owen (1893–1918; killed a week before the armistice). Owen wrote brilliant yet terrifying poems such as "Dulce et Decorum Est," "Strange Meeting," and "Anthem for Doomed Youth." W. H. Auden (1907–1973) was a British poet from the next generation.

387. **(E)** The Dreyfus Affair refers to the controversy surrounding the treason conviction (1894) of Captain Alfred Dreyfus (1859–1935), a French officer. The French army was a stronghold of monarchists and antisemitic Catholics, and they accused Dreyfus, an Alsatian Jew, of spying for Germany. Dreyfus insisted he was innocent, but he was court-martialed, convicted, and deported to Devil's Island for solitary confinement. However, in 1896, Colonel Georges Picquart and Mathieu Dreyfus (Alfred's brother) independently discovered evidence that Major Ferdinand Esterhazy, who was deep in debt, was the actual traitor. Over tremendous obstacles, they forced the reopening of the case. Yet when Esterhazy was court-martialed in 1898, he was acquitted in minutes. Émile Zola (1840–1902), a leading supporter of Dreyfus, published an open letter entitled "J'accuse" to the president of the French republic, citing a list of military lies by highly placed government officials to falsely convict Dreyfus. Zola was tried for libel, sentenced to jail, and had to flee to England. The case divided the French into irreconcilable factions between royalist, militarist, and nationalist elements on one hand and republican, socialist, and anticlerical elements on the other. In 1898, it was discovered that the evidence against Dreyfus had been forged by Hubert-Joseph Henry of army intelligence. Henry committed suicide and Esterhazy fled to England. Yet a new court-martial in 1899 still found Dreyfus guilty and sentenced him to 10 years in prison. In 1906, Dreyfus was finally exonerated. The Dreyfus Affair brought the French political left wing to power; army influence declined, and in 1905, church and state were separated in France.

388. **(D)** In an effort to unite the Japanese nation, the leaders of the Meiji Restoration consciously created an ideology centered around the emperor. Although the Japanese emperor had little political power, he was viewed as a symbol of Japanese culture and historical continuity, especially as the head of the Shinto religion. One of Shinto's beliefs was that the emperor was semidivine. The Meiji reformers used this history to bring the emperor into national prominence. By associating Shinto with the imperial line, Japan had not only the oldest ruling house in the world but also a powerful symbol of national unity. In the 1900s, Japanese nationalism and militarism were closely linked to the legends of foundation and emperors. Students were required to recite an oath to protect the imperial family, and the state distributed imperial portraits for veneration. This so-called State Shinto came to an abrupt end in August 1945 when Japan lost World War II. Although the United States demanded unconditional surrender, they allowed the Japanese to keep the imperial system. Soon after the war, Emperor Hirohito issued a statement renouncing his claims to the status of "living god."

389. (C) Nazi ideology asserted that German Aryans were a superior race and therefore needed *Lebensraum*, or "living space," to thrive. This space, according to Adolph Hitler's book *Mein Kampf,* would be taken from inferior Slavic peoples (such as the Poles) or the Bolsheviks, who would be moved to Siberia or serve as slaves to the Aryans. The entire urban population was to be exterminated, thus creating an agricultural surplus to feed Germany and allowing their replacement by superior Germans. The concept of *Lebensraum* served as the motivation for the aggressive expansionism of Nazi Germany, just as Manifest Destiny had helped motivate 19th-century Americans to expand westward and take Native American and Hispanic land. The term *Lebensraum* was actually coined by Friedrich Ratzel in 1901, but with a different meaning.

390. (E) Alice Paul (1885–1977) worked for women's suffrage (the Nineteenth Amendment) in the United States. Paul was also the original author of a proposed Equal Rights Amendment to the Constitution in 1923. Emmeline Pankhurst (1858–1928) organized the Women's Social and Political Union (WSPU) in Great Britain, an all-women suffrage advocacy organization dedicated to "deeds, not words"; its members smashed windows, assaulted police officers, and staged hunger strikes in prison. Lida Gustava Heymann (1868–1943) was a German women's rights activist. Heymann, with Anita Augspurg and Marie Stritt Cauer, founded the German Union for Women's Suffrage, which also fought against state-regulated prostitution. Ichikawa Fusae (1893–1981) was a Japanese advocate for women's political rights. With Hiratsuka Raichō, she helped establish the New Woman Association in Japan and was eventually elected to Japan's House of Councilors in the 1950s. Mary Augusta Ward (1851–1920) was a noted British novelist who wrote under her married name as Mrs. Humphry Ward. She was the first president of Britain's Anti-Suffrage League and wrote that constitutional, legal, financial, military, and international problems were problems only men could solve.

391. (C) Sun Yat-sen (1866–1925) was a political leader who played a key role in the overthrow of the Qing dynasty in 1911. He was educated in Hawaii and Japan and promoted nationalism, democracy, and socialism in China. Sun was the first provisional president of the Republic of China in 1912. He later cofounded the Kuomintang (KMT), a quasi-political party, and served as its first leader. When China collapsed into political anarchy, Sun advocated Chinese reunification and he began a self-proclaimed national military government in Guangzhou in southern China. To develop the military power needed for the Northern Expedition against the warlords at Beijing (successfully concluded from 1926 to 1928), he established the Whampoa (present-day Huangpu) Military Academy with Chiang Kai-shek as its commandant. In 1924, he began a policy of active cooperation with the Chinese Communists, and he also accepted the help of the Soviet Union in reorganizing the Kuomintang. After Sun's death in 1925, the Communists and the Kuomintang split, each claiming to be Sun's true heirs. Sun Yat-sen remains unique among 20th-century Chinese politicians for retaining a high reputation in mainland China and in Taiwan as Father of the Nation, and Forerunner of the Revolution.

392. (A) Sigmund Freud (1856–1939) was an Austrian neurologist who founded the discipline of psychoanalysis. Freud's treatment of emotional disorders led him to believe they sprang from unconscious dynamics, which he sought to analyze through the use of free association and dreams. Freud believed personality was composed of pleasure-seeking psychic impulses (the id), a reality-oriented executive (the ego), and an internalized set of ideals (the superego). Tensions between the demands of the id and superego cause anxiety. The ego copes by using defense mechanisms such as repression, projection, and denial. He suggested that children develop through psychosexual stages (oral, anal, phallic, latency, general), during which the id's pleasure-seeking energies focus on distinctive pleasure-sensitive areas of the body called erogenous zones. The *collective unconscious* is Carl Jung's (1875–1961) concept of a shared, inherited reservoir of memory traces from human history.

393. (B) The Fashoda Incident (1898) was a diplomatic dispute between France and Great Britain. Britain wanted to establish a continuous strip of territory from Cape Town to Cairo (south to north), while France desired to establish an overland route from the Red Sea to the Atlantic Ocean (west to east). Obviously, these goals conflicted with each other. In 1897, despite a British warning, the French dispatched a small force from Brazzaville. After crossing 2,000 miles of Africa, they reached the village of Fashoda (present-day Kodok) on the Nile in the southern Sudan. Meanwhile, Lord Kitchener led his Anglo-Egyptian army to Fashoda and claimed the town for Egypt. The French government, fearing war, ordered its mission to withdraw in 1899. France gave up its claim to the upper Nile area and accepted part of the Sahara in return. The Fashoda Incident was the last major colonial dispute between Great Britain and France. In 1904, the French and British made an agreement that guaranteed British claims to Egypt and French claims in Morocco. This began the British-French alliance sometimes called the Entente Cordiale; the enemies of more than 500 years fought as allies in World War I.

394. (D) The League of Nations was an intergovernmental organization founded after World War I. The League was an idea dear to President Woodrow Wilson and was the first permanent international organization whose principal mission was to maintain world peace; yet the United States rejected the Treaty of Versailles and never joined the League. The organization had many notable successes in the 1920s but lacked its own armed force and depended on Europe's powers to enforce its resolutions, keep its economic sanctions, or provide an army when needed. However, these nations were reluctant to do so in major crises. The tipping point was the League's failure to act when Japan invaded Manchuria in 1931; Japan reacted to international criticism by simply quitting the League in 1933. Italy attacked Ethiopia in defiance of League economic sanctions (1935), and Adolf Hitler remilitarized the Rhineland (1936). Faced by problems on all sides, the League of Nations collapsed; it was officially dissolved in 1946 and replaced by the new United Nations.

395. (D) Modernism refers to a cultural movement that developed from the enormous changes to European society in the late 1800s and early 1900s. In general, modernism reflected the belief that the traditional forms of art, architecture, literature, religious faith, and daily life were outdated in the new conditions of the industrialized world. Modernism rebelled against the supposed conservative values of realism. It rejected the optimism and certainty of the Enlightenment, especially as Sigmund Freud's theories of the unconscious spread through the intellectual classes. In addition, Charles Darwin's theory of natural selection and evolution seemed to undermine the belief in a compassionate and all-powerful creator God. The movement was boosted by the horrific death toll in World War I, a war that seemed meaningless to many people even as it was being fought. Modernists distrusted nationalism and argued for cultural relativism and multiple ways of looking at the world. In art, modernism tended toward abstraction, with geometric shapes and works filled with symbols. In architecture, it deified functionality and the removal of "outdated" ornamentation. In literature, modernists rejected a linear storyline or a sweeping subject. In philosophy, the ideology of *positivism* suggested that anything that could not be proved to be empirically true should be abandoned; the result was essentially the end of metaphysics.

Chapter 15: The Cold War Era

396. (A) The administration of US President Dwight Eisenhower and Secretary of State John Foster Dulles (1953–1959) promoted containment in the Cold War with a few new ideas. Both Eisenhower and Dulles viewed atheistic Communism as a moral evil to be avoided at all costs. The United States advocated the liberation of Eastern Europe, although no means were proposed. The new look of the American military emphasized air power and nuclear weaponry and deemphasized conventional forces. The American threat of massive retaliation with nuclear weapons was intended to deter hostile Soviet behavior. The huge arsenal led to brinkmanship, the idea that the United States should not back down in a crisis even if it meant going to the brink of war. The domino theory asserted that small, weak nations would fall to Communism one by one if not propped up by the United States. The Eisenhower administration tried to hold the line against the Soviet Union, Communist China, neutralism, Communism, socialism, nationalism, and revolution everywhere. Détente refers to an easing of strained relations, especially in the relations between the Soviet Union and the United States in the 1970s.

397. (B) The Potsdam (Germany) Conference was held in July and August 1945. For the United States, President Harry Truman replaced the recently deceased Franklin Roosevelt. Clement Attlee was the British representative, and Joseph Stalin the only constant from the other meetings. The Big Three agreed on general policies, but the vague wording and tentative provisions of agreements at Potsdam allowed for an extremely wide range of interpretations. Truman disliked Stalin and was emboldened after the successful atomic bomb test, but he knew he had little leverage in Eastern Europe, which was already occupied by Soviet forces. The Big Three agreed that postwar Germany would be completely disarmed, its monopolies broken, and its economy decentralized. Germany and Berlin would both be divided into four zones (agreed in principle at the Yalta Conference), and each occupying nation would extract reparations from its own zone. All ex-German territory east of the Oder and Neisse Rivers was transferred to Polish and Soviet administration pending a final peace treaty; the German population in many parts of Europe was transferred to Germany. Truman conceded that a democratic Poland was a lost cause and so recognized the Warsaw government. The Potsdam Declaration (July 26, 1945) presented an ultimatum to Japan, offering that nation a choice between unconditional surrender and total destruction (without mentioning the atomic bomb).

398. (A) The Chinese Civil War (1927–1950) was fought between the Kuomintang (or Nationalists) and the Communist Party of China. It began in the late 1920s, but the two sides engineered a temporary truce after Japan invaded China in 1937. There was almost no cooperation between the Kuomintang and the Communists in fighting the Japanese. However, the Communist guerilla war against the Japanese won them much popular support in Japanese-occupied areas. After Japan was defeated in 1945, China's full-scale civil war resumed almost immediately. The United States government aided the Nationalists with economic loans but no military support. After four years of war, the Chinese Communists under Mao Zedong (1893–1976) led the Red Army to victory over Chiang Kai-shek's (Jiang Jieshi) unpopular and corrupt Nationalist government. Chiang Kai-shek and approximately two million Nationalist Chinese retreated from mainland China to the island of Taiwan, where they established the Republic of China (ROC), while the newly founded People's Republic of China (PRC) controlled mainland China. As of 2012, no peace treaty was signed; the PRC still claims Taiwan as part of its territory.

399. (D) After Joseph Stalin died in March 1953, a power struggle ensued within the Soviet government. In 1955, Nikita Khrushchev (1894–1971) outmaneuvered other rivals to emerge as the undisputed leader of the Soviet Union. The next year, he gave a speech at the Twentieth Party Congress in which he listed what he called Stalin's "perversions" of the Communist Revolution. Khrushchev denounced the "cult of personality" that Stalin had built about himself and announced that Stalinism did not equal socialism. The "secret speech" was not published in the Soviet Union until 1989, but it became widely known both within the country and internationally. Khrushchev's speech stunned the people of the Soviet Union, who had lived through 25 years of relentless propaganda and praise of the genius of Stalin. It also astonished communist parties around the world.

400. (C) The Three Rules of Discipline were written in 1928 by Mao Zedong for the Chinese Communist Army that was fighting against the capitalist Kuomintang. The rules emphasized respect for the civilians during wartime and as a result made the Red Army popular in China. Their behavior contrasted positively with the Nationalist Kuomintang armies, led by Chiang Kai-shek (Jiang Jieshi). The Kuomintang often boarded in civilian houses without permission, tended to be disrespectful toward civilians, and sometimes confiscated supplies from peasants. On the other hand, Red Army soldiers avoided looting peasant homes, and many people gave them supplies and shelter voluntarily. Eventually, many villagers and their sons and daughters joined the Communists, providing the Red Army with sufficient manpower to combat the Kuomintang. Mao's insistence on Red Army discipline was a major reason for winning popular support, and thus the victory of the Red Army over the Kuomintang in 1949.

401. (D) The Marshall Plan began in July 1947; its purpose was to encourage economic recovery in Europe after World War II. The plan was named after US Secretary of State George C. Marshall. In April 1948, President Harry Truman approved the creation of the Economic Cooperation Administration (ECA) to administer the program. The Marshall Plan was supposed to contain the spread of Communism in western Europe by easing austerity conditions after the war. Sixteen nations, including Germany, became part of the program and received nearly $13 billion in aid including shipments of food, staples, fuel, and machinery from the United States. The program lasted until 1951, when its activities were transferred to the Mutual Security Agency. The Soviet Union denounced the Marshall Plan as American economic imperialism; it was especially unhappy with aid to rebuild Germany only three years after Nazi rule. The Soviet Union forced the nations in its Eastern European sphere of influence to refuse Marshall Plan aid. The years 1948 to 1952 saw the fastest period of growth in European history; there is debate over how much of this should be credited to the Marshall Plan. In some cases, European nations used the American money to try (unsuccessfully) to reestablish their empires in the Dutch East Indies and French Indochina.

402. (B) Postindustrial society transformed young people's lives. A century earlier, teens had been full-time wage earners. Now, most were students, financially dependent on their parents and sometimes remaining financial minors into their twenties. These young people now filled a new social role as consumers. In the 1960s, long hair, blue jeans, and rock music supposedly announced young people's rejection of middle-class values. With the widespread availability of the birth control pill, sexual abstinence became unnecessary as a method of birth control and a revolution in sexual values ensued. Young people of the 1960s constructed a subculture based on "sex, drugs, and rock 'n' roll," complete with its own rituals, songs, and gathering places. Yet this subculture did not exist outside capitalism; businesses made billions of dollars selling clothing, music, and stereo equipment as well as packaging and managing the stars of youth culture. By 1970, the revolutionary aspects of the youth culture had faded away; instead, it contributed to social assimilation by instructing young people in very orthodox ways of consumption.

403. (E) The administration of US President Dwight Eisenhower and Secretary of State John Foster Dulles (1953–1959) wanted to win over newly independent nations in Africa and Asia to the "Western" side. However, Eisenhower and Dulles considered neutralism immoral and the first step toward Communism. Dulles praised repressive South Korea as part of "the great design of human freedom," while he denounced democratic India as indifferent to human freedom. Racism in the United States was also a problem; dark-skinned diplomats from third world nations personally experienced segregation and discrimination in the United States, especially around Washington, D.C. In addition, the United States typically supported its European allies in their attempts to regain their foreign empires, or sided with the conservative propertied classes in the developing world against anticolonialists and land reformers. The United States often misinterpreted anti-imperialism, political instability, and attacks on foreign-owned property as part of the "Communist menace." American policy makers tended to believe that all revolutions were Soviet-inspired rather than expression of nationalism or internal divisiveness.

404. (C) The *Red Scare* after World War II was known as *McCarthyism* after its most famous supporter, Wisconsin Senator Joseph McCarthy (1908–1957). In 1947, President Harry Truman created the Federal Employees Loyalty Program; this established political-loyalty review boards who determined the "Americanism" of federal employees and recommended termination of those suspected of being "un-American." The Hollywood blacklist began in November 1947 after 10 writers and directors (the Hollywood 10) were cited for contempt of Congress for refusing to give testimony to the House Committee on Un-American Activities (HCUA). Eventually, more than 300 directors, radio commentators, actors, and screenwriters were boycotted by the studios. In 1950, Nevada Senator Pat McCarran introduced the McCarran Internal Security Act, which restricted civil liberties in the name of security. The Palmer Raids were associated with the Red Scare after World War I, in November 1919 and January 1920.

405. (B) Socialist realism was developed in the Soviet Union in the late 1920s and became a dominant style in many Communist countries. Artists who followed the socialist realist philosophy believed that successful art should depict and glorify the proletariat's struggle toward socialist progress. In the 1920s, Soviet artists had embraced a wide variety of art forms; this position was rejected by the Communist Party in the 1930s. They criticized modern styles such as impressionism, cubism, and abstract expressionism as unintelligible, pessimistic, and "decadent bourgeois art." Socialist realism was a reaction against modern abstract art that made no sense to the majority of people. Socialist realism became Soviet state policy in 1932. Painters such as Aleksandr Deyneka (1899–1969) depicted happy, muscular peasants and workers in factories and collective farms. During the Stalin period, they also produced numerous heroic portraits of the dictator for his cult of personality.

406. (C) In October 1962, the United States reported the installation of Soviet medium-range missiles and nuclear bombers in Cuba. Cuba's leader, Fidel Castro, claimed they were needed to deter further American invasions after the Cubans defeated the American-sponsored invasion at the Bay of Pigs in 1961. Soviet motives for sending the missiles to Cuba included a desire to trigger negotiations over Berlin, force the withdrawal of American missiles from Turkey, and give the Soviet Union the same access to enemy territory enjoyed by the United States in Europe. President John Kennedy, chastened by his failure to act regarding the building of the Berlin Wall (1961), now acted forcefully. Kennedy called for a blockade of ships heading to Cuba and threatened nuclear war if the missiles were not removed. For several days, the world seemed on the brink of nuclear disaster. Then, between October 25 and 27, Kennedy and Soviet leader Nikita Khrushchev negotiated an end to the crisis. The Soviets removed the missiles in return for an American pledge to respect Cuban sovereignty; President Kennedy also privately agreed to remove missiles from Turkey.

407. (E) The Korean War (June 25, 1950, to July 27, 1953) began with the North Korean invasion of South Korea. Despite the help of United Nations forces (90 percent American), by September 10, soldiers defending South Korea were besieged on the tiny Pusan peninsula. However, General Douglas MacArthur's daring amphibious landing of 18,000 soldiers behind North Korean lines at Inchon (September 15) achieved complete surprise and enabled the United States to push the North Koreans out of South Korea. American war aims then changed. President Harry Truman now supported the reunification of Korea by force; Communism would not only be contained but rolled back. By November 24, UN forces had driven the North Koreans to the Yalu River on the Chinese border. The Chinese were nervous that the United States would continue to advance and invade China and warned that the UN advance northward should stop. An overconfident MacArthur ignored the warnings. On November 26, 300,000 Chinese troops poured across the border, completely surprising UN troops and driving them southward. Embarrassed, MacArthur demanded massive air attacks on China. Truman refused, and when MacArthur made reckless statements in public, Truman fired him (April 11). The battle lines stabilized in April 1951 near the 38th parallel where the war had begun. About 37,000 Americans died in the Korean War (150,000 casualties), more than 140,000 South Korean soldiers (1 million casualties), and about 400,000 Chinese and North Koreans (1.2 million casualties). An estimated 2.5 million civilians also lost their lives.

408. (A) In 1956, Nikita Khrushchev (1894–1971) gave his famous "secret speech" in which he condemned Stalin's "cult of personality." De-Stalinization encouraged Eastern Europeans that it might be possible to liberalize Soviet-dominated rule. In Poland, Wladyslaw Gomulka (1905–1982) initiated a more moderate national Communism. Inspired by the Polish example, Hungarians rebelled in October 1956. Announcements of reduced wages sparked some of the first outbreaks of violence, but the protest soon targeted the entire Communist system. A popular Hungarian hero, Imre Nagy (1896–1958), took control of the government. When Nagy announced he might leave the Warsaw Pact, Soviet troops invaded Hungary. More than 2,500 Hungarians and 700 Soviet troops were killed in the conflict, Nagy was hanged, and 200,000 Hungarians fled as refugees. The United States' refusal to intervene showed that despite its rhetoric of "liberation," America would not risk World War III by militarily challenging the Soviet Union in its sphere of influence.

409. (C) According to one study, there have been 99 accidents at nuclear power plants as of 2010; 57 percent have occurred in the United States. Serious nuclear power plant accidents include the Fukushima Daiichi disaster (Okuma, Japan; 2011), the Three Mile Island accident (Pennsylvania, US; 2011), the KS-150 accident (Jaslovské Bohunice, Czechoslovakia; 1977), and the SL-1 accident (Idaho Falls, US; 1961). However, by far the worst accident was the Chernobyl disaster on April 26, 1986, in the Ukraine in the Soviet Union. An explosion and fire released large quantities of radioactive contamination into the atmosphere, eventually necessitating the evacuation of 300,000 people from Kiev. The radioactive material spread over much of the western Soviet Union and then Western Europe. At least 64 people died directly as a result of the accident; estimates on additional premature cancer deaths range from 4,000 to one million. The accident raised concerns about the safety of the Soviet nuclear power industry as well as of nuclear power in general.

410. (D) The British nation supported Prime Minster Winston Churchill's coalition cabinet during World War II until the surrender of Germany. However, despite Churchill's exalted reputation, Great Britain's desire for rapid social reform after the war led to a Labour Party electoral victory in July 1945, and Churchill became leader of the opposition. He also became the leader of European and American politicians who were concerned with Soviet influence in eastern Europe. This quotation comes from a controversial speech that Churchill made (while out of power) at Westminster College in Fulton, Missouri, on a visit to the United States in March 1946. The speech is often seen as the breakpoint from wartime cooperation between the Soviet Union and the "Western" Allies to a period of ideological and political "Cold War."

411. (E) The *military-industrial complex* refers to the close connection between politicians, armed forces, and the industries that support them. The term specifically refers to the situation in the United States; the quotation is from the farewell address of President Dwight Eisenhower in January 1961. The idea of a military-industrial complex includes corporate campaign contributions from industry, political approval for almost all defense spending, and legislation that favors the military and reduces oversight of it. In the United States, retired military officers often become consultants to defense contractors, and some are later appointed to important civilian positions in the Pentagon. Corporations such as General Electric own important media outlets (NBC) and also serve as major subcontractors for lucrative defense contracts. These relationships perpetuate excessive military spending and hinder arms reduction efforts. By 2010, the United States government spent about $1 trillion annually on "defense-related" purposes.

412. (A) The earliest experiments to create a working "television" were in the 1920s, but the device did not become popular until after World War II. In the United States, there were 8,000 televisions in 1946, 4 million in 1950, and 46 million in 1960. By 1970, 95 percent of American households had at least one television. Europeans underwent the same conversion slightly later; in France, 1 percent of households had televisions in 1954, 40 percent by 1964, and 80 percent by 1974. By 1960, many television viewers watched five hours a day, leading to a decline in the audience for theater and newspapers and seducing the population off the streets and moving people indoors. In the United States, television was bankrolled by advertising: $171 million in 1950, $1.6 billion in 1960, and $3.6 billion in 1970. In western Europe, governments funded television broadcasting with tax dollars and attempted to avoid what they considered substandard American commercial fare. Both state-sponsored and commercial television tried to avoid controversy to keep sponsors happy. Governments used the new media to project propaganda; politicians now needed to cultivate a successful media image.

413. (B) Antarctica is the earth's fifth-largest continent, comprising about 5.5 million square miles. Because Antarctica has no permanent population, it has no sovereignty, citizenship, or government. People on Antarctica are always citizens of some other place. The Antarctic Treaty, written in 1959, was originally signed by 12 nations; it had 48 signatory nations as of 2011. It set aside Antarctica as a scientific preserve, established freedom of scientific investigation, and banned military activity (but not the presence of military personnel). It also prohibited nuclear explosions and the disposal of radioactive wastes in Antarctica. This was the first arms control agreement established during the Cold War. The hope was that Antarctica would be used exclusively for peaceful purposes.

414. (B) The United States' war against Vietnam destabilized all of southeastern Asia. The US invasion of Cambodia (Kampuchea) in 1970, and the carpet-bombing of Cambodia in 1973 (500,000 tons of bombs dropped) led to hundreds of thousands of casualties. When the US-backed Prince Norodom Sihanouk (b. 1922) was deposed in a coup in 1970, a civil war broke out, and he made an alliance with the Khmer Rouge (the Communist Party of Cambodia) to regain power. The chaos allowed the Khmer Rouge, led by Pol Pot, to rule Cambodia between 1975 and 1979. The Khmer Rouge are remembered for their policies of social engineering that ended in mass murder. They closed schools, hospitals, and factories, abolished banking and currency, outlawed all religions, confiscated private property, and relocated people from cities to collective farms where forced labor was widespread. The *killing fields* refers to several sites in Cambodia where large numbers of people were killed and buried by the Khmer Rouge. The death toll is estimated between 1.4 million and 2.5 million (out of a population of 8 million) with about half the deaths by execution and the rest from starvation and disease. In 1979, Communist Vietnam invaded Cambodia and toppled the Khmer Rouge regime.

415. (C) The dropping of the atomic bomb on Nagasaki on August 9, 1945, which killed about 70,000 people, was the last use of nuclear weapons in war as of 2012. The United States had already dropped an atomic bomb three days earlier on Hiroshima, killing about 100,000 people. In both cities, almost all of the dead were civilians. The Soviet Union had agreed at the Yalta Conference (February 1945) to attack Japan within three months of the end of the war in Europe. On August 9, 1945, exactly three months after the German surrender, 1.6 million Soviet infantry launched a surprise attack on the Japanese forces occupying Manchuria. This invasion came in between the dropping of the atomic bombs on Hiroshima and Nagasaki. The Soviet entry into the war dashed any hopes of the Japanese that they could end the war through Soviet mediation. The atomic bombing of Nagasaki occurred the next day, when the Japanese had still not fully comprehended the devastation at Hiroshima or the implications of the Soviet attack. The lack of time between the bombings has led some historians to believe that the second bombing was actually meant to intimidate the Soviet Union and forestall any Communist advance into Asia. Six days after the detonation over Nagasaki, Japan surrendered. The role of the bombings in Japan's surrender, the United States' ethical justification for them, and their strategic importance are still hotly debated.

416. (A) The quotation is the Equal Rights Amendment (ERA) to the US Constitution, first written by Alice Paul (with slightly different wording) and proposed to Congress in 1923. It was reproposed every year until the wording in the question passed both houses of Congress in 1972. However, the amendment failed to gain ratification from three-quarters of the states (38 states) before its June 30, 1982, deadline. At first, the pace of state ratifications was very quick, with 30 ratifications by the end of 1973. However, as the nation became more conservative in the 1970s, the pace of ratifications slowed to a crawl: three in 1974, one in 1975, none in 1976, and one in 1977. That made 35 states that ratified the ERA; however, five states rescinded their ratifications before the deadline: Idaho, Kentucky, Nebraska, South Dakota, and Tennessee. The Republican Party supported the ERA in every presidential platform from 1940 until 1976, when vast numbers of Republicans began to oppose its passage. As public opinion shifted, politicians listened and the ERA was defeated. The amendment has been reintroduced in every session of Congress since 1982 but shows little sign of passage as of 2012.

417. (E) In 1966, Mao Zedong unleashed the Cultural Revolution, a movement to remake individual personality according to Mao's vision of socialism. Mao wanted the Chinese to experience revolution on a permanent basis instead of stagnating in Soviet-style bureaucracy and corruption. China's youth were empowered to haul away people of every class for *reeducation*. This usually meant personal humiliation, incarceration, and often death (estimates range from 500,000 to 20 million). One of the goals of the Cultural Revolution was to bring an end to the so-called Four Olds—Old Customs, Old Culture, Old Habits, and Old Ideas—and this resulted in the widespread destruction of priceless Chinese cultural artifacts. The revolution marked the return of Mao Zedong to a position of absolute power after the failed economic and social campaign known as the Great Leap Forward (1958–1961). The 10 years of the Cultural Revolution brought China's education system to a virtual halt; university entrance exams were cancelled after 1966 and were not restored until 1977. Mao officially declared the Cultural Revolution to have ended in 1969, but the movement paralyzed the country politically and socially at least until Mao's death and the arrest of the Maoist Gang of Four in 1976.

418. (B) In vitro fertilization is known by the acronym IVF. *In vitro* literally means "in glass," as in a test tube. An IVF cycle begins when doctors give a woman a series of hormone injections or drugs to stimulate the ovaries to produce 10 or more eggs (*ova* or *oocytes*). The eggs are removed surgically and fertilized with donor sperm in the laboratory. Doctors then transfer the resulting embryos into a woman's uterus. Several eggs are usually implanted because some of them may not develop. Nine months later, a so-called *test-tube baby* is born. The first successful human pregnancy achieved through IVF occurred in 1977 when gynecologist Patrick Steptoe and research physiologist Robert Edwards pioneered the technique. The conception resulted in the world's first IVF baby—Louise Brown—on July 25, 1978, in Manchester, England. The first successful IVF in the United States was performed in 1981. In the 21st century, IVF has become the final solution for most fertility problems. About 50,000 babies are born through IVF in the United States every year (slightly more than 1 percent of all American births). More than a million people are believed to have been conceived using IVF since 1978.

419. (C) In the 1950s, the US Central Intelligence Agency (CIA) began to bribe foreign politicians, subsidize foreign newspapers, hire mercenaries, conduct sabotage, dispense false information, plot assassinations, and stage coups to influence foreign governments toward a pro-American position. In Guatemala, Jacobo Árbenz Guzmán's government expropriated United Fruit Company's (an American corporation) uncultivated land. The CIA initiated a coup that deposed Árbenz from power in June 1954 and replaced him with a military dictatorship. In Iran, Mohammad Mosaddeq ordered the seizure of Iran's oil wells from British companies in 1951. The CIA helped overthrow the democratically elected government of Mosaddeq (1953) and replaced him with the young shah, Mohammad Reza Pahlavi, who allowed American oil companies access to Iranian oil reserves. In 1973, the CIA sponsored a coup that overthrew the democratically elected president of Chile, Salvador Allende, whom it deemed a threat to American interests; he was replaced by a military dictatorship headed by Augusto Pinochet, who ruled Chile until 1990. In Brazil, the CIA spent $20 million to influence the 1962 elections against President João Goulart (1918–1976), who had promoted socialist reforms. When Goulart won anyway, his government was overthrown in 1964 with American help. For the next 15 years, Brazil was a military dictatorship without free speech or civil rights.

420. (D) Immediately after World War II, coalition governments, which included liberals, socialists, Communists, and peasant party leaders predominated in Hungary, Poland, and Czechoslovakia (although Joseph Stalin imposed Communist rule almost immediately in Bulgaria and Romania). However, after the Marshall Plan, the Soviet Union suppressed the remaining coalition governments and assumed complete control in central and eastern Europe. In Poland, where the government found the possibility of Marshall Plan aid attractive, Stalin purged Peasant Party leader Stanislaw Mikolajczyk in 1947 and created a Communist-controlled state. In Hungary, the prime minister and head of the Smallholders Party were deposed while on a trip to Switzerland in 1947. Czechoslovakia, which had prospered under a Communist-led coalition, was purged of non-Communist officials in late 1947. In June 1948, socialist president Edvard Beneš resigned and was replaced by a Communist figurehead. By 1948, the Soviet Union had created a buffer of satellite states in Eastern Europe to protect the Soviet Union from an American or another German invasion. Stalin capped his victory by organizing the Cominform, a centralized association of Communist parties of the world under Moscow's direction.

421. (D) Enlightenment writers believed in the idea of *progress*. They thought that science and reason would inevitably bring happiness to the world as time passed, and that attitude predominated in the 19th century. However, the 20th century presented one disaster after another. The Battle of the Somme (1916) symbolized the waste of World War I; the British suffered 60,000 casualties in a few hours for no meaningful purpose. An estimated 15 million people were killed in the war and 20 million wounded. The Holocaust refers to the murder of six million Jews in World War II for no rational reason. The American use of the atomic bombs against civilian populations in World War II killed 150,000 people instantly and meant the possible future use of even stronger weapons that could destroy the world. The popularity of Sigmund Freud's theory of the unconscious implied that human actions did not depend on rationality but were instead controlled by darker nonrational forces. However, *Sputnik*, the first artificial satellite to be launched from Earth (1957), suggested that human intelligence and rationality might still be used for peaceful purposes (although space technology was quickly applied to the creation of intercontinental nuclear missiles).

422. (A) Simone de Beauvoir (1908–1986) was a French existentialist philosopher. Her 1949 treatise, *The Second Sex*, presented a dispassionate and detailed analysis of women's oppression; it is widely considered the foundational book of Second Wave feminism. Betty Friedan

(1921–2006) wrote *The Feminine Mystique* (1963) about what she called "the problem that has no name." This was the sense that many middle-class women led useless existences in postindustrial societies, allowing their talents to stagnate while laborsaving devices, fewer children, and their children's daily presence in school made a woman's presence at home largely redundant. Susan Brownmiller (b. 1935) is best known for her 1975 book *Against Our Will: Men, Women, and Rape*, in which she emphasized rape as a crime of power, not passion, and discussed its use as a weapon of war. Alice Schwarzer's (b. 1942) *The Little Difference and Its Huge Consequences* became a bestseller in 1975 and has been translated into 11 languages. In it, she wrote, "It is not penis and uterus that make us into men and women, but power and powerlessness." Phyllis Schlafly is an American conservative activist; millions of copies of her self-published book, *A Choice, Not an Echo*, were distributed in support of Barry Goldwater's 1964 presidential campaign. Schlafly was the most outspoken opponent of the Equal Rights Amendment during the 1970s.

423. (C) Minimalists simplified music by using repetition and sustained notes as central elements of their compositions. They rejected the masterpiece tradition of lush classical compositions and instead wrote music with a steady pulse (if not a drone) and the repetition and gradual transformation of musical phrases. Some minimalists stressed the use of modern technology; they introduced tape recordings and tape loops into vocal pieces and used computers and synthesizers to compose and to perform their works. Minimalist music began in the early 1960s in San Francisco and New York and spread to become a popular experimental music style of the late 1900s. In the United States, minimalism is associated with Steve Reich (b. 1936), Terry Riley (b. 1935), Philip Glass (b. 1937), and John Adams (b. 1947). In Europe, some minimalists include the Polish composer Henryk Górecki (1933–2010), the Estonian Arvo Pärt (b. 1935), and the British composer John Tavener (b. 1944). Minimalism is not popular, and most audiences dislike it; critics claim that minimalism is passionless, passive, and emotionally blank.

424. (E) The Non-Aligned Movement (NAM) was primarily a Cold War group of nations that refused to align themselves formally with or against any major power bloc. The movement originated at the Bandung Conference (1955), a meeting of 29 Asian and African states (comprising about 1.5 billion people), most of which were newly independent. The conference aimed to promote Afro-Asian economic and cultural cooperation and to oppose colonialism and imperialism by either the United States or the Soviet Union in the Cold War. In 1961, the Non-Aligned Movement was founded in Belgrade. The driving forces were Josip Broz Tito of Yugoslavia, Jawaharlal Nehru of India, Gamal Abdel Nasser of Egypt, Sukarno of Indonesia, and Kwame Nkrumah of Ghana. All five national leaders were known for their support of a "middle course" for developing nations between the "Western" and "Eastern" blocs in the Cold War. Australia was a member of the British Commonwealth and supported the "Western" bloc.

425. (C) The Angolan Civil War took place from 1975 (Angola's independence) to 2002. The war was one of the most prominent Cold War proxy wars, with the United States, South Africa, the Soviet Union, and Cuba all sending massive amounts of weapons into the area. Angola had three competing guerilla groups: the National Union for the Total Independence of Angola (UNITA), the National Front for the Liberation of Angola (FNLA), and the People's Movement for the Liberation of Angola (MPLA). After initial fighting in the late 1970s, the FNLA took over the Angolan government and was recognized internationally. However, the United States refused to recognize the FNLA and instead, with the support of the apartheid regime in South Africa, backed UNITA, led by Jonas Savimbi. Over 27 years, more than a million people died and hundreds of thousands became refugees. Slums called *musseques* stretched for miles around Luanda as a result of the enormous migration of civil war refugees. The fighting did not stop until Savimbi was killed in combat with government troops in 2002. A cease-fire was finally arranged, with the MPLA victorious and UNITA surrendering its armed wing.

426. (B) Ronald Reagan (1911–2004), a former movie actor and governor of California, served as US president from 1981 to 1989. Reagan promoted the values of a so-called moral majority and vowed to promote values such as commitment to Bible-based religion, dedication to work, sexual restraint, and unquestioned patriotism. In domestic affairs, "Reaganomics" produced a huge income tax cut of 25 percent combined with large reductions in federal spending for student loans, school lunch programs, and mass transit. Reagan believed that tax cuts would lead to investment and a reinvigorated economy ("trickle-down economics"). This would make federal welfare programs, which Reagan believed only encouraged laziness, unnecessary. In foreign policy, Reagan labeled the Soviet Union an "evil empire" and sponsored huge military budgets; the combination of tax cuts and military expansion pushed the federal deficit to $200 billion in 1986. The impact of Regan's domestic and foreign policies is disputed, but he remains popular with Americans and his presidency symbolizes a renaissance of the Republican Party.

427. (B) Josip Broz Tito (1892–1980) had a distinguished career in World War I and joined the Communist Party of Yugoslavia after the war. He effectively led the Yugoslav guerilla movement, known as the Partisans, against the Nazis in World War II. He served as premier (1945–1953) and then president (1953–1980) of Yugoslavia. Tito's Yugoslavia represented the only successful exception to the Soviet sweep in eastern Europe, benefitting from its lack of a common border with the Soviet Union. Tito backed *national communism* and was one of the founders and promoters of the Non-Aligned Movement between the two hostile blocs in the Cold War. Tito's successful political and economic policies allowed Yugoslavia to prosper in the 1960s and 1970s. Tito was a popular public figure both in Yugoslavia and abroad and was viewed as a unifying symbol for the nations of the Yugoslav federation. Tito forcefully suppressed nationalist sentiment, and his presidency was been criticized as authoritarian. However, after Tito's death in 1980, tensions between the Yugoslav republics exploded and in 1991 the country disintegrated and went into a decade of civil wars and unrest.

428. (D) In the United States, most states abandoned the death penalty for sodomy in the early 1800s. However, homosexuals remained a despised minority for the next century. Things did not begin to change until the publication of the Kinsey Reports in 1948, which publicized sexual subjects that had previously been taboo. The Mattachine Society, founded in 1950, was one of the earliest organizations in the United States to protect the rights of homosexuals. In 1961, the American Bar Association suggested that the government drop all laws regulating private consenting relations between adults. The sexual revolution of the 1960s liberalized American attitudes toward homosexuality. The modern gay rights movement in the United States began in 1969 when a police raid on a gay bar led to the Stonewall riot in New York City. A number of groups immediately formed to work for the repeal of laws prohibiting consensual sex, for legislation barring discrimination against gays in housing and employment, and for greater social acceptance of homosexuals. In 1973, the American Psychiatric Association declassified homosexuality as a mental disorder and declared it a normal variation of human sexual orientation. However, in 1986, the US Supreme Court in *Bowers v. Hardwick* upheld the constitutionality of a Georgia sodomy law criminalizing sex in private between consenting adults when applied to homosexuals. Sixteen states still had antisodomy laws on the books in 2003 when the US Supreme Court in *Lawrence v. Texas* decriminalized consensual homosexual sex in the United States.

429. (C) The Battle of Dien Bien Phu took place between March and May of 1954 and was the decisive battle of the war between French imperialists and Vietnamese nationalists. The battle was a total French defeat that led to the end of France's Asian empire. Dien Bien Phu was a French outpost deep in the hills of northwestern Vietnam. Despite its precarious position, the French supported the soldiers there, hoping to draw the Vietnamese into a major battle that would cripple them. However, the French had underestimated their opponents. The Vietnamese, under Vo Nguyen Giap, surrounded and besieged Dien Bien Phu, occupying the highlands and bombarding French positions at will. The French repeatedly repulsed Vietnamese assaults on their positions while supplies and reinforcements were delivered by air. The garrison was overrun after a two-month siege, and most French forces surrendered. In the 1954 Geneva Accords, France agreed to withdraw from its former Indochinese colonies.

430. (A) The Tet Offensive, in January and February 1968, was an attempt by the Vietnamese communists to strike American and South Vietnamese military and civilian centers throughout South Vietnam. The Tet Offensive dramatically turned American public opinion against the Vietnam War by exposing the lies of the American generals and government about the state of the war. Martin Luther King was assassinated by a white racist on April 4, 1968; more than 100 cities in the United States erupted in racial violence and riots. In the months surrounding May 1968, France experienced the largest general strike in history (11 million workers), massive student protests, and several riots in Paris. Prague Spring describes the liberalization of Czechoslovakia in 1967–1968. Its leader, Alexander Dubcek (1921–1992), liberalized the Communist government by ending censorship, instituting secret ballots for party elections, and allowing competing political groups to form. On August 20, 1968, Soviet tanks rolled into Prague and crushed the nascent democratic movement. The United States' *Apollo 11* was the first human mission to land on the moon on July 20, 1969; there were six human landings between 1969 and 1972.

Chapter 16: Global Liberation and Independence Movements

431. (E) Many Poles had resisted Soviet-imposed Communism for decades. Catholics, who made up 80 percent of Poland's population of 35 million, opposed socialist secularization. In the 1970s, steep energy prices, scarce consumer goods, and inflation worsened the conditions of everyday life and led to worker protests. Karol Wojtyla, the former archbishop of Cracow who became Pope John Paul II in 1978, lent his authority to the anti-Communist cause. Workers in the Gdansk shipyards, led by electrician Lech Walesa (b. 1943) and crane operator Anna Walentynowicz (1929–2010), created an independent labor movement called Solidarity in 1980. It was the first non-Communist Party-controlled trade union in Poland. By September 1981, Solidarity had reached 9.5 million members, about one-third of the total working age population of Poland, when it was outlawed by the Polish government. However, the Polish government could not revive the economy or gain Soviet support for further repression. In the spring of 1989, the Polish government again legalized Solidarity and promised free elections. In the June elections, Solidarity candidates easily defeated Communists. By 1990, Lech Walesa was president of Poland and the country was converted to a market economy.

432. **(D)** Harry Thuku (1895–1970) was an early Kenyan independence leader who cofounded the East African Organization in 1921 opposing the colonial rule. The Mau Mau Uprising (1952–1956) was an armed Kenyan movement (primarily Kikuyu) directed against the colonial government and the European settlers. Killings, assassinations, and atrocities were committed on both sides, reflecting the ferocity of the movement and the British brutality in suppressing it. As many as 50,000 people may have died. Jomo Kenyatta (c. 1899–1978) led Kenya to independence and served as president from 1964 to 1978. As Kenyan leader, he set up a relatively prosperous capitalist state, following a moderate anti-Communist economic philosophy and foreign policy. When Kenyatta died, Daniel arap Moi (b. 1924) became president of Kenya from 1978 to 2002. Moi had been a leader of the independence movement, but his regime was condemned for massive corruption, repression, and torture. Idi Amin (c. 1925–2003) was dictator of Uganda from 1971 to 1979; his rule was known for its human rights abuse and corruption.

433. **(A)** Muhammad Ali Jinnah (1876–1948) was a member of the All-India Muslim League from 1913 until Pakistan's independence in 1947. He originally supported Hindu-Muslim unity and a one-state solution. However, Hindu-Muslim cooperation broke down in the 1920s, and Jinnah advocated the two-nation theory embracing the goal of creating a separate Muslim state. From 1934 until his death, he headed the Muslim League and guided its struggle for an independent Pakistan composed of the predominantly Muslim areas of northern India. His support of the British during World War II increased his authority after the war. Jinnah's influence and widespread Hindu-Muslim riots forced the Indian National Congress to accept the establishment of the separate state of Pakistan. In August 1947, the subcontinent of India was partitioned. Jinnah was appointed the first governor-general of the dominion of Pakistan; he died shortly afterward.

434. **(C)** Tibet was subject to the laws and decisions of the Yuan and Qing rulers, but it was not attached to China; the Ming dynasty (1368–1644) had no control over Tibet. When the Qing dynasty collapsed in 1911, Tibet became independent; from 1912 until the founding of the People's Republic of China (PRC) in 1949, no Chinese government controlled Tibet. In 1950, the PRC government led by Mao Zedong moved into the area. The Chinese quickly abolished slavery and serfdom, reduced taxes and unemployment, established secular schools (breaking the educational monopoly of the monasteries), and constructed water and electrical systems. However, many Tibetans viewed them as invaders, and China's military crackdown on rebels in 1959 led to the Lhasa Uprising. Resistance spread through Tibet, and the Dalai Lama fled to India. The Chinese occupied Tibet in force, demolishing most of Tibet's more than 6,000 monasteries between 1959 and 1961 and breaking up the monastic estates. In the late 1960s, the Chinese began destroying Tibetan cultural sites, and thousands of Buddhist monks and nuns were killed or imprisoned. As of 2012, most governments recognize the PRC's sovereignty over Tibet, and none have recognized the Government of Tibet in Exile in India.

435. **(B)** The majority of Muslim women who became active participants in Algeria's War for independence (1954–1962) supported the National Liberation Front (FLN). They were mostly rural women who provided food, provisions, and safe houses for the guerrillas. In cities, women who joined the FLN were often young, middle-class graduates of French schools. French-educated women, who had never worn the traditional veil, adopted it as a military strategy in order to carry bombs, money, or messages in the Battle of Algiers (1957) without being detected. A number of women, such as Djamila Boupacha and Louisette Ighilahriz, were captured by the French police or army, imprisoned, and subjected to horrible tortures. Djamila Bouhired, who was recruited by her older brother, became internationally famous after her arrest in 1957 for carrying a bomb. These women were eventually released because of worldwide pressure from human rights groups. However, most women were more involved in feeding and nursing FLN soldiers. The FLN used women in the Algerian War for propaganda purposes, trying to create a myth of a female warrior. However, women in Algeria, regardless of their involvement, remained in their prewar subservient position after independence as a result of the prevailing societal, religious, and cultural conditions.

436. (C) The Tamil people are an Indian ethnic group that are primarily Hindu. About 13 percent of Sri Lanka's 21 million people are Tamils, but the vast majority of the Sri Lankan population is Sinhalese and Buddhist. The Tamil Tigers (LTTE) is a separatist organization founded in 1976 to create an independent Tamil state in northeastern Sri Lanka. The civil war lasted more than 30 years and cost almost 100,000 lives. The Tamil Tigers pioneered the use of suicide bombing and carried out many attacks on civilians. The LTTE was militarily defeated in 2009, and the future of the movement is uncertain.

437. (A) Sukarno (1901–1970) was the leader of the radical nationalist movement founded in 1927 in the Dutch East Indies. He was jailed and exiled several times by the Dutch in the 1930s. During World War II, Sukarno cooperated with the Japanese but continued working for Indonesian independence. After the war, Sukarno and Mohammad Hatta (1902–1980) played a crucial part in the establishment of the Republic of Indonesia (1945). The Netherlands tried to reestablish its rule, and a bitter armed and diplomatic struggle ended only in 1949 when the Dutch recognized Indonesian independence. As first president of Indonesia, Sukarno established (1956) a guided democracy system based on discussion and consensus within a cabinet that represented all political parties. In 1959, Sukarno assumed full dictatorial powers. When a coup failed in 1965, communists were scapegoated. Anticommunists, encouraged by the army and the United States, killed more than 500,000 people. The purge led to a military takeover in Indonesia by General Suharto (1921–2008), who became the second president of Indonesia. Suharto headed a corrupt, military-dominated dictatorship from 1966 to 1998.

438. (E) Despite Sikh protests, the 1947 partition of the Indian subcontinent divided their homeland in the Punjab between India and Pakistan. After the partition, militant Sikhs and Hindus fought the Muslims of Punjab in a struggle that caused more than a million casualties. About 2.5 million Sikhs migrated from West Punjab (in Pakistan) into East Punjab (in India). The 1950s and 1960s were a period of relative stability. However, militant Sikhs in the 1970s and 1980s called for an autonomous Sikh state, to be called Khalistan, within or separate from India. Religious hostility and communal violence erupted in the early 1980s; the most dramatic incident occurred in 1984 when the Indian Army stormed the Sikh Golden Temple at Amritsar, which had been taken over by militant Sikhs. Many Sikhs believed that the attack desecrated the holiest Sikh shrine. In retaliation, Indian Prime Minister Indira Gandhi (1917–1984) was assassinated in 1984 by her Sikh bodyguards. After this, mobs massacred Sikhs throughout India with the suspected collusion of the Indian government. As of 2012, a nonviolent movement for independent Khalistan continues, but in a state of reduced popularity among Sikhs.

439. (C) Negritude was a literary movement of French-speaking African and Caribbean writers who lived in Paris during the 1930s, 1940s, and 1950s. Noted adherents of Negritude included Senegalese poet Léopold Sédar Senghor (1906–2001) and French poet Léon Damas (1912–1978). Aimé Césaire (1913–2008), a poet from Martinique, is credited with coining the term in 1935; it is often translated into English as "blackness." Some basic characteristics of Negritude were a denunciation of Europe's colonial devastation of Africa, an attack on the inhumanity of Western culture, and a corresponding pride in the humane qualities found in African cultures. The Negritude writers preached the benefits of black identity and self-esteem as the best tool to fight European political and intellectual domination. These writers borrowed many of the themes of the Harlem Renaissance in the United States (1920s and 1930s) by asserting their pride in African history and traditions. Senghor later served as the first president of Senegal (1960–1980).

440. (D) Patrice Lumumba (1925–1961) was a Congolese leader who helped the country win its independence from Belgium in June 1960. He then became the first prime minister (1960) of the Republic of the Congo. Lumumba was an outspoken advocate of pan-African unity, and his vision of a strong and united Congo gained him many enemies. Both Belgium and the United States actively sought to have him killed simply because they did not like his policies. Within months of Lumumba's taking power, the army mutinied and the mineral-rich province of Katanga declared independence under Moise Tshombe (1919–1969) with support from the Belgian government and powerful multinational mining companies. Lumumba appealed for aid from the United Nations, which sent troops to reestablish order. In September 1960, Lumumba's government was deposed in a coup by Joseph Kasavubu (c. 1910–1969), his rival for power. Shortly afterward, Lumumba was imprisoned by Joseph Mobutu (1930–1997), later dictator of the Congo from 1965 to 1997. In January 1961, Lumumba was executed by firing squad with the support of the governments of the United States and Belgium. The Belgian government apologized in 2002, admitting their "irrefutable portion of responsibility in the events that led to the death of Lumumba."

441. (A) In 1957, the Gold Coast became the first sub-Saharan African nation to achieve independence from Great Britain; the name Ghana was chosen for the new nation to reflect the ancient empire of Ghana. The country was formed from the merger of the Gold Coast and British (formerly German) Togoland by a United Nations–sponsored vote in 1956. The Ghanaian independence movement intensified after World War II, and Kwame Nkrumah (1909–1972) formed the Convention People's Party with the motto of "self-government now." Nkrumah's campaign gained the support of rural and working-class people, and the British left Ghana without a fight. On March 6, 1957, Nkrumah declared Ghana "free forever" and took office as the first prime minister and then president of the country. Sierra Leone (1961), Uganda (1962), Kenya (1963), and Zambia (1964) all won their independence after Ghana.

442. (B) Yugoslavia was a conglomeration of six regional republics (Slovenia, Croatia, Bosnia and Herzegovina, Macedonia, Montenegro, and Serbia) and two autonomous provinces within Serbia (Kosovo and Vojvodina). After Joseph Tito died in 1980, ethnic tensions intensified in Yugoslavia when Slobodan Milošević, a Serb nationalist, won the presidency of his republic and began to press for Serb control of the country. Other nationalities resisted, and Slovenia and Croatia seceded in 1991. The Croats soon lost almost a quarter of their territory to the Serb-dominated Yugoslavian army. A devastating civil war engulfed Bosnia, where the republic's Muslim majority tried to create a multicultural and multiethnic state. Many Bosnian Serbs formed a guerilla army, backed by support by the Serbian government, and took control. The Serbs often pursued a policy known as *ethnic cleansing* (genocide) against other nationalities. In the late 1990s, Serb forces began attacking people of Albanian ethnicity living in the Yugoslav province of Kosovo. NATO pilots bombed the region and UN peacekeeping forces became involved, but tens of thousands of civilians had already died. (The creation of Albania dates to the early 1900s.)

443. (D) The African National Congress (ANC) was founded in 1912 to increase the rights of the black South African population. At the Sharpeville Massacre in 1960, the South African police opened fire on a crowd of protesters, killing more than 60 people. The Soweto Uprising in 1976 was a series of high school student–led protests against the introduction of Afrikaans as the language of instruction in local schools. Again, the white police reaction was out of control, and more than 150 people were killed. Stephen Biko (1946–1982) was a noted antiapartheid activist in the 1960s and 1970s. He was murdered by the police in 1982 while under police custody. In 1990, the moderate South African leader F. W. de Klerk released political leader Nelson Mandela (b. 1918), who had been imprisoned for almost three decades. In 1993, De Klerk's government and the ANC agreed to a new election with universal suffrage. In 1994, the ANC won a landslide victory and Mandela, now the country's president, endorsed a new constitution that promoted a multiracial democracy.

444. (B) Nigeria is the world's seventh largest exporter of oil, mainly to the United States and Europe. The oil is extracted by the state-run Nigerian National Petroleum Corporation and eight powerful multinational oil companies (especially Shell). Money from oil has poured into Nigeria over the last 40 years, yet 70 percent of the population live in poverty. Residents of the Niger Delta, living above some of the richest oil deposits in the world, sleep in mud houses without electricity and drink dirty water from rivers. The oil companies pollute the air and degrade the ecology of the Niger Delta and then bribe the Nigerian government to suppress opposition by razing villages, detaining people illegally, and executing activists (most famously the Ogoni 9 in 1995). The annual production of both cash and food crops dropped significantly in Nigeria in the late 1900s. In the 1990s and 2000s, the Niger Delta's minority ethnic groups protested continuously against their exploitation by foreign oil corporations. The failure of the Nigerian government to invest in industry or education indirectly benefited Islamic fundamentalists who claimed to speak for the oppressed masses.

445. (E) India (1950), Malaysia (1957), Ecuador (1967), and Portugal (1976) all granted women the right to vote before Saudi Arabia. In 2011, King Abdullah of Saudi Arabia granted women the right to vote and run for office in the 2015 local elections. Before this decree, Saudi Arabia was the only country in the world that did not allow women to vote. Most gender roles in Saudi society are based on Shari'ah (Islamic law) and tribal culture; purdah (the separation of women and men) is widely practiced. In Saudi Arabia, all women, regardless of age, are required to have a male guardian, and it is the only country in the world that prohibits women from driving a car (as of 2011).

446. (C) In the 1960s, Panamanian demands to gain greater control over the Panama Canal intensified. This led to the Torrijos–Carter Treaties (1977), which guaranteed that Panama would control the Panama Canal after 1999, ending American domination that dated from the country's foundation in 1903. The treaties were named after US President Jimmy Carter and Panamanian General Omar Torrijos (who had seized power in a coup in 1968). The treaties were easily ratified in Panama by a referendum. In the United States, after extended and rancorous debate, the Senate ratified the treaties in 1978 by 68 to 32 margins (one vote more than the two-thirds needed). The treaties were extremely controversial in the post–Vietnam War era, where they were seen as another blow to American power and prestige. On December 31, 1999, the United States relinquished control of the Panama Canal and all areas in what had been the Panama Canal Zone.

447. (A) Robert Mugabe (b. 1924) was a leader of the liberation movement against white minority rule in Rhodesia (later renamed Zimbabwe). Mugabe was held as a political prisoner in Rhodesia by the white minority government between 1964 and 1974. Upon release, he rejoined the Zimbabwe Liberation Struggle based in Mozambique. Mugabe became an African hero, and when the war ended he became the first prime minister of Zimbabwe in 1980. Mugabe's early rule emphasized reconciliation between white residents and rival political groups. After 2000, however, the Mugabe-led government began a controversial fast-track land reform program intended to correct the unfair land distribution created by colonial rule. When Zimbabwe gained independence, 46 percent of the country's arable land was owned by about 6,000 farmers; white farmers, who made up less than 1 percent of the population, owned 70 percent of the best farming land. Mugabe's land reform was a failure, alienating both the white farmers and the international community. The result hurt Zimbabwe's economy and led to hyperinflation as well as increased political repression. As of 2012, Mugabe was 88 and the future was unclear.

448. (C) Václav Havel (b. 1936) was a Czech writer and politician. He was the last president of Czechoslovakia (1989–1992) and the first president of the Czech Republic (1993–2003). Havel wrote more than 20 plays and many works of nonfiction. In 1977, Havel's involvement with the human rights manifesto Charter 77 made him a leader of the anti-Communist opposition in Czechoslovakia; he was imprisoned several times. In November and December 1989, the Velvet Revolution nonviolently overthrew the Communist government in Czechoslovakia. In 1990, when Czechoslovakia held its first democratic election since 1946, Havel became president of Czechoslovakia. His 13 years in office saw major changes in the nation, including its split with Slovakia (which Havel opposed but was unable to prevent), the development of a market economy, and the nation's entry into NATO.

449. (D) Botswana is one of the most successful democracies in sub-Saharan Africa. Since its independence from Britain in 1966, it has consistently held free and fair democratic elections. However, it is basically dominated by one party, the Botswana Democratic Party, a coalition representing the eight Setswana-speaking tribes that make up nearly 80 percent of the population. Botswana is a landlocked country of about two million people and one of the most sparsely populated countries in the world. It was one of the poorest countries in Africa when it gained independence, with a GDP per capita of about $70. Botswana has since become one of the fastest-growing economies in the world with a GDP per capita of about $14,800 (in 2010). Mauritania (2008), Guinea (2008), Madagascar (2009), and Niger (2010) all suffered recent coups.

450. (E) Akinwande "Wole" Soyinka (b. 1934) is a Nigerian writer, poet, and playwright. He was awarded the 1986 Nobel Prize in Literature, the first African in Africa to win the honor. Soyinka wrote about the tension between the spiritual and material worlds and the benefits and difficulties when individuals depend on each other. His plays often highlight the problems of daily life in Africa; the best known are *Death and the King's Horseman* (1975) and *A Play of Giants* (1984). His most famous novel is probably *The Interpreters* (1965), which considers the problems of a young Nigerian in an increasingly corrupt society. Soyinka was an outspoken critic of many Nigerian military dictators and of political tyrannies worldwide, regardless of skin color. He was jailed in Nigeria several times and forced to flee the country in the 1990s; the military government sentenced him to death in absentia. The South African writers J. M. Coetzee (2003) and Nadine Gordimer (1991) also won the Nobel Prize in literature. Chinua Achebe (b. 1930) is a Nigerian novelist known for *Things Fall Apart* (1958), probably the most widely read book in modern African literature. Ben Okri (b. 1959) is a Nigerian novelist; his best-known work, *The Famished Road*, is a magical realist novel set in western Africa.

451. (C) Biafra was an oil-rich area of southeastern Nigeria that seceded from Nigeria in May 1967. The inhabitants of Biafra were mostly the Igbo people, and the country took its name from the Bight of Biafra (an arm of the Atlantic Ocean). The state was led by Chukwuemeka Ojukwu, and the original capital was Enugu. The creation of the country led to a civil war that lasted until January 1970; Biafra was defeated and reabsorbed into Nigeria, and about a million civilians died from fighting and famine.

452. (B) Euskadi Ta Askatasuna (ETA) fought for the independence of Spain's northern Basque region. Since 1968, the ETA has killed more than 800 people and been involved in dozens of kidnappings. The Chechens are a Muslim ethnic minority who live in Russia's Caucasus region. In 1999, Chechen bombings of a shopping arcade and apartment building in Moscow killed 64 people. In 2002, Chechen fighters seized a theater in Moscow; more than 120 people died in a rescue attempt. In Northern Ireland, the Irish Republican Army (IRA) has fought for the area's independence from Great Britain since 1916. Between 1969 and 1999, the IRA was responsible for more than 1,700 deaths including British police, soldiers, and civilians. The Armed Islamic Group (GIA) is a Muslim organization advocating the overthrow of the Algerian government and its replacement with an Islamic state. In the 1990s, the GIA conducted a violent campaign of brutal civilian massacres, especially in the villages of Sidi Moussa, Hais Rais, Ben Talha, and Ami Moussa. The Cluster Munition Coalition (CMC) is an international movement campaigning against the production and use of cluster munitions such as land mines.

453. (E) Ferdinand Marcos won the presidency of the Philippines in 1965, but he declared martial law in 1972 and became a dictator. His rule was increasingly corrupt, the Philippine economy collapsed, educated Filipinos left the country, and opponents were imprisoned. However, American support kept him in power. Benigno Aquino Jr., a rising opposition politician, was arrested in 1973 and imprisoned for seven years but allowed to go to the United States to seek medical treatment. In August 1983, Aquino returned to the Philippines; he was assassinated as he disembarked from the plane at Manila Airport. The collusion of Marcos's government in Aquino's murder incited mass demonstrations. International criticism forced Marcos to hold a presidential election in 1986 in which Corazon Aquino, Benigno's widow, was elected. Marcos tried to steal the election through fraud and violence, but the Filipino Army and the US government refused to support him any longer. Marcos fled to Hawaii, taking millions of dollars with him. The Philippine Revolution of 1986 is sometimes known as the People Power Revolution or the EDSA Revolution. EDSA stands for Epifanio de los Santos Avenue, the main highway in Manila where a million Filipinos assembled in a nonviolent mass demonstration against Marcos for four days. The Orange Revolution was in the Ukraine in 2004; the Singing Revolution in the Baltic republics between 1987 and 1991; the Velvet Revolution in Czechoslovakia in 1989; and the Rose Revolution in Georgia in 2003.

454. (B) Until the Berlin Wall was built by East Germany in 1961, the divided city had served as an escape route by which some three million people fled Communist rule and moved to western Europe. The Berlin Wall was the most tangible symbol of the Cold War between the United States and the Soviet Union and symbolized the lack of freedom in the Soviet bloc. When Austria and Hungary opened their common border in 1989, thousands of East Germans pretended to vacation in Hungary and then fled into neighboring West Germany. This made the Berlin Wall irrelevant. In November 1989, the East German government permitted passage through the Berlin Wall. It turned into a giant celebration as Berliners assaulted the wall with sledgehammers; all signs of the Berlin Wall had virtually disappeared by the fall of 1990. The full political reunion of the two Germanies took place on October 3, 1990.

455. (D) Benazir Bhutto (1953–2007) was prime minister of Pakistan (1988–1990; 1993–1996) and the first woman elected to lead a Muslim state, but she was assassinated in 2007. Corazon Aquino (1933–2009) was the first female president of the Philippines. She led the 1986 People Power Revolution that toppled dictator Ferdinand Marcos and restored democracy in the Philippines. Ellen Johnson Sirleaf (b. 1938) was elected president of Liberia in 2005. Sirleaf received the 2011 Nobel Peace Prize for her "nonviolent struggle for the safety of women and for women's rights to full participation in peace-building work." Michelle Bachelet (b. 1951) was the first female president of Chile (2006–2010). She campaigned on a platform of continuing Chile's free-market policies while increasing social benefits to help reduce the gap between rich and poor. Toni Morrison is an American novelist who won the Nobel Prize in Literature in 1993.

Chapter 17: The Middle East Since 1900

456. (A) In the late 1800s, Jews in Europe began organizing resistance to pogroms and anti-Semitic politics. Intellectuals drew on Jewish folklore, philology, and history to establish a national identity similar to that of other Europeans. In the 1880s, the Ukrainian physician Leon Pinsker (1821–1891) experienced a number of pogroms in Russia and concluded that humanism and enlightenment alone would not defeat anti-Semitism. Pinsker saw the lack of a national territory as fundamental to the persecution heaped on Jews, and he advocated the migration of Jews to Palestine. In 1896, Theodor Herzl (1860–1904) published *The Jewish State*, which called for the creation of a Jewish state. Herzl searched Europe for financial backing and advice for the venture. With the backing of poorer eastern European Jews, Herzl called the first International Zionist Congress in 1897. This conference endorsed settlement in Palestine and gained financial backing from the Rothschild banking family. By 1914, about 85,000 Jews had resettled in Palestine.

457. (D) Thomas Edward Lawrence (1888–1935), also known as Lawrence of Arabia, was a British soldier and scholar. While a student at Oxford, he went on a walking tour of Syria and joined a British Museum archaeological expedition. After World War I began, Lawrence served with the British army in Egypt. In 1916, he joined Arab forces under Faisal I and became a leader in their revolt against the Ottoman Turks. Lawrence's use of small and rapid assaults with an Arab force of a few thousand occupied larger Ottoman armies, and he helped capture Damascus in the final weeks of the war. Lawrence envisioned Damascus as the capital of an Arab state and helped establish an Arab government under Faisal. Faisal's rule as king, however, ended abruptly after the French victory over the Syrians in the Battle of Maysalun (1920). After the war, Lawrence was a delegate to the Paris Peace Conference, where he tried unsuccessfully to negotiate for an independent Arabia. He died in a motorcycle accident in 1935.

458. (A) The Arab Spring of 2011 refers to a wave of protests in several countries in the Arab world that aimed at overthrowing or reforming government dictatorships. The protests usually involved techniques of civil resistance such as strikes, demonstrations, marches, and rallies. The Arab Spring was also noteworthy for the use of the Internet and cell phone photography as a way to organize, communicate, and raise awareness in the face of state attempts at repression and censorship. Many demonstrations drew violent crackdowns from authorities, progovernment militias, and/or counterdemonstrators. The protests enjoyed considerable success in Tunisia and Egypt, where revolutions brought down the existing governments. In Libya, the protests led to a civil war that also resulted in regime change. Civil uprisings also occurred in Bahrain, Syria, and Yemen.

459. (B) Mustafa Kemal Atatürk (1881–1938) was a Turkish army officer and the first president and founder of modern Turkey. In 1908, Atatürk took part in the successful Young Turk revolution as chief of staff of Enver Paşa. In World War I, he fought bravely and effectively at Gallipoli, Armenia, and Palestine. In 1921–1922, he organized the brilliant campaign that defeated the Greek invasion of Anatolia. On November 1, 1922, Kemal proclaimed the abolition of the sultanate, and in the Treaty of Lausanne (1923), the European powers recognized an independent Turkey. Atatürk served as president of Turkey from 1923 until his death. In those 15 years, he embarked on a staggering range of political, economic, and cultural reforms to transform the former Ottoman Empire into a modern secular nation. Atatürk regarded Islam as a conservative force, and so he abolished the caliphate (1924) and disestablished Islam as the state religion; Islamic law was separated from secular law and restricted to matters of religion. Women were given new freedoms, including equality in inheritance, divorce, and education. Most amazingly, he implemented a Latinized alphabet for the written Turkish language to replace Arabic script. Atatürk wanted to eliminate the old Ottoman social system based on religious affiliation, and so he banned religion-based clothing such as the fez, veil, and turban.

460. (E) The Iranian Revolution of 1979 refers to the overthrow of Shah Mohammad Reza Pahlavi and the creation of an Islamic government under Ayatollah Ruhollah Khomeini, the leader of the revolution. Demonstrations against the shah and his hated secret police began in October 1977, and in 1978, strikes paralyzed the country. The shah fled Iran in January 1979, and Ayatollah Khomeini returned to Tehran to wild acclaim by several million Iranians. Iran voted to approve a new theocratic constitution whereby Khomeini became supreme leader of the country. The revolution replaced a modernizing monarchy with an Islamic theocracy, was popular with both the people and the armed forces, and generally surprised the world. Khomeini's new regime required women to cover their bodies in special clothing, restricted their right to divorce, and eliminated other rights. These restrictions were intended to restore the pride and Islamic identity that imperialism had stripped from Middle Eastern culture. In October 1979, the dying shah was admitted into the United States for cancer treatment. In Iran, groups demanded the shah's return to Iran for trial. On November 4, 1979, young Islamists invaded the US embassy and seized its staff as hostages. The Iranians refused to release the hostages for more than a year; the hostage crisis was a major cause of the collapse of Jimmy Carter's presidency and the election of Ronald Reagan.

461. (E) In May 1967, Egypt's President Gamal Abdel Nasser mobilized units in the Sinai and closed the Gulf of Aqaba to Israel; Israel responded by mobilizing its own armed forces. The escalation of threats and provocations on both sides continued until June 5, 1967, when Israel launched a massive preemptive air assault that crippled Arab air capability. With air superiority protecting its ground forces, Israel controlled Gaza and the Sinai Peninsula within three days, and then captured Jerusalem's Old City and the "West Bank" from Jordan. On the Syrian border, Israel occupied the Golan Heights. This war, which ended on June 10, is known as the Six-Day War. Israel subsequently declared that it would not give up Jerusalem and that it would hold the other captured territories until significant progress had been made in Arab-Israeli relations. Although Israel won a stunning victory in the Six-Day War, the territorial acquisitions proved to be a major impediment to even a temporary peace in the area for at least the next 45 years.

462. (D) The Persian Gulf War (1990–1991) was waged against Iraq by a United Nations–authorized coalition force from 34 nations. The war was a response to Iraq's invasion (August 1990) and annexation of the oil-rich state of Kuwait. Iraq claimed that Kuwait was an Iraqi territory improperly created after World War I by British imperialists. In the United States, the war is sometimes called Operation Desert Storm after the name of the military response. Most soldiers in the coalition were from the United States, with Saudi Arabia, the United Kingdom, and Egypt also contributing. The United States was concerned with the territorial integrity of Kuwait, but also wanted to support Saudi Arabia, whose role as a crucial supplier of American oil made its safety extremely important. The coalition forces won a decisive victory in February 1990, liberating Kuwait and advancing into Iraqi territory; they then ceased their advance and declared a cease-fire 100 hours after the ground campaign started. Although Kuwait was liberated, Saddam Hussein remained in power in Iraq until the 2003 American invasion of Iraq.

463. (B) Naguib Mahfouz (1911–2006) was probably the best known and most widely read modern writer in Egypt and the entire Arab world; in 1988, Mahfouz became the first writer in Arabic to win the Nobel Prize in Literature. Mahfouz's novels realistically depict Egyptian social and political life and explore controversial issues such as the position of women and political prisoners. Mahfouz's most famous work is probably the Cairo Trilogy, an immense work of 1,500 pages set in the parts of Cairo where Mahfouz grew up. The three novels depict the life of a family over three generations, from World War I to the 1950s when King Farouk I was overthrown. The *Children of Gebelawi* (1959), a semibiblical allegory, includes characters identified with Muhammad and Jesus. The book is often considered blasphemous by Islamic fundamentalists and was banned in Egypt until 2006. Mahfouz's defense of the author Salman Rushdie, when Iranian fundamentalists condemned Rushdie to death in 1989 for *The Satanic Verses*, made him a target for radical Islamists. In 1994, at age 82, Mahfouz was stabbed in an unsuccessful assassination attempt by an Islamic fundamentalist.

464. (C) The term *Young Turks* referred to the members of Ottoman society in the early 1900s who were progressive, modernist, and opposed to the status quo. These Turkish nationalists rejected Sultan Abdülhamid II's (reigned 1876–1909) pan-Islamic solution to stem the decline of the Ottoman Empire. Instead, the Young Turks built their movement on the uniqueness of the Turkish culture, history, and language in the same way as other European ethnic groups. They attempted to build nationalism by purging their language of words from Arabic and Persian and popularizing Turkish folklore and history. In 1909, the Young Turk movement helped the parliament depose the sultan and put Muhammad V on the throne. Ironically, once in power, the Young Turks tried to suppress nationalist uprisings in Egypt, Syria, and the Balkans that their own success had encouraged. In the two successive Balkan Wars (1912–1913), the Ottoman Empire/Turkey lost nearly its entire territory in Europe to Bulgaria, Serbia, Greece, and Albania. By 1913, Enver Paşa, the leader of the Young Turks, gained virtual dictatorial power by a coup and aligned the Ottoman Empire with Germany in World War I.

465. (E) The Lebanese Civil War (1975–1990) was extremely complex but originated in the political compromises of Lebanon's colonial period. The Lebanese constitution created a balance of power between various religious groups, but the president was required to be a Christian. On the basis of the 1932 census, parliamentary seats were divided according to a six-to-five Christian/Muslim ratio. The constitution gave the president veto power over any legislation, almost ensuring that the six-to-five ratio would never be revised. Yet by 1960, Muslims were a majority of the population. After the bloody suppression of the Palestinian Liberation Organization in Jordan in 1970 (Black September), more than 300,000 Palestinians fled to Lebanon. There, they set up a state-within-a-state, launched guerilla raids against Israel, and fought with the Lebanese government. In late 1975, Lebanon became embroiled in civil war among the Christians, Muslims, and Palestinians, made worse by Syrian and then Israeli invasions of Lebanon. Every new upheaval in the Middle East—the Iranian Revolution, Palestinian militancy, Islamic fundamentalism, Israeli aggression, the Iran-Iraq War—had repercussions in Lebanon. By the time the war ended in 1990, more than 100,000 people had been killed, at least 200,000 wounded, and hundreds of thousands displaced from their homes.

466. (B) Al-Qaeda is an international organization formerly led by Osama bin Laden (1957–2011). He established the group in 1988 with Muslims who fought in Afghanistan against the invasion by the Soviet Union. Al-Qaeda wants to unite Muslims to overthrow non-Islamic governments, especially in Asia and the Middle East. Al-Qaeda's ultimate goal is to establish Islamic government—a so-called Islamic Caliphate—from Spain to Indonesia. Al-Qaeda believes the United States has insulted Islam by establishing military bases in Saudi Arabia, using Islamic nations to acquire Middle Eastern oil, and continuing to support Israel against Islamic countries. The members of al-Qaeda believe these actions constitute a declaration of war against God and therefore justify a holy war against the United States. Al-Qaeda is responsible for numerous violent actions against civilians. The most infamous is the September 11, 2001, hijacking attacks of four American passenger planes. Two of the planes crashed into the World Trade Center in New York City and a third into the Pentagon outside Washington, D.C.; about 3,000 people were killed. Al-Qaeda is also linked with other incidents such as the 1998 bombings of the US embassies in Nairobi, Kenya, and Dar es Salaam, Tanzania; the 2002 suicide bombing of a synagogue in Tunisia; the 2004 bomb attacks on Madrid commuter trains; and the 2005 bombings of the London public transportation system.

467. (A) In 1952, Gamal Abdul Nasser (1918–1970) became Egypt's president after the ouster of King Farouk. One of Nasser's prime goals was reclaiming the Suez Canal from Great Britain, which he nationalized in July 1956. Britain demanded the canal's return and invaded Egypt in October with help from France and Israel. The United States refused to back the invaders and pressured them to withdraw from Egyptian territory, which they did. Nasser's triumph inspired confidence in the Arab world that they could confront Europe and win. Nasser was also instrumental in the establishment of the international Non-Aligned Movement, an attempt to avoid taking sides in the Cold War. His version of pan-Arabism had many followers during the 1950s and 1960s. Nasser engineered a union between Egypt and Syria in 1958 known as the United Arab Republic, but it dissolved in 1961. Nasser helped to organize military opposition to Israel, but his reputation was damaged by Egypt's crushing defeat in the Six-Day War.

468. (D) When World War II began, 600,000 Jewish settlers and about twice as many Arabs lived in British-controlled Palestine. In 1947, an exhausted Britain ceded the area to the United Nations to work out a settlement between Jews and Arabs. In the aftermath of the Holocaust, the UN voted to partition Palestine into an Arab region and a Jewish region. On May 14, 1948, the State of Israel came into existence for the first time in 2,000 years. Arab forces immediately invaded Israel, but Jewish military forces prevailed after fierce fighting. After the armistice, Israel acquired all of Galilee west of the Jordan River and a five-mile-wide corridor leading to Jerusalem. They did not receive any of Jerusalem, however, which remained under Jordanian control. After the War of Independence, Israel encouraged Jewish immigration, driving its ambitions against those of its neighbors.

469. (D) According to a 2007 study, five of the nine countries with the greatest estimated oil reserves (using figures that are admittedly guesswork) are in the Middle East (in billions of barrels): Saudi Arabia (265); Venezuela (212); Canada (175); Iran (151); Iraq (143); Kuwait (102); United Arab Emirates (98); Russia (74); and Libya (47).

470. (A) In September 1970, known as Black September by some Arabs, King Hussein of Jordan moved to crush Palestinian organizations and restore his monarchy's rule over the country. In 1950, Jordan had annexed the "West Bank" of the Jordan River. At the time, the population east of the Jordan River contained more than 400,000 Palestinians who made up one-third of the population of Jordan; another third of the population was now Palestinians on the West Bank. Only one-third of the population of the nation consisted of the original inhabitants of Transjordan, meaning the Jordanians had become a ruling minority over a Palestinian majority. Because the Palestinians were obsessed with the West Bank as a center of their territorial aspirations, Jordan's domestic and foreign policy was increasingly affected by Palestinian demands. King Hussein, the target of numerous Palestinian assassination attempts, feared that an independent West Bank under Palestinian administration would threaten his own Hashemite kingdom. As a result, he launched a brutal three-week war in September 1970 against the Palestine Liberation Organization (PLO) in Jordan. He aimed to end the PLO's state-within-a-state in Jordan as well as its guerilla attacks on Israeli-occupied territory in the West Bank. Hussein's forces won the conflict and expelled Yasser Arafat and the PLO in July 1971. Thousands of Palestinian fighters migrated to Lebanon, quickly destabilizing that country.

471. (E) *Intifada* is an Arabic word which means "shaking off," although it is usually translated into English as "uprising" or "rebellion." The First Intifada was a Palestinian uprising in the Gaza Strip and West Bank, beginning in 1987 and continuing into the early 1990s, to protest Israeli occupation of these territories. The Second Intifada, also known as the Al-Aqsa Intifada, refers to a period of intensified Palestinian-Israeli violence that began in September 2000. Al-Aqsa is the name of the mosque at the Temple Mount in Jerusalem, the holiest site in Judaism and third holiest in Islam. The conflict began when Ariel Sharon (b. 1928), a candidate for Israeli prime minister, entered the Temple Mount guarded by hundreds of Israeli policemen, an action viewed as intentionally provocative by Palestinians. Riots erupted, and over the next four years, the military and civilian death toll is estimated at about 5,500 Palestinians and 1,100 Israelis. Many Palestinians viewed the Second Intifada as part of their struggle for national liberation and justice. Many Israelis considered it to be nothing more than a wave of preplanned Palestinian terrorism instigated by Palestinian leader Yasser Arafat (1929–2004). When Arafat died in 2004, the Intifada lost momentum and Palestinian factions such as Hamas and Fatah began to fight among themselves. Israel's unilateral disengagement from the Gaza Strip in August 2005 also led to a gradual decline in violence.

472. (B) In September 1980, Iraq's President Saddam Hussein launched an attack on oil-rich Iran, hoping to gain territory and take advantage of Iran's disarray after the revolution that overthrew the shah in 1979. However, Iraq made only limited progress into Iran; within several months the Iraqis were repelled by the Iranians, who regained virtually all lost territory by 1982 and then took the offensive. The tactics in the Iran-Iraq War mirrored World War I: large-scale trench warfare, machine-gun posts, bayonet charges, barbed wire, and human-wave attacks across no-man's-land. Most distressing was the extensive use of chemical weapons by the Iraqi government against Iranian troops and civilians as well as Iraqi Kurds. The United States, more angry with Iran than with Iraq at the time, prevented the United Nations from condemning Iraq's use of poison gas. After eight years of combat, the war's primary outcome was a massive loss of life. Anywhere from 500,000 to 1.5 million Iraqi and Iranian soldiers and civilians died, but the fighting brought no change in borders. The financial loss was also enormous, estimated at the time at more than $600 billion for each country.

473. (C) The Balfour Declaration of November 2, 1917, was a 67-word letter from British Foreign Secretary Arthur Balfour to Baron Walter Rothschild, a leader of the British Jewish community, for transmission to the Zionist Federation of Great Britain and Ireland. The Balfour Declaration essentially committed the British government to the establishment in Palestine of a national home for the Jewish people. The Balfour Declaration was later incorporated into the Treaty of Sèvres with Turkey and the Mandate for Palestine. The Declaration was controversial as soon as it was issued, mainly because of its own imprecise and contradictory wording. The Balfour Declaration did not refer to Palestine as *the* site of the Jewish homeland, but that of *a* Jewish homeland. That left Britain's commitment to an independent Jewish nation open to question. The second part of the Declaration—that "nothing shall be done which may prejudice the civil and religious rights of the existing non-Jewish communities"—could be (and was) read by Arabs as an endorsement of Arab autonomy and rights.

474. (D) The Arab states were humiliated by their crushing defeat by Israel in the Six-Day War and vowed to reverse that outcome. On October 6, 1973, they launched a surprise attack on Yom Kippur, the holiest day of the Jewish year. In a two-pronged assault, Egyptians pushed eastward across the Suez Canal, while the Syrians advanced from the north. The attacks caught Israel by surprise, and it was several days before the country was fully mobilized. Israel then forced the Syrians and Egyptians back and crossed to the west bank of the Suez Canal. United States and Soviet diplomatic pressures led to an eventual cease-fire in November; Israel eventually gave back the territorial gains it had made. Despite the ambiguous outcome of the war, Egyptian pride was restored by the army's performance. In Israel, regardless of the ultimate success, the war ended the nation's sense of invincibility since the Six-Day War. The war ultimately led to the signing of the Camp David Accords, the return of Sinai to Egypt, and a 40-year peace between Israel and Egypt.

475. (A) The Kurds are an Iranian people who live in Kurdistan, which includes parts of Iran, Iraq, Syria, and Turkey. They speak the Kurdish language and, as of 2010, numbered about 30 million; about 1.3 million Kurds live in western Europe, 100,000 in the United States, and 50,000 in Canada. The Kurds are one of the largest ethnic groups without a country of their own, and the push for a Kurdish nation state has intensified since the 1970s. Kurds make up about 15 percent of the population of Iraq and were violently suppressed by Saddam Hussein, including his use of poison gas on civilian Kurdish populations. After Hussein's fall in 2003, Iraqi Kurds enjoyed considerable local autonomy. Kurds make up about 20 percent of the population of Turkey, and the Turkish government has often repressed Kurdish nationalism, fearing the loss of its eastern provinces. As a result, the Partiya Karkerên Kurdistan (PKK) formed advocating violence to achieve an independent Kurdish state. As of 2012, the United States, European Union, and NATO have labeled the PKK a terrorist organization.

Chapter 18: Global Interdependence Since 1900

476. (C) Acquired immune deficiency syndrome (AIDS) was first identified in the 1970s and spread through the world in the 1980s. AIDS shuts down a person's immune system, leaving the body vulnerable to life-threatening infections and cancers. The virus can be transmitted through sexual contact, blood, and from mother to child through pregnancy or breast milk. AIDS begins with HIV infection. People who are infected with HIV may have no symptoms for many years, but they can still transmit the infection during this time. The spread of AIDS reinforced stereotypes and prejudices about some of its most vulnerable victims. As of 2012, there is no cure for AIDS. However, a variety of treatments can improve the quality of life for people who have developed symptoms. In 2009, the World Health Organization estimated that more than 25 million people have died from AIDS since the beginning of the epidemic. In addition, there were about 33 million people living with HIV/AIDS, more than two million new HIV infections per year, and about two million annual deaths caused by AIDS. Sub-Saharan Africa remains by far the worst-affected region. In 2007, it contained 68 percent of all people living with AIDS, 76 percent of all AIDS deaths, and 11 million AIDS orphans. Unlike other regions, most people living with HIV in sub-Saharan Africa were women. The highest prevalence percentage rate for adults (age 15–49) was Swaziland (26 percent), Botswana (25 percent), Lesotho (24 percent), South Africa (18 percent), and Zimbabwe (14 percent).

477. (C) Global warming describes an increase in the earth's average atmospheric temperature; this warming causes corresponding changes in climate. According to the vast majority of scientists, the main reason the climate is changing is because people are adding greenhouse gases to the atmosphere. The most important greenhouse gas is carbon dioxide, which is released when people burn fossil fuels to drive cars, heat buildings, and make electricity. As greenhouse gases build up in the atmosphere, they cause the earth to trap extra heat, making the planet warmer. There is no dispute that global warming exists, although some people suggest that the change is natural and not caused by humans. However, regardless of cause, 21st-century society will have to deal with widespread changes in climate. Some possible repercussions from global warming include rising sea level, stronger storms, droughts, increased wildfires, animal and plant migration and extinction, and degradation of farmland.

478. (A) Al-Qaeda is an international organization that was established in 1988 by Muslims who fought in Afghanistan against the invasion by the Soviet Union. Al-Qaeda wants to unite Muslims to overthrow governments that are not Islamic, especially in Asia and the Middle East, and establish a so-called Islamic Caliphate from Spain to Indonesia. Al-Qaeda is responsible for numerous actions against civilians. The most infamous is the September 11, 2001, hijackings of four American passenger planes, killing more than 3,000 people. Al-Qaeda is also linked to all the answer choices except the 1999 bombing of a shopping arcade and apartment building in Moscow. These bombings have been attributed to Chechen separatists; there are other theories, but al-Qaeda is not associated with them.

479. (D) Magical realism is a literary style (also prevalent in film and art) in which magical elements blend with the real world. These magical elements are presented in a straightforward manner that equates real and magical aspects. In many cases, authors using magical realism hope readers will ignore plot advancement, chronology, or scientific reason in order to gain a heightened awareness of life's connectedness or hidden meanings. Magical realism is often associated with Latin American writers, especially the novels of Colombian-born Gabriel García Márquez (b. 1928) such as *One Hundred Years of Solitude* (1967) and *Love in the Time of Cholera*. Márquez won the Nobel Prize in Literature in 1982. The Guatemalan writer Miguel Ángel Asturias (1899–1974) also won the Nobel Prize (1967) for novels such as *Mulata* that combine traditional storytelling with mystical elements, Guatemalan legends, and Mayan culture. The Argentine writer Jorge Luis Borges (1899–1986) juxtaposed dreams, labyrinths, libraries, animals, and religion in his fiction. Isabel Allende was the first Latin America woman writer recognized outside the continent; her first novel, *The House of Spirits* (1982), is her best known. Salman Rushdie (b. 1947) is an Indian-British novelist who often writes about the Indian subcontinent. Jorge Amado (1912–2001) was the best-known modern Brazilian writer; his work often dealt with the poor urban black and mulatto communities of Bahia.

480. (D) The South African Truth and Reconciliation Commission (TRC) was an attempt in the late 1990s to heal the wounds of apartheid in a nation attempting to create a democratic government. In a court-like setting, victims of human rights violations between 1960 and 1994 were invited to give statements about their experiences, and some were selected for public hearings. Perpetrators of violence could also give testimony and request amnesty from civil and criminal prosecution. The TRC's relative success and effectiveness are disputed. The TRC, supported by Nelson Mandela, had many respected members and was chaired by South African Nobel Peace Prize Winner (1984) Archbishop Desmond Tutu. Many black South Africans were angered at amnesty being granted for abuses committed by the apartheid government. The highest-profile critics were the family of prominent antiapartheid activist Stephen Biko, who was murdered by white security police in 1977. On the other side, former apartheid President P. W. Botha defied a subpoena to appear before the commission, calling it a "circus." Nonetheless, many South Africans supported the reconciliatory approach of the TRC in revealing the evils of apartheid without the confrontation of actual trials.

481. (B) Desertification refers to the degradation of dryland ecosystems; it is one of the world's most significant environmental problems. Drylands were home to about a third of the earth's population in 2010 and take up almost half of its land area. In drylands, water scarcity limits the production of crops, forage, and wood. These ecosystems, especially in the sub-Sahara and central Asia, are very fragile and cannot sustain the pressure that results from intense population growth. Yet about 90 percent of the inhabitants of drylands live in developing countries where land is often at a premium. Many drylands are inappropriately opened to development and then overcultivated. One of the most troubled regions is the Sahel, the zone of transition that stretches across Africa between the Sahara Desert in the north and the savannas in the south. The Sahel covers parts of the territory of Senegal, southern Mauritania, Mali, Burkina Faso, southern Algeria, Niger, northern Nigeria, Chad, southern Sudan, northern Ethiopia, and Eritrea. São Tomé and Príncipe is a Portuguese-speaking island nation in the Gulf of Guinea.

482. (E) *Postmodernism* is an ambiguous and difficult-to-define term used to describe many different trends in the arts, philosophy, religion, technology, and literary criticism after about 1980. In general, the postmodern view can be described as ironic and accepting of the fragmentation of contemporary existence. Postmodernism tends to mix influences from many different time periods and cultures in a playful way, without a unifying theme or privileged canon. To postmodernists, no single style or culture is valued over any others, and very little is claimed to be valid for all groups, cultures, or traditions. Postmodernism tends to blur the distinctions between high and low culture and challenge traditional cultural values. Interpretation is everything, and reality is basically considered an individual and social construct.

483. (C) The United States invaded Afghanistan in 2001; the primary cause of the invasion was the attacks by al-Qaeda on the United States on September 11, 2001. The United States aimed to end al-Qaeda's use of Afghanistan as a base. The United States also wanted to remove the Taliban, a fundamentalist Islamic regime, from power and create a democratic state. Finally, the United States hoped to find and kill Osama bin Laden and other high-ranking al-Qaeda members. In the first phase of the war, the United States ousted the Taliban regime from power in a matter of weeks; most Taliban leadership fled to neighboring Pakistan. A quasi-democratic republic was established under Hamid Karzai. However, as early as 2003, the Taliban began to mount an insurgency campaign against the new Afghan government and the American troops that supported it. As of 2012, the United States continued to battle a widespread Taliban insurgency with mixed success, and the war expanded into areas of neighboring Pakistan. The war in Afghanistan is the United States' longest war and, according to one estimate, the cost of the war in Afghanistan reached $455 billion by the end of 2011 (and another $800 billion for the war in Iraq). Osama bin Laden was not killed until May 2, 2011, when he was assassinated in a private residence in Abbottabad, Pakistan, by US operatives in a covert operation ordered by US President Barack Obama.

484. (A) Many industrialized countries desire Africa's mineral wealth and other raw materials. As a result, many African countries are dangerously dependent on mineral exports. In 2005, Africa produced 46 percent of the world's diamonds (Botswana produced 35 percent of Africa's total); 21 percent of the world's gold (South Africa produced 56 percent of Africa's total); 16 percent of the world's uranium (Namibia produced 46 percent of Africa's total); and 5 percent of the world's copper (Zambia produced 65 percent of Africa's total). Although the Congo was once the greatest rubber producer in the world, in 2010, Asia was the main source of natural rubber, accounting for 94 percent of the total. Africa accounts for only 4 percent of the world's rubber production, and its leading producers are not the Congo, but Ivory Coast and then Nigeria.

485. (D) There was a massive movement of people around the world in the last third of the 20th century and continuing into the 21st century. Uneven economic development, political persecution, and warfare sent tens of millions in search of safety and opportunity. The turmoil of decolonization sent millions of migrants and refugees to Europe and North America to earn desperately needed income for family members who remained in the native country. A 2009 survey found that roughly 700 million adults would like to migrate to another country permanently if they had the chance. In 2010, Europe hosted the largest number of immigrants, with about 71 million people. The treatment of migrants and immigrants in host countries by governments, employers, and the native population is a topic of continual debate and criticism. In Europe, foreign workers became a target for native peoples suffering from unemployment caused by economic downsizing. Political parties with racist programs sprang up in Europe, where unemployment was often in double digits in the 1990s and 2000s. The National Front Party in France, the Progress Party in Norway, and the Party for Freedom in the Netherlands all thrived by exploiting tensions between foreigners and natives.

486. (B) The world's population has been increasing steadily since about 1400 after the catastrophes of the Great Famine and the Black Death. At that time, the world's population was about 370 million, although there is obviously a great deal of guesswork in such conjectures. It is thought that the population of the world reached one billion for the first time in 1804. It would be another 122 years before it reached two billion in 1927, but it took only 33 years to rise by another billion people (1960). The world's growth rate peaked at about 2.2 percent in 1963 but declined to 1.1 percent by 2009. However, by then, the global population reached four billion in 1974, five billion in 1987, six billion in 1999, and by most estimates, seven billion in 2011. The future is obviously hard to predict, but some projections show a continued increase in population, reaching eight billion by about 2030 and nine billion by about 2050.

487. (E) The Tiananmen Square protests of 1989 (known in China as the June Fourth Incident) were a series of demonstrations in and near Tiananmen Square in Beijing, China, from April to June 1989. The protests began with an outpouring of grief over the death of Hu Yaobang, a Communist Party official who had supported political liberalization. By the eve of Hu's funeral, 100,000 people had gathered at Tiananmen Square. Demonstrations began to encourage continued economic and political reform and attack corruption and nepotism in the government. Protests also occurred in other cities throughout China. The movement used mainly nonviolent methods and was led mostly by students and intellectuals. Martial law was declared, but no military action took place until June 4, when tanks and troops moved into the streets of Beijing and fired live ammunition to clear the area of protesters. Estimates of civilian deaths range from several hundred to thousands. The government then conducted widespread arrests of protesters, banned the foreign press from China, strictly censored domestic news, and purged officials considered sympathetic to the protests.

488. (C) The Advanced Research Projects Agency Network (ARPANET) was the world's first operational packet switching network and the core network of a set that eventually composed the global Internet. The packet switching concept of the ARPANET system was based on designs by Lawrence Roberts (b. 1937). ARPANET was primarily developed by scholars to link research computers around the world. It also had potential military uses; the network was funded by the US Department of Defense for use by its projects at research laboratories in the United States. Through the development of HyperText Markup Language (HTML), computer code could be translated and viewed by computers around the world via phone modems. The first message on the ARPANET was sent in 1969; the system was formally decommissioned in 1990.

489. (B) Aung San Suu Kyi (b. 1945) was the daughter of Aung San (1915–1947), often considered the founder of modern-day Burma (Myanmar). She became an opposition political party leader and was placed under house arrest by the government in 1989. In the 1990 election, her party won 59 percent of the vote and 81 percent of the seats in Parliament, but she remained under arrest for nearly 15 of the next 21 years until her release in November 2010. Aung San Suu Kyi received the Nobel Peace Prize in 1991 "for her non-violent struggle for democracy and human rights." The other four choices are all winners of the Nobel Peace Prize for other reasons.

490. (A) The North American Free Trade Agreement (NAFTA) is an agreement signed by the governments of Canada, Mexico, and the United States in 1994. NAFTA created a trilateral bloc in North America to eliminate barriers to trade and investment between the three nations. The agreement passed the US Congress after considerable argument. Its implementation led to the immediate elimination of tariffs on more than half of American imports from Mexico and more than one-third of American exports to Mexico. However, there is tremendous dispute over NAFTA's environmental impact, as well as where and how many (if any) jobs were created by the agreement.

491. (B) Internal migration usually involves people moving from rural to urban areas, often to find better employment opportunities. By definition, internal migration takes place within a nation. *Favela* is a term for a shantytown in Brazil. Most modern favelas appeared in the 1970s as a result of the movement from the countryside to the city. From 1980 to 1990, the favela population of Rio de Janeiro increased by 41 percent. A 2004 study estimated that 19 percent of Rio's population lived in favelas. Rocinha is the largest favela in Rio de Janeiro, with an estimated population of 250,000.

492. (A) The Rwandan Genocide refers to the 1994 mass murder of an estimated 800,000 people in the eastern African nation of Rwanda. In little more than 100 days, as much as 20 percent of the country's total population may have been killed. The murders were the culmination of long-standing competition and tensions between two groups, the Tutsi and the Hutu. The minority Tutsi had been favored by European colonizers and had controlled the nation for decades. The majority of Rwandans were Hutu peoples who had come to power in the rebellion of 1959–1962 and overthrown the Tutsi monarchy. This genocide had been planned by members of the Hutu national government and was supported by local military and civil officials and mass media. Almost all of those killed were Tutsis. The fighting eventually spilled over into neighboring nations, causing chaos in eastern and central Africa.

493. (D) Deng Xiaoping (1904–1997) was a Chinese revolutionary and government leader. He was a veteran of the famous Long March and rose rapidly in the government after World War II. During the Cultural Revolution, he was attacked as a capitalist stooge, thrown out of the Communist Party, and sent to work in a tractor factory (1966). He was reinstated as deputy premier by Zhou Enlai in 1973 and helped to implement Zhou's Four Modernizations. After Mao Zedong's death in 1976, Deng became, from 1980 to 1987, the most powerful Chinese leader. Deng tried to loosen government control of the economy in order to promote development, yet simultaneously insisted on tight Communist Party control of the government and politics. Deng's reforms led China toward a market economy. He opened China to foreign investment and the global market and allowed limited private competition. He helped turn China into one of the world's fastest-growing economies and raised the standard of living for hundreds of millions of Chinese. He resigned from his last party post in 1989 after the Tiananmen Square demonstrations.

494. (E) Vicente Fox Quesada (b. 1942) served as president of Mexico from 2000 to 2006. His election in 2000 was a milestone in Mexican history; Fox was the first president elected from an opposition party since Francisco Madero in 1910. Fox was also the first president in 71 years (1929) to defeat the dominant Institutional Revolutionary Party (PRI). From 1929 to 1982, the PRI won every presidential election by more than 70 percent of the vote. These voting margins were usually obtained by massive electoral fraud and patronage abuses. Beginning in the 1980s, Mexican elections became more competitive. In 2000, Fox, running on the Alliance for Change party, received 42.5 percent of the vote; his PRI opponent, Francisco Labastida, won 36.1 percent of the vote. The Alliance for Change also became the largest faction in the congressional elections. In 2009, the PRI regained control of the Mexican Congress.

495. (A) According to a 2008 survey (CNN-Money), the top five multinational corporations by revenue were: (1) Wal-Mart Stores, (2) Exxon-Mobil, (3) Royal Dutch Shell, (4) British Petroleum, (5) Toyota Motor. In this survey, General Electric was ranked 12. United States Steel, once the largest corporation in the world, was now ranked only 495. A different survey (Forbes), also from 2008, had different rankings but the same general result: (2) General Electric, (5) Exxon-Mobil, (6) Royal Dutch Shell, (8) Toyota Motor, (16) Wal-Mart, (535) United States Steel.

496. (D) As of 2012, the European Union (EU) is an economic and political union of 27 independent countries in Europe. The first steps to create a European Union were taken after World War II based on the theory that countries that trade with one another will avoid conflict. With the collapse of Communism in the early 1990s, the idea of a unified Europe gathered steam. The Maastricht Treaty in 1992 (amended by the Treaty of Amsterdam in 1999) officially created the European Union and led to the creation of the single European currency, the euro. The eurozone comprised 17 member states as of 2012. The EU, with a combined population of more than 500 million people (7 percent of the world population) generates an estimated 20 percent of global GDP. The EU abolished border controls between EU countries and made it easier for people to travel, trade, or work across most of Europe. However, not all European nations joined. In 1992 and 2001, Swiss voters turned down proposals to consider joining the EU.

497. (D) Since 1970, more than 200,000 square miles of Amazon rainforest have been destroyed. Between 2000 and 2006, Brazil lost more than 50,000 square miles of tropical rainforest, an area larger than Greece. Unlike in some tropical countries, the majority of deforestation in Brazil is not caused by poor subsistence farmers. A larger portion is caused by the clearing of land for cattle grazing by commercial and speculative interests. These wealthy people are supported by the Brazilian government in the form of tax subsidies and the World Bank in the form of loans.

498. (B) During the 20th century, South America was transformed from a largely agriculture-based society to one of the world's most urbanized regions. In 1900, nearly 90 percent of South Americans lived in rural areas. By 1950, about 41 percent of the region's population lived in urban areas. Between 1950 and 2000, Latin America's urban population grew at an average annual rate of 3.5 percent, while the rural population barely grew at all. Because of massive internal migration, Latin America's urban population swelled from about 65 million people in 1950 to 380 million in 2000, when urban residents accounted for about three-quarters of the region's population. In 1950, Buenos Aires was the only Latin American city with a population over five million. By 2010, there were seven cities (but not 20) with five million or more residents: Buenos Aires, São Paulo, Mexico City, Lima, Bogotá, Santiago, and Rio de Janeiro.

499. (E) A mobile phone (also known as a cell phone) is a device that can make and receive telephone calls over a radio link while the owner moves around a wide geographic area. The first handheld mobile phone was demonstrated by Martin Cooper in 1973, using a handset weighing about 2.5 pounds. The first commercially available mobile phone appeared in 1983, and it became one of the most widely adopted pieces of technology in history. From 1990 to 2010, worldwide mobile phone subscriptions grew from 12 million to more than 4.6 billion, spreading across the entire world; China alone has more than a billion mobile phones, followed by India, the United States, Brazil, and Russia.

500. (A) Beginning in 2009, many investors began to fear a debt crisis in European states such as Greece, Ireland, Italy, Spain, and Portugal. This made it difficult or impossible for these nations to borrow money. Outside investors demanded that governments drastically cut expenditures, but this infuriated many people who felt it was unfair that the majority of citizens should have to suffer for the mistakes of bankers and politicians. Countries with stronger economies, such as Germany, also became resentful of propping up weaker economies; these possibilities were not fully considered by economists when the eurozone was created. In 2011, Greece was unable to pay its debts but the Greek people rejected austerity measures and expressed their dissatisfaction through protests and riots. As of 2012, the situation still had not been resolved.